Early Buddhist Teachings

Early Buddhist Teachings

A Foundation for Counseling

Kin Cheung George Lee
Adrian J. Davis
Sabin Maharjan

HKU
PRESS
香港大學出版社

Hong Kong University Press
The University of Hong Kong
Pok Fu Lam Road
Hong Kong
https://hkupress.hku.hk

ISBN 978-988-8876-84-6 (*Hardback*)

British Library Cataloguing-in-Publication Data
A catalogue record for this book is available from the British Library.

Digitally printed

Contents

Figures and Tables

Figures

Tables

Preface

Ye keci osadhā loke vijjanti vividhā bahū,
dhammosadhasamaṁ natthi; etaṁ pivatha bhikkhavo.

(*Anumānapañho*, *Milindapañha*)

"Of the many kinds of medicines in the world, none is greater when compared to the medicine of the Dhamma. Drink this, O monks."

This book presents our humble interpretations of Early Buddhist Teachings in the form of a theoretical framework for Buddhist counseling. In so doing, our ultimate aim is to invite scholars, mental health professionals, students, and other interested individuals to explore and embody the wise and compassionate teachings of the Buddha, leading to the use of skillful means for alleviating suffering in the world.

We thank you for opening this book and walking this path with us. Together, let us navigate the teachings and insights within as we seek to cultivate wisdom and compassion in ourselves and others.

In the shadows of our minds,
Where doubts and fears reside,
The ancient teachings of the Buddha,
Are a beacon of light to guide.
Buddhist counseling is a means,
To spread this light in modern times,
To expose the Dhamma's wisdom,
To those who seek to find.

Abbreviations

ACT	acceptance and commitment therapy
AN	*Aṅguttara-nikāya*
BTBI	Buddhist teaching–based interventions
CBT	cognitive behavioral therapy
DBT	dialectical behavioral therapy
Dhp	*Dhammapada*
Dhs	*Dhammasaṅgaṇī*
DN	*Dīgha-nikāya*
Khp	*Khuddakapāṭha*
KhpA	*Khuddakapāṭha-aṭṭhakathā (Paramatthajotikā)*
MBCT	mindfulness-based cognitive therapy
MBSR	mindfulness-based stress reduction
MBIs	mindfulness-based interventions
MN	*Majjhima-nikāya*
PTS	Pāli Text Society
SN	*Saṃyutta-nikāya*
Sn	*Suttanipāta*

1
Introduction

Early Buddhist teachings, consisting of the fundamental insights and theories revealed by the historical Buddha as documented in the Pāli *Nikāya*s, Chinese *Āgama*s, and *Gandhāran* texts, provide the key principles and practices required in attaining liberation from suffering. This wisdom from more than 2,500 years ago has been adapted over the centuries in numerous ways, one recent form being the secularization and inclusion of Buddhist mindfulness into psychological techniques for counseling purposes. Regardless of the success and popularity of mindfulness, however, there have been increasing criticisms and doubts expressed regarding the secularization of mindfulness in particular and Buddhism in general. In response, a number of scholars and practitioners in psychology and Buddhism started to examine whether Buddhism can work alone as a counseling method to alleviate suffering in the contemporary world, thereby giving rise to new Buddhist-teaching based interventions, such as the Awareness Training Program (Wu et al. 2019) and Cognitively-Based Compassion Training (Negi et al. 2014). However, even these interventions did not address the essence of an archetypal counseling model: a valid and comprehensive theoretical orientation with which to understand different presenting problems and intervene in a specialized and individual manner for a given client and their particular situation. The aim of this book therefore is to integrate Early Buddhist teachings into the development of a theoretical counseling orientation, with the present introductory chapter providing the reader with an overview of the entire therapeutic journey by introducing the background, methodology, and summary of all the chapters of the text.

1.1 Background and Rationale of the Study

In recent times, professional psychology has experienced heated controversy over secularized Buddhist-derived interventions, especially mindfulness-based ones (Lee et al., 2017, 113). Buddhist-derived interventions are an attempt to extract certain components of Buddhist-inspired theories and practices in order to apply them to a secular mental health treatment model. Noteworthy progress has been made in the development of evidence-based treatments that incorporate Buddhist concepts and practices—including mindfulness-based stress reduction (MBSR), mindfulness-based cognitive therapy (MBCT), trauma-focused cognitive behavioral therapy (CBT), and dialectical behavior therapy (DBT)—for various psychological disorders (Lee et al. 2017, 113–15). Neurological, quantitative, and qualitative research findings have also provided promising evidence showing the benefits of mindfulness-based interventions for a variety of mental health disturbances (e.g. Fix and Fix 2013; Luders, Cherbuin, and Gaser 2016). However, critics of these partial applications of Buddhist practice have noted several challenges in doing so: the danger of dissociating mindfulness practice from the Buddhist ethical framework (Harrington and Dunne 2015, 621), the oversimplification of original Buddhist practice (Sun 2014, 395–96), the possibility of causing harm to clients through improper guidance and practice (Shonin, Van Gordon, and Griffiths 2013, 131), and the dilution of treatment effects (Neale 2011, 2–3). For example, Dobkin, Irving, and Amar (2012, 46) conducted a literature review on MBSR, the most common secular mindfulness intervention, and demonstrated such possible adverse effects as increased anxiety, depressed mood, and perceived stress after the MBSR program. These voices at each pole of the discussion have created significant ambiguity in the application of Buddhism to mental health treatments.

Perhaps one reason for the ambiguity is the question of how much of the Buddhist teachings a contemporary intervention model should adopt. Regardless of acceptance and integration of Buddhist concepts and practices into different treatment approaches, most of the contemporary psychotherapy models, such as MBCT, acceptance and commitment therapy (ACT), and DBT, maintain an approach which selectively extracts relevant components of Buddhism instead of using all Buddhist tenets as the foundation for treatment. Van Gordon and Shonin (2013) termed such interventions as mindfulness-based interventions (MBIs), which are secularized treatment approaches that have emerged from different Buddhist schools, although the integration of key Buddhist doctrines is limited (2–3). In addition to Edo Shonin and William Van Gordon, a number of scholars in psychology and Buddhism, such as Alan Wallace, Andreas Schmidt, Bhikkhu Bodhi, and Ron Purser have participated in an ongoing dialogue about the MBIs and their relationship to Buddhist teachings, as well as the potentiality to develop intervention models primarily based on those teachings.

Ron Purser was one of the first researchers to harshly criticize the oversimplification and overuse of mindfulness that began with the emergence of MBSR. Using the catchy term "McMindfulness," Purser criticized the secularization of mindfulness into a business product which has been decontextualized from the original Buddhist teachings (Purser and Loy 2013, 14). The article pinpointed the difference between Right Mindfulness and wrong mindfulness by assessing whether the practice of mindfulness encompasses the quality of awareness characterized by wholesome intentions and positive mental qualities leading to optimal wellness for self and others. Such a conscious consideration contrasts with the McMindfulness applications that are mainly marketable projects without ethical concern, such as fostering one-pointedness concentration to support the violent work of terrorists or assassins. The article also implied that certain therapies could be considered part of the McMindfulness approach, thereby criticizing certain mindfulness-based interventions. Such arguments are some of the most blatant criticisms of the secularization of mindfulness to date. Furthermore, in his book *McMindfulness: How Mindfulness Became the New Capitalist Spirituality*, Purser (2019) shared his observation that mindfulness had been commodified, leading to a capitalization of spirituality in the world (9–13). He even made references to leading global corporates, such as Google's mindfulness program known as "Search Inside Yourself" (Purser 2019, 96), as well as the use of mindfulness by the military establishment (Purser 2019, 150) to illustrate the application of mindfulness for financial, political, or other inappropriate reasons. In addition, in a direct attack on MBSR, Purser wrote the following criticism of Jon Kabat-Zinn (Purser 2019, 177):

> Calling this (mindfulness) a theory of social change, as Kabat-Zinn does, is not only misleading, it encourages people to bury their heads in the sand.

In response, Purser proposed the solution of teaching mindfulness within the Buddhist context, thereby disillusioning people with the fairy tale of secular mindfulness and moving towards the realization of the emptiness of self (Purser 2019, 183–89). In summary, Purser's viewpoint is that mindfulness should not be treated as a solitary cure-it-all technique; rather, it was time to go beyond McMindfulness by returning to the original Buddhist teachings.

As one of the most prolific scholars in evaluating MBIs, Edo Shonin and his team criticized many applications of mindfulness as misappropriations of Buddhist teaching, which can easily misguide and confuse practitioners (Van Gordon and Shonin 2020, 1). Shonin, originally trained as a Buddhist monk as well as a chartered psychologist in the UK, developed meditation awareness training (MAT), which claims to "incorporate practices that would be traditionally followed by meditation practitioners" (Shonin, Van Gordon, and Griffiths 2013, 852–53). As a group-based intervention consisting of guided meditation, workshops, seminars, and one-on-one support sessions, MAT integrates key Buddhist concepts such as impermanence, emptiness, and compassion as part of its treatment (Shonin, Van Gordon, and Griffiths 2013, 853). Such efforts move beyond the existing secularized mindfulness interventions and promote initiatives that incorporate some of the core Buddhist teachings.

Indeed, the debate on mindfulness as a therapeutic intervention tends towards situating MBIs back into a more comprehensive Buddhist framework, although there are opposing voices. Andreas Schmidt, a scholar in politics and philosophy, made a bold assertion that MBIs can be considered as liberal neutral, which fits the needs of contemporary society, and hence such a practice should be used without any affiliation with a religious worldview or ethical framework (Schmidt 2016, 454). Most of the states in the US maintain liberal neutrality to avoid promoting any particular religions (Schmidt 2016, 451). Although most of the MBIs are designed to be secular in nature, the integration of Buddhist values could become a significant hindrance to the acceptability of this intervention in mainstream society. Instead of seeing the insufficient integration of key Buddhist teachings in MBIs as a shortcoming, Schmidt proposed that it be considered a positive feature in promoting mindfulness regarding health policy, educational settings, and different organizations (Schmidt 2016, 453). Moreover, he argued that even though MBIs may be less effective than traditional Buddhist meditation, this constraint should not limit the practical application of the Buddhist tradition into MBIs. In response to common criticisms of MBIs lacking Buddhist ethical values, Schmidt questioned the reason for using the Buddhist worldview to judge such a practice (Schmidt 2016, 452–53). For example, a non-Buddhist worldview may deem the practice of using mindfulness for military purposes as ethical. Therefore, he generally did not see much value in reintegrating MBIs back into a Buddhist context.

Besides criticisms and support for MBIs, there are still more open-minded voices. Alan Wallace, an expert on Tibetan Buddhism and a renowned scholar in the dialogue between Buddhism and science, has also shared similar concerns with Edo Shonin in that contemporary applications of mindfulness distort Buddhism. In an interview on his position on the contemporary application of mindfulness, Wallace stated (2008):

> But the more I looked into this, the more it appeared to me that traditional Theravada and Mahayana sources are largely in accord with each other, and it was the modern accounts of mindfulness that departed from both traditions.

Furthermore, when asked about the pitfalls of MBIs in viewing mindfulness as bare attention, Wallace responded (2008):

> When mindfulness is equated with bare attention, it can easily lead to the misconception that the cultivation of mindfulness has nothing to do with ethics or with the cultivation of wholesome states of mind and the attenuation of unwholesome states.

It is clear that Wallace's stance leans towards the use of traditional Buddhist meditation instead of simplified MBIs. However, when he expressed such concerns in a dialogue with Bhikkhu Bodhi, Bodhi replied with a somewhat different perspective, quoting a statement the Buddha made in the *Mahāparinibbāṇa-sutta* (DN 16):

> in this present age we should take the attitude: "The Tathāgata has no closed fist of a teacher," interpreting this statement to mean that we should let others take from Buddhism what they find useful for secular purposes.[1]

In this exchange of ideas, Bhikkhu Bodhi stated that it is fine for psychotherapists, clinicians, and others to integrate Buddhist mindfulness practice to help others. This is perhaps one of the most open-minded attitudes among scholars in this dialogue.

In reviewing this dialogue, many scholars lean towards a more comprehensive development of Buddhism into a standalone treatment model instead of an extracted or reductionist treatment technique. We will also argue for the benefits of developing and using a comprehensive intervention model based on Early Buddhist teachings, although we will address areas that were missing in the previous dialogues.

First, almost all of the discussions we have read take the perspective of a theoretician while the most important perspective, we argue, is that of the mental health of clients or other receivers of the interventions. When we discuss whether to put mindfulness in its Buddhist context or develop a model based on Buddhism, the key question to answer for a counselor should be: what is best for my clients? We argue that one answer to this question is: the best intervention is the one that matches with a client's worldview. We will briefly explore this idea of matching as found in the Buddhist *sutta*s and in psychology.

In the former, many scenarios illustrate that a particular Buddhist teaching was disseminated in a different way in order to match the background and level of understanding of the hearers. For example, the *Dhanañjāni-sutta* (MN 97) documented a dialogue between Sāriputta and the Brahmin Dhanañjāni who held a view of the existence of the creator *Brahma*. Early Buddhist teachings do not focus on or align with a belief in Brahma, so Sāriputta focused on and explained the Four Immeasurables meditation—the meditation on loving kindness, compassion, joy, and equanimity—as a path leading to the company of Brahma.

The issue of such "matching" has been an ongoing and heated discussion in the field of mental health. Starting in the US, there has been advocacy for cultural

---

1. B. Alan Wallace and Bhikkhu Bodhi, "The Nature of Mindfulness and Its Role in Buddhist Meditation: A Correspondence between B. Alan Wallace and the Venerable Bhikkhu Bodhi" (unpublished manuscript, Winter 2006), 15–16, Santa Barbara Institute for Consciousness Studies, Santa Barbara, CA.

competency in order to address disparities in the quality of services delivered to ethnic minority groups over the last forty years (Sue et al. 2009, 525). The Sue brothers are two of the most prominent researchers in the development of cultural competency models[2] in the field of mental health. They also explain that one key reason for the cultural competency movement stemmed from inadequate mental health services for ethnic minorities in the US in the 1970s (Sue 2003, 964–65). As the treatment models and service delivery were designed for a mainstream population (Caucasian or White American), there was bias, racism, insensitivity to sociocultural needs, and a lack of requisite skills among mental health professionals to provide quality services to clients from different cultural backgrounds (Sue 2003, 965). In support of such an observation, Jerome Frank and Julia Frank, prominent scholars in counseling and psychotherapy training and education, explicitly described psychotherapy as a very culturally specific healing practice (Frank and Frank 1991, 192–93). In particular, they asserted that psychotherapy is created from and designed for specific cultural contexts which have culturally specific assumptions of psychopathology, the role of healers, healing settings, and methods of healing (Frank and Frank 1993, 21–25). Frank and Frank used the first psychotherapy model, psychoanalysis, as an example of a culturally encapsulated treatment approach (Frank and Frank 1993, 192): "Like every other form of psychotherapy, psychoanalysis was and is a cultural enterprise, best understood in the context of its particular cultural and historical setting."

According to Frank and Frank, psychotherapy models rooted in one culture and designated for that specific milieu will work best. This idea resonates with Sue and Sue's pursuit of cultural competency in the provision of more sensitive and culturally congruent treatments for ethnic minorities. Such a standpoint has been influential in the development of psychotherapeutic models by considering cultural competency when applying interventions to clients from different cultures. In a more recent research article, Sue and his team summarized years of experience on this topic and provided reasons for why cultural competency is so important (Chu et al. 2016, 18): "Cultural competency works because it creates: (a) a contextual match with clients' external realities; (b) an experiential match in the microsystem of the therapeutic relationship or framework; and (c) an intrapersonal feeling of being understood and empowered within the client."

We see these reasons as highly relevant to the receivers of psychotherapy, that is, by matching the contextual and cultural worldviews of a mental health professional and client to achieve successful treatment. Such congruence in

---

2. There are numerous definitions of cultural competencies in the literature and the definition and meaning continue to evolve. As this book is not a study of cultural competency, we will use a commonly recognized definition from Stanley Sue as follows: "cultural knowledge and skills of a particular culture to deliver effective interventions to its members" (Sue 2006, 237).

worldview allows the professional to understand a client's view of reality and to connect with them using that client's culturally accepted ways of being and interacting. Cultural competence also has empirical support, as the following key study indicates.

In a meta-analysis of 1,242 clients from fifty-nine studies on culturally adapted psychotherapy (published and unpublished), Benish and his team evaluated whether culturally adapted psychotherapy (using a psychotherapy model developed within mainstream culture and then adapting it to a client's cultural background) is more effective than non-adapted ones (Benish, Quintana, and Wampold 2011, 279–80). One major finding was that "culturally adapted psychotherapy produces superior outcomes for ethnic and racial minority clients over conventional psychotherapy" (Benish, Quintana, and Wampold 2011, 285). This meta-analysis provided clear evidence that adapting an intervention to a client's culture constitutes an important difference in psychotherapy.

Coming back to the discussion on MBIs and the subsequent question of whether there is a need to develop an intervention based on Buddhist teachings, we believe the literature on cultural competency has given a clear answer. The best form of psychotherapy is one rooted in and designated for a particular culture. From the eastward transition of the *Dhamma* since the Buddha's time, Buddhism has been a highly influential school of thought, having become part of the cultures of millions of individuals in the world, especially in Asian cultures (Tamura 2000, 56–57; Xue 1994, 1–3). For example, Xue Ke-qiao (薛克翘) wrote in his book *Buddhism and Chinese Culture* that the transmission of Buddhism had a huge impact on Chinese culture: in philosophy, literature, art, and science (Xue 1994, 1–6). Similarly, Yoshirō Tamura shared the observation in his book *Japanese Buddhism: A Cultural History* that Buddhism continues to remain highly influential in contemporary Japanese culture, with many individuals using film, fiction, poetry, comics, architecture, and other means to express Buddhist thought (Tamura 2000, 171–75). These examples are just a few instances of plentiful evidence of how various Buddhist teachings have planted "seeds" of influence in various Asian cultures. Given such a historical feature, we believe Buddhism can be a very effective source theory for the creation of counseling interventions, as it is highly congruent with many cultures, especially in Asian countries.

Nevertheless, scholars such as Schmidt have doubted whether an intervention should include a worldview. We can agree with Schmidt's position that mindfulness itself can be a neutral practice without any religious ties or particular value. However, when, why, and how to intervene in a client's presenting problem is a clinical judgment which is already driven by a professional's worldview. Take anxiety as an example of treatment target—if a counselor believes the cause of anxiety is the arising of self-critical thoughts, and that the way to cease such suffering is to disengage from such thoughts, the counselor may guide a client to practice mindful breathing in order to shift attention away from such thoughts. If another counselor views the cause of anxiety as primarily based on bodily tension, the counselor may guide the client to use mindfulness for a body scan to alleviate tension in the body. If a third counselor sees anxiety as a product of unresolved conflicts from childhood, that counselor may use mindfulness as a transitional tool to soothe the client's anxiety and then process their childhood experiences. In other words, the same problem of anxiety and the same practice of mindfulness can give rise to very different uses according to the therapist's worldview. Therefore, we argue that no psychotherapy or counseling approach can be completely free from an implicit worldview simply because every psychotherapist or counselor is born into and acquires a certain worldview with associated values and perspectives.

Assuming that the development of a culturally congruent treatment approach can be an effective practice to benefit numerous individuals affiliated with Buddhism, the next question is: can Buddhism be appropriated into a mental health treatment modality?

According to its doctrine, Buddhism has provided comfort and healing to countless individuals over the last 2,500 years. With its own epistemological assumptions about human nature, psychopathology, ideal health, and associated practices and interventions, this book argues that Early Buddhist teachings offer a comprehensive system of human psychology and is thus well qualified in providing an independent theoretical orientation for professional counseling.

Since the advent of the Buddha and throughout the history of the dissemination of Buddhist ideas, Buddhism has been interpreted and elaborated in many different forms in response to cultural, political, and historical environments. To capture this tradition's most fundamental and original ideas and discuss the teachings that are common to all schools of Buddhism, this book will make use of Early Buddhist teachings, particularly the Buddha's discourses in the Pāli *Nikāya*s, as primary sources of information in order to establish its position as a theoretical orientation. Since its inception, Buddhism has invigorated various cultures with certain ideas and practices in response to the specific needs of each population. Chinese Buddhism, Theravāda Buddhism, Tibetan Buddhism, Chan Buddhism, Zen Buddhism, recent Buddhist-derived interventions in psychology, and many other traditions and applications exemplify such culturally adaptive forms of Buddhism, all of which have the same goal: to make a wholesome contribution to alleviating and ending human suffering. However, the most original form of Buddhism enshrines an essential status as a commonly accepted tradition by all schools of Buddhism, making Early Buddhist philosophy a primary model in the development of a theoretical orientation. Therefore, based on the Pāli *Nikāya*s, this book aims to appropriate Early Buddhist teachings in its framework for a theoretical orientation that will support a model of Buddhist counseling.

1.2 Literature Review

Between the years 1960 and 1980, a new technique started to emerge in the research literature on mental health treatment. Scholars such as Richard Davidson and Daniel Goleman (1965, 235) studied the impact of meditation on anxiety and found that this practice can reduce automatic arousal when feeling anxious. Furthermore, Gary Deatherage (1975, 133) was one of the very first researchers to use mindfulness techniques, as based on the *Satipaṭṭhāna-sutta*, on mental health patients. In addition, Daniel Brown and Jack Engler (1980, 143) compared practitioners of different levels of Buddhist meditation on their Rorschach[3] responses, thereby initiating a series of social science investigations of the Buddhist practice of mindfulness by either integrating it into contemporary psychology or comparing it with similar psychological constructs. However, mindfulness studies did not garner much attention in the field until the emergence of Jon Kabat-Zinn.

Using chronic pain as a treatment target, Kabat-Zinn (1982, 34) designed a ten-week stress reduction and relaxation program based on Theravāda Buddhist meditation, Mahāyāna Buddhist meditation, Zen traditions, and Western Yogic practices. In these 10 weeks, participants received instruction on mindfulness and practiced mindfulness meditation and yoga in a group format. The result was surprisingly effective: 50% of participants reported a 50% reduction of pain symptoms after the program. Since then, mindfulness has been a hot topic of research and has given rise to a trend of integrating mindfulness into mental health treatment models.

The following section will briefly review several common MBIs and their theoretical foundations.

Mindfulness-based stress reduction. After his first successful study, Kabat-Zinn coined the term MBSR as an intervention designed to reduce distress and enhance quality of life using mindfulness, a program that yielded significant empirical support for this innovative model of treatment (Kabat-Zinn 2003, 145). It was one of the earliest psychotherapy methods to incorporate Buddhist ideas, demonstrating high efficacy in different clinical studies. The success of MBSR led to a wave of MBIs across the world, with the founder Jon Kabat-Zinn becoming a prominent figure in mindfulness research. In his book on MBSR, *Full Catastrophe Living: Using the Wisdom of Your Body and Mind to Face Stress, Pain, and Illness*, first published in 1990 and revised in 2013, Kabat-Zinn became the first scholar to secularize Buddhist meditation. He described mindfulness as paying attention (2013, 70):

3. Rorschach is a projective psychological assessment tool to measure a number of characteristics, such as personality, cognitive variables, perceptions, and other domains.

> the very word meditation tended to evoke eyebrows and thoughts about mysticism and hocus-pocus in many people. In part, that was because people did not understand that meditation is really about paying attention.

Utilizing the important Buddhist concept of Right Mindfulness while minimizing the position of other Buddhist teachings, the treatment program Kabat-Zinn developed attempts to help clients achieve nonjudgment, awareness, attention, and compassion through the four main mindfulness practices: sitting meditation, walking meditation, hatha yoga, and body scans (Kabat-Zinn 2003, 146). The foundation of MBSR is to cultivate present moment awareness in clients, thereby relaxing the body and mind and providing the potentiality to relate to things differently (Kabat-Zinn 2013, 74). Through MBSR practices, practitioners are expected to foster greater awareness and compassion toward themselves and, consequently, reduce their suffering.

In a meta-analysis on the efficacy of MBSR, Grossman, Niemann, Schmidt, and Walach reviewed twenty studies on MBSR involving 1,605 participants (Grossman, Niemann, Schmidt, and Walach 2004, 35). They found that MBSR can be considered a reliable intervention for a variety of chronic disorders and problems, especially stress management and chronic pain (Grossman, Niemann, Schmidt, and Walach 2004, 43). They found consistently strong effects across different samples, which indicate the benefits of MBSR for coping with distress and disability in everyday life (Grossman, Niemann, Schmidt, and Walach 2004, 39–40).

Researchers such as Ron Pursuer have expressed doubts about MBSR. Some criticism is directed at the practice of secularized mindfulness, extracting it from the Buddhist context (Harrington and Dunne 2015, 622). Even so, the scientific data is highly promising and MBSR can be an effective tool for symptom reduction, especially for the alleviation of chronic pain and stress. We observe that MBSR represents an important step in the application of Buddhist teachings to relieve suffering in thousands of individuals. Another potential success that could not be captured by scientific data is the recognition of Buddhism in the field of mental health. Recognition by the field allows Buddhism to be considered a viable psychotherapeutic means. Instead of criticizing MBSR, our approach is to take it one step further and develop interventions for particular symptoms or disorders; indeed, it could be even more beneficial to develop a comprehensive treatment approach that allows deeper and more transformative changes in clients.

Mindfulness-based cognitive therapy. Cognitive therapy and CBT are arguably the most popular mental health treatments of choice in contemporary society. MBCT, a treatment that combines mindfulness techniques and cognitive therapy, was developed to treat recurrent depression (Segal, Williams, and Teasdale 2002, 44). It aims to teach clients to gain more awareness of their thoughts, emotions, and bodies and to develop improved coping mechanisms by building new relationships between their thoughts and emotions (Segal, Williams, and Teasdale 2002, 45). Again, the notion of mindfulness in MBCT is similar to that of Right Mindfulness (*sammā sati*) in Early Buddhist teachings, since both emphasize becoming more cognizant of one's mind and body. This was proven to be effective in treating recurrent major depressive disorder. Jacob and Hougaard conducted a meta-analysis to evaluate the effectiveness of MBCT on the relapse of major depressive disorder, studying six randomized controlled trials with a total of 593 participants (Jacob and Hougaard 2011, 1032). They concluded that MBCT significantly reduced the risk of relapse, with risk reduction being 43% higher for participants who experienced three or more previous relapses in comparison to control groups. Therefore, MBCT can be seen as at least as effective as antidepressant medication (Jacob and Hougaard 2011, 1033). Furthermore, in a recent meta-analysis, McCartney and his team evaluated 23 studies on MBCT for depression-related symptoms that involved 2,077 participants (McCartney et al. 2021, 6–7). Similarly, they found that MBCT showed statistically significant advantages when compared to conventional treatments for depression relapse (McCartney et al. 2021, 18–19).

We observe that MBCT—with its integration of CBT and mindfulness—is a leap forward in psychotherapy, serving as a role model of how to integrate mindfulness into a mainstream treatment approach. Since the emergence of MBCT, some practitioners of traditional theoretical orientations have integrated mindfulness into their treatment repertoire, including practitioners of the highly traditional approach of psychodynamic therapy (Simone, Barilaro, and Palmieri 2016, 552). At the same time, MBCT also makes use of a traditional theoretical orientation as its base but enriches it by adding the component of mindfulness as a secular tool. The core theoretical origin of CBT is rooted in Stoic philosophy, a Western philosophical tradition that emphasizes the importance of rational thinking and asserts that our thoughts significantly shape our perceptions of reality (Robertson 2020, 71). Mindfulness itself helps foster mental distance from thoughts in order to see the transient nature of mental processes, supplementing the CBT rationale regarding cognitive processes. While this integration has proven to be scientifically sound, it has a Western root, leading some Eastern scholars and mental health professionals to make cultural adaptations when applying MBCT to clients from different cultural backgrounds. Thapaliya et al. conducted a meta-analysis to evaluate research studies of MBIs with Asian participants, which is the only meta-analysis focusing on Asian populations (Thapaliya, Upadhyaya, Borschmann, and Kuppili 2018, 10). One interesting finding was that the positive outcomes may be partly ascribed to cultural adaptations. In fact, a number of studies adopted cultural adaptations to match MBCT with their respective populations (Thapaliya, Upadhyaya, Borschmann, and Kuppili 2018, 16):

> Few studies highlighted the cross-cultural adaptations of the MBIs e.g. by translating the manual into the local language or giving flavor of the local culture, like incorporation of Korean meditation or Iranian poems, incorporation of Tai Chi exercise in China. Some studies slightly modified the standard MBI e.g. exclusion of "Hatha" Yoga for Chinese elderly participants and replacement of home sessions with group mindfulness meditation for Chinese prisoners.

CBT and MBCT are generally compatible with Asian cultures when supplemented with mindfulness, although their Western origin entails a theoretical framework with cultural assumptions and worldviews differing from those in Asian populations. We believe this mismatch is a sign that the best treatments should be rooted in and designed for a particular culture. If this idea is valid, the implication is clear—instead of taking psychotherapeutic models from other cultures and using Buddhist theories and practices to enhance them, the development of a new model founded on Buddhism makes more sense.

Dialectical behavior therapy. Established by Marsha Linehan, DBT is a cognitive-behavioral treatment developed to address parasuicidal behaviors among women with borderline personality disorder (BPD) (Linehan 1993, 4). The core treatment modes of DBT include individual therapy, skills training, client and therapist consultations, and therapist consultation meetings. The aim of DBT is to teach clients to regulate their emotions, improve their interpersonal skills, tolerate distress more effectively, and employ self-management skills. In addition, DBT incorporates the core tenets of Zen Buddhism: mindfulness, nonjudgement, and observation (Linehan 1993, 144). These tenets, which are used to help clients increase their awareness of body, feelings, and thought processes, are similar to the notion of Right Mindfulness in Buddhism (Linehan 1993, 144–45). Acceptance, a crucial component of DBT that encourages therapists to accept clients as they are while teaching them to change and accept themselves, also resonates with the Buddhist practice of observing, accepting, and discerning internal experiences in the present moment (Linehan 1993, 146).

Two meta-analyses of the efficacy of DBT have been carried out. The first, by Panos, Jackson, Hasan, and Panos, evaluated five randomized controlled trials of DBT to specifically evaluate its effectiveness in reducing suicide attempts, parasuicidal behavior, attrition, and symptoms of depression in adult clients suffering from BPD (Panos, Jackson, Hasan, and Panos 2014, 213). Results showed that DBT is a marginally better treatment than traditional ones like CBT. The second meta-analysis by DeCou, Comtois, and Landes evaluated the efficacy of DBT for suicidal behaviors using eighteen clinical trials (DeCou, Comtois, and Landes 2019, 60). They concluded that DBT is effective in reducing self-directed violence and the frequency of crisis hospitalization (DeCou, Comtois, and Landes 2019, 69). In general, DBT is an evidence-based and efficacious treatment for patients suffering from BPD while promising to be particularly effective for reducing suicidal behaviors.

In our observation, DBT is one of the earliest empirically-supported treatment intervention models that acknowledges the integration of certain Buddhist teachings. Furthermore, while DBT is silent about whether the co-opted Buddhist component has been secularized or not, the founder Marsha Linehan does not shy away from making her affiliation with Zen Buddhism public (she is an ordained Zen master).[4] We believe DBT is one of the very few recognized psychotherapy approaches to acknowledge its Buddhist root, even going beyond mindfulness to integrate Mahāyāna principles, such as non-dualism (*advayatā*), in its treatment plan. In contrast to MBSR, DBT is designed for more severe mental illnesses, particularly suicidal behaviors and BPD. The success of DBT provides evidence for the applicability of Buddhism to counseling and psychotherapy practice. However, DBT is specifically aimed at a particular problem and was not designed as a general treatment approach for a variety of psychological disturbances. In this regard, Reddy and Vijay conducted a review of research evidence for the efficacy of DBT and made the following conclusion: "DBT has specific utility in addressing suicide attempts in borderline personality without being generally effective in the overall personality management" (Reddy and Vijay 2017, 107).

Moreover, they also criticized the long-term commitment required by this treatment, the necessity of advanced training for therapists, and the limited research evidence that mainly supported DBT's high effectiveness for managing suicidal behaviors, although the actual benefits may not be significantly better than other treatments of choice. In view of the successful integration of Buddhist components, albeit with limited efficacy, it is reasonable to experiment with a more comprehensive, or even complete, integration of Buddhist teachings, especially the core principles. If Buddhism claims to be a practical method for the cessation of all suffering (Somaratne 2021, 6), a counseling approach based on Buddhism should be able to treat a wider variety of mental health problems.

Acceptance and commitment therapy. Founded by Steven C. Hayes, ACT is a psychotherapy method based on two theoretical frameworks: namely, relational frame theory and functional contextualism (Twohig 2012, 499). Functional contextualism utilizes empirically based concepts and principles to predict and influence behavioral events within their environmental and contextual frameworks. This approach emphasizes understanding the relationship between behavior and context, enabling practitioners to tailor interventions that effectively address specific situations and outcomes (Twohig 2012, 450–499). In its clinical application, functional contextualism sees the purpose of an action as highly

4. Pranada McBurnie, "The Secret Dr. Marsha Linehan Kept for Five Decades," Parvati Magazine, August, 2020, https://parvatimagazine.com/the-secret-dr-marsha-linehan-kept-for-five-decades/.

important in order to successfully intervene in that behavior (Twohig 2012, 500). Relational frame theory proposes that human cognition and communication are developed through our ability to create relational responses to stimuli, such that language and concepts are contextualized with different associations of concepts and trained responses (Twohig 2012, 501). A clinical implication is to decontextualize behaviors from trained responses and relate them to the concepts and language more functionally (Twohig 2012, 500–501).

Based on these two theories, ACT starts from the assumption that psychological problems are rooted in a person's psychological rigidity. The treatment method attempts to increase the client's psychological flexibility, which includes one's ability to implement positive actions when faced with unfavorable emotions or experiences instead of avoiding them (Hayes, Strosahl, and Wilson 1999, 10–11). To enhance one's psychological flexibility, ACT emphasizes six concepts: acceptance, diffusion, self as context (observing self), contact with the present moment, values, and committed action (Hayes, Strosahl, and Wilson 1999, 201–327). The emphasis on contact with the present moment together with the practice of mindfulness classifies ACT as an MBI (Van Gordon and Shonin 2020, 2). Treatment aims to "help clients move forward in valued directions by developing behavior that is sensitive to the current context", that is, by increasing the functionality of each of the six aspects (Webster 2011, 311). Moreover, the six components are not linear in nature but are interrelated to create a fluid model in order to foster psychological flexibility (Webster 2011, 311–12).

Since 1986, there have been more than 250 randomized controlled trials demonstrating the effectiveness of ACT on different clinical problems (Yavuz and Çelik 2019, 360). For example, A-Tjak and his team conducted a meta-analysis on the efficacy of ACT that consisted of thirty-nine randomized controlled trials involving 1,821 patients with mental disorders or somatic health problems (A-Tjak et al. 2015, 30). In their evaluation of these studies, they concluded that ACT is as effective as conventional treatments (e.g. CBT) in treating anxiety disorders, depression, addiction, and somatic health problems. In addition to their comparison of treating symptoms and disorders, they found that ACT has demonstrated higher efficacy in increasing life satisfaction or quality of life (A-Tjak et al. 2015, 33). Promising data from these research studies have made ACT a highly convincing treatment approach in the contemporary field of mental health.

From our observation of MBIs, most models do not incorporate a large amount of theoretical material from Buddhism to sustain their treatment approach; indeed, they usually shy away from adopting core Buddhist teachings such as impermanence (*anicca*), dependent co-arising (*paṭicca samuppāda*), suffering (*dukkha*), and non-self (*anattā*). However, we believe the central assumptions about human nature behind ACT resonate with the Buddhist perspective on the causes of suffering, which is usually explained as rigidly clinging to the delusion of self and craving to satisfy infinite and insatiable personal desires. As we understand them, the six core concepts of ACT are similar to certain concepts in Early Buddhist teachings as follows: acceptance aligns with the idea of accepting current experiences; diffusion aligns with detachment from clinging to a self; the concept that the self is context explicable in relation to the idea of non-self; that personal values align with Buddhist ethics; that contact with the present moment concerns mindfulness; and that committed action aligns with Right Effort as explained in the Eightfold Path. Perhaps due to these similarities, Steven Hayes published an article in which he compared and contrasted ACT and Buddhism. While pinpointing several compatible aspects between the two school of thoughts, he made clear a possible difference in understanding a sense of self: "There may be a point of divergence, however, because while the person is alive, a sense of perspective is not known by that person to change once it emerges (in the preschool period). Indeed, in ACT this sense of self as context is argued to be critical therapeutically because it means that there is at least one stable, unchangeable, immutable fact about oneself that has been experienced directly and is not just a belief or a hope or an idea" (Hayes 2002, 65).

Such a "stable, unchangeable, immutable" sense of self may or may not differ from Buddhist teachings, as Hayes further explained (Hayes 2002, 65):

> I am not sure whether this concept diverges from Buddhist teachings . . . By a transcendent self I do not mean the belief in such a self or the belief in immutability, but the experience of from-here-now and the essential continuity it provides for all verbally known events from the point of view of the knower. The claim is simply that all verbal knowing is known "from here now." That experience is an important sense of the word "I"—namely, that in one important sense 'I' am from-here-now. This sense of perspective is immutable from the point of view of the knowing person. It is not immutable in the sense that it assumes a form that cannot or does not change. It is immutable in the sense that it has no form at all. It has no limits that can be known by the knower, by definition. In that sense, it is not a thing, and only things can change. No thing cannot.

We see this interpretation of sense of self as partially in alignment with the non-self doctrine, which states that a sense of self is a provisional existence that falls under the Law of Dependent Co-arising. His statement also carries an implication of impermanence in that everything—including sense of self—changes. However, he still infers a "stable, unchangeable, immutable" deeper foundation of self, which does not seem to align with the Law of Dependent Co-arising. We interpret his description of self as a deep-seated and immutable consciousness that has malleable features and outer layers. Despite our interpretation and the similarities we observe between ACT and Buddhism, Steven Hayes has denied any theoretical root in Buddhism and connection between the two. In this case, there is a lack of a comprehensive theoretical orientation using the Buddhist teachings as source information.

In reviewing these MBIs and outcome studies, MBIs are no doubt empirically supported as effective treatment programs for an array of psychological symptoms. As previously mentioned, albeit briefly, MBIs have received increasing criticism for their secularization and decontextualization from Buddhist teachings. The following section will describe the criticism in more detail. Such criticisms can be categorized into three domains:

(1) A diluted effect due to decontextualized mindfulness. McWilliams stated that MBIs have tended to utilize a reductionist approach that divorces mindfulness from the spiritual paradigm of Buddhism, which may undermine the essence of the Buddhist teachings themselves (McWilliams 2011, 269). In support of the same viewpoint, Huxter regarded this reductionist approach as a possible limit on effectiveness when he claimed, "It is understandable that many psychologists wish to distance themselves from Buddhism in order to make mindfulness scientifically acceptable, culturally relevant, and not confused with religion. However, separating mindfulness from its spiritual connection could be diluting its psychological effectiveness" (Huxter 2007, 44).

    Similarly, as the first scholar to use the term "McMindfulness," Miles Neale decried the secularization of mindfulness for ignoring the important context of the threefold training and Four Noble Truths of Buddhism (Neale 2011, 1–3). In effect, such titration of Right Mindfulness into a superficial calming technique may not bring lasting changes to clients (Neale 2011, 3). Last but not least, Jessie Sun, one of the earliest scholars to openly criticize MBIs, pointed out that MBIs do not differentiate between Right Mindfulness and Wrong Mindfulness, which can lead to a probable abandonment of the transformative potential of Buddhist mindfulness (Sun 2014, 399).

(2) Risks of practicing mindfulness without the guidance of Buddhist principles. Shonin et al. argued that these psychotherapies may not incorporate the essence of Buddhist principles and theories, and that such MBIs can carry potential risks for clients who use the practices inappropriately (Shonin, Van Gordon, Slade, and Griffiths 2013, 124). They used a highly critical tone when describing the nature of MBIs: "Such comportment and usage of mindfulness amounts to the misappropriation of Buddhist teachings, with damaging consequences for scientific, social scientific and healthcare disciplines, as well as Buddhism more generally . . ." (Van Gordon and Shonin 2020, 2).

To expand their criticisms, researchers identified three potential risks or weaknesses. First, applying mindfulness solely as a relaxation technique may lead practitioners into dullness and hence hinder the progress of meditation (Britton et al. 2014, 64–65). Second, Van Gordon and Shonin (2020) reviewed the development of MBIs and pointed out the risks of practicing mindfulness without the guidance of ethics (Van Gordon and Shonin 2020, 1). In fact, while mindfulness practices can enhance the quality of awareness, they do not naturally result in compassion or morality (Sun 2014, 401). Sun, in her article examining mindfulness in its historical context and up to its contemporary application, asserted that one can easily apply mindfulness when engaging in violent or criminal behaviors. This is illustrated by the US Marine Corps' utilization of mindfulness skills to optimize combat performance (Sun 2014, 402). Third, most mindfulness research has been conducted as quantitative studies, which measured symptom reduction in relation to short-term MBIs (e.g. Spinhoven, Huijbers, Ormel, and Speckens 2017, 112). In other words, little is known about long-term practitioners' experience of a secularized version of mindfulness and possible differences between them and Buddhist practitioners of mindfulness. Moreover, empirical evidence indicates some aversive effects of secularized mindfulness practices. For example, Dobkin, Irving, and Amar conducted a literature review on the attrition and adverse effects of the MBSR program, finding that a number of participants in several studies reported relaxation-induced anxiety, perceived stress, and depression (Dobkin, Irving, and Amar 2012, 44). Finally, some scholars and counselors using contemporary mindfulness may integrate it with different other theories and practices (Thapaliya, Upadhyaya, Borschmann, and Kuppili 2018, 16). Bhikkhu Bodhi (2011), a recognized Buddhist scholar and the president of the Buddhist Publication Society, pointed out the potential danger in integrating theories or techniques from different schools of thoughts, the reason being that the theoretical assumptions of each school can differ. The dissonance created may produce short-term benefits, but is unlikely to result in long-term beneficial effects. This viewpoint implies the importance of matching techniques with their theoretical assumptions in any practice. Therefore, we can conclude that the extraction of either compassion or mindfulness from Buddhism, a holistic religion, may sabotage and reduce their effectiveness, resulting in potential risks.

(3) Potential benefits of the traditional practice of meditation. A traditional Buddhist approach to psychological healing may promote more lasting

positive changes; cultivate a different, keener, wiser kind of attention (Hyland 2015, 220); or provide more interventions that help mental health professionals better address the needs of different clients (Lee et al. 2016, 3). Consequently, experts in both Buddhism and psychology have recommended that practitioners and researchers acquire a foundation in Buddhist teachings and an understanding of the Buddhist rationale for mindfulness in order to deliver effective Buddhist Derived Interventions (BDIs) to clients. For example, Sun is in favor of the current direction of mindfulness movement, describing the movement as "leaving the cultural baggage behind" and letting Buddhism silently benefit more people (Sun 2014, 408–9). She described the development of MBIs as the contemporary interpretation of the *Dhamma* in a culturally and socially accepted manner. However, the secularization of mindfulness should acknowledge the Buddhist teachings behind it; as Sun (2014) stated, "if the Dharma is understood as the nature of reality, or a set of ideas that can be universally applicable, then perhaps it is not something that Buddhists can 'copyright' and be possessive over. Even so, it would only be decent to tread respectfully on such sacred territory, which must require a basic appreciation for the roots of the practice and the meanings it holds" (409).

Echoing this point, Van Gordon and Edo Shonin both observed that the trend of MBIs is moving toward further integration of Buddhist teachings as well as a more authentic application of mindfulness within its Buddhist context (Van Gordon and Shonin 2020, 1–4). They also developed a mindfulness program which is more closely in line with the Threefold Training in Buddhism (Van Gordon and Shonin 2020, 2), a feature which will be discussed in later sections. In fact, the founder of MBSR, Jon Kabat-Zinn, has not proposed a divorce between mindfulness and Buddhism; instead, his attitude seems to be the removal of the "Buddhism" label while disseminating the same message through the teaching of mindfulness. In an article published almost 30 years after the establishment of MBSR, Kabat-Zinn wrote (Kabat-Zinn 2011, 298):

> when we work with people in a medical or psychological setting, using 'stress' and the suggestion that 'stress reduction' might be possible as the core invitational framework, we can dive right into the experience of dukkha in all its manifestations without ever mentioning dukkha; dive right into the ultimate sources of dukkha without ever mentioning the classical etiology, and yet able to investigate craving and clinging first-hand, propose investigating the possibility for alleviating if not extinguishing that distress or suffering (cessation), and explore, empirically, a possible pathway for doing so (the practice of

> mindfulness meditation writ large, inclusive of the ethical stance of sila, the foundation of samadhi, and, of course, prajna, wisdom—the eightfold noble path) without ever having to mention the Four Noble Truths, the Eightfold Noble Path . . . In this fashion, the Dharma can be self-revealing through skillful and ardent cultivation.

According to our interpretation, Kabat-Zinn initiated the secularization of Right Mindfulness as a skillful means to introduce the *Dhamma* to many people. At the same time, his work is permeated with unacknowledged Buddhist teachings in order to avoid cultural or religious resistance. However, the later development of MBIs and their incorporation and adaptation of mindfulness went further by cutting this practice away from its Buddhist roots and principles. While this shift may not have been Kabat-Zinn's original intent, which was to increase the reach of *Dhamma* through a non-religious approach, it has nonetheless led to a broader acceptance of mindfulness.

To summarize this section, William Van Gordon and Edo Shonin's review of the trend of mindfulness development in psychology offers a viable way forward for healing purposes. They categorized the development of MBIs into two generations: first generation mindfulness-based interventions (FG-MBIs) and second-generation mindfulness-based interventions (SG-MBIs) (Van Gordon and Shonin 2020, 1). FG-MBIs refer to mental health treatment interventions that integrate the Buddhist practice of mindfulness as a core component of treatment while they may not include any Buddhist theories, such as MBSR and MBCT (Van Gordon and Shonin 2020, 1–3). In general, the FG-MBIs have several characteristics: (1) being silent about the spiritual or religious aspect or even explicitly claiming to be a secularized approach; (2) employing particular meditative techniques, and; (3) generally divorcing the meditative techniques from a related Buddhist framework, such as the emphasis on ethics (Van Gordon and Shonin 2020, 1). In general, FG-MBIs are the ones which have received the aforementioned criticisms.

William Van Gordon and Edo Shonin also made the observation that a second generation of MBIs developed because they: (1) are explicitly psycho-spiritual or spiritual in nature; (2) integrate a greater range of Buddhist meditative techniques; (3) acknowledge ethics as a key component of the program while attempting to put mindfulness back into the Buddhist context by guiding mindfulness along with other Buddhist teachings such as ethical awareness, impermanence, emptiness/non-self, loving-kindness and compassion meditation; and (4) employ an instructor training program that requires several years of supervised mindfulness practice (Van Gordon and Shonin 2020, 4). However, they only mentioned their development of MAT as one of the SG-MBIs because they did not discuss other specific interventions that can be included in this category. We will now briefly review MAT as an SG-MBI category.

Meditation awareness training. In response to the specific criticism of MBIs applying mindfulness outside of their Buddhist roots, Shonin, Van Gordon, and Griffiths (2014) developed the MAT to incorporate more Buddhist concepts and techniques in various treatments, such as fostering clients' understanding of impermanence and emptiness. MAT is designed to be an eight-week group-based secularized program applying Buddhist principles to foster emotional regulation, ethical awareness, patience, generosity, and compassion in participants. The themes of the eight sessions include introduction to meditation and mindfulness, introduction to impermanence and emptiness, cultivation of joy and equanimity, generosity towards self and others, ethical awareness and patience, revisiting impermanence and emptiness, loving-kindness and compassion, and letting go. With a combination of didactics, assigned self-practice for participants, one-on-one support sessions, and a series of guided meditation, participants gradually learn and practice different meditative skills and techniques. MAT has demonstrated its effectiveness in enhancing emotional regulation ability in higher education students with issues of stress, anxiety, and low mood (Van Gordon 2014); improving levels work-related stress, job satisfaction, psychological distress, and employer-rated job performance (Shonin 2014); and ameliorating fibromyalgia symptomatology and pain perception (Van Gordon 2017, 186).

While MAT successfully integrates more Buddhist principles in its intervention model, we have two comments. First, MAT is a group-based intervention with a specific focus instead of a theoretical orientation. It also allows a practitioner to provide tailor-made treatments to address clients' specific needs. In other words, it is not designed to provide individual psychotherapy or counseling, nor does it provide any theoretical foundation to assess and conceptualize the presenting problems of clients. Second, MAT successfully reintegrated Buddhist components into meditation training while not acknowledging any specific Buddhist lineage or texts. Moreover, MAT chose to use the term "spiritual" to represent the nature of its meditation practice, which may or may not align with Buddhist teachings. For these reasons, we see MAT as an advancement upon FG-MBIs while not seeming to move beyond the general approach of other MBIs.

Based on the classification system proposed by Van Gordon and Shonin, we would interpret the definitions in a slightly different, and perhaps more concise, manner. As interventions integrating secularized mindfulness, FG-MBIs decontextualize Buddhist teachings. Examples of this include MBSR and MBCT. On the other hand, SG-MBIs are interventions that openly adopt Buddhist principles and practices in its model. However, SG-MBIs use a traditional psychological framework or theoretical foundation as the basis of treatment, with DBT and MAT falling into this category. We would now like to propose a third generation of MBIs which have evolved into Buddhist teaching–based interventions (BTBIs). The first scholars to use this term were Bonnie Wu, Venerable Sik Hin Hung, and their team who published an article on the Awareness Training Program (ATP), one of the first BTBIs in the field (Wu et al. 2019, 1280). In their article, they defined BTBIs as an intervention that comprises Buddhist teachings and practices in a way that the characteristics of BTBIs are "textually aligned" and have "coherent theory and praxis" and that can also be scientifically studied (Wu et al. 2019, 1291). In addition, Venerable Sik Hin Hung introduced his intervention model of Dharma therapy, describing it in the following manner (Sik and Yim 2021, 305):

> Dharma therapy is a Buddhist teaching-based therapeutic intervention which utilizes the Buddhist model of ending suffering to help clients to deal with psychological issues.

As a BTBI, Dharma therapy is built on the Buddhist teaching, the Law of Dependent Co-arising, and has given rise to different counseling tools, such as "spiritual oasis," to help clients who are suffering from psychological problems (Sik and Yim 2021, 306–10). In our opinion, the blossoming of such interventions reveal a trend of MBIs evolving towards BTBIs.

Taking the above definition from Venerable Hin Hung and his team, we will now summarize several BTBIs that have received increasing clinical attention and research interest.

Cognitively-based compassion training. Cognitively-based compassion training (CBCT) is a secularized mind training program based on Tibetan Buddhist compassion meditation practices (Negi et al. 2014, 24). The program includes six modules of meditative practices and contemplative exercises including attentional stability and clarity, insight into the nature of mental experience, self-compassion, cultivating impartiality, appreciation and affection, and empathic concern and engaged compassion with two meditation strategies: (1) stabilizing meditation and (2) analytical meditation (Ash et al. 2019). Moreover, the program emphasizes fostering participants' skills across three levels: content knowledge, personal insight, and embodied understanding. CBCT has shown strong efficacy for various psychological disturbances. For example, CBCT was found to increase hopefulness and decrease generalized anxiety in at-risk adolescents (Reddy 2013, 219), reduce psychological stress in infants and young children (Poehlmann-Tynan 2020, 126), and reduce depressive symptoms and increase self-compassion for African-American suicide attempters (Sun 2019).

In our observation, CBCT is the BTBI that has gained by far the most empirical support. Although it is a secularized intervention and not a full-blown model that allows a practitioner to assess, conceptualize, and intervene in the specific problems of clients, it clearly has identifiable Buddhist roots and a theoretical foundation. We believe CBCT is one of the first to go beyond MBIs and explicitly and skillfully integrate core Buddhist teachings into its intervention model.

Awareness training program. Based on Mahāyāna Buddhist teachings, the ATP is the first group-based program to foster wisdom and compassion in participants (Wu et al. 2019, 1293). Using the *Sandhinirmocana-sūtra* as its theoretical foundation, the ATP helps to release participants from their delusionary attachment to the concept of self through the development of tranquility and observation. In six three-hour workshops and two whole-day weekend retreats, participants learn and memorize the mantra "*Oṃ maṇi padme hūṃ*," attend lectures, engage in meditation practices, and make use of experiential and reflective learning activities as well as group discussions to actualize the meaning of the mantra (Wu et al. 2019, 1294). Results have so far shown that participants reported a reduction in stress and an improvement in sense of coherence and psychological well-being (Wu et al. 2019, 1296). Nevertheless, unlike CBCT and MAT, which have already been developed over a few years, the ATP is a brand new development and the founders have only published one article to date indicating its effectiveness.

We see two important features of ATP that make it stand out from other intervention models. ATP may be the first empirically supported intervention that acknowledges its theoretical foundation in a particular *sutta*. Moreover, the content of the workshop involves the traditional learning, contemplation, and practice of Chinese Buddhism, such as reciting "*Oṃ maṇi padme hūṃ*." Such practices show that ATP is not a secularized intervention.

Dharma therapy. Venerable Sik Hin Hung (2010, 353) developed a counseling model named as Dharma therapy based on Early Buddhist teachings. Following the Buddha's path to liberation, Dharma therapy provides an individual approach involving a seven-step model to help clients eliminate suffering (Sik and Yim 2021, 306–7). These steps are as follows:

1. Introduction and preparation session.
2. Become aware of suffering and the unsatisfactory conditions of the current situation.
3. Develop a desire to be liberated from suffering.
4. Question and investigate the cause of suffering.
5. Observe and learn by paying careful attention to suffering and the cause of suffering.
6. Develop insight and wisdom on how to bring an end to suffering and the cause of suffering.
7. With insight and wisdom, take the necessary steps to bring an end to suffering.

Although the founder, Venerable Hin Hung, has not yet published any clinical trial data using this model, Jennifer Yim, the director of the first Buddhist counseling center in the history of Hong Kong (Tsz Shan Monastery Buddhist Spiritual

Counselling Centre), has started using this model for mental health treatment and has reported highly satisfactory outcomes in a public presentation.[5]

In our understanding, Dharma therapy is the first theoretical orientation based on Buddhist teachings that uses a comprehensive theoretical framework to assess, conceptualize, and intervene in the specific problems of clients. The emergence of Dharma therapy may signify a new trend of using Buddhism as a full treatment model instead of specific interventions for particular problems or group-based interventions. However, there needs to be empirical studies to evaluate its efficacy.

Note, Know, Choose. One of this book's authors has developed a Buddhist counseling model using Early Buddhist teachings as a theoretical orientation. Based on the Early Buddhist Cognitive model discussed in the *Madhupiṇḍika-sutta*, the Note, Know, Choose approach reflects the essence of mental processes and provides the main ingredients for therapeutic change in action terms (Lee and Ong 2019, 327–28). In contrast to many psychotherapies or counseling models, Note, Know, Choose is a flexible framework that can include a range of mental activities, from a moment of mindfulness to a comprehensive treatment process (Lee and Tang 2021). The Note, Know, Choose model uses an iterative three-phase process with interventions that (a) Note: raise clients' ability to concentrate, (b) Know: increase clients' insight into the causes of their suffering, and (c) Choose: reveal ways to reduce suffering and strengthen clients' ability to make better decisions at every moment. It is designed as a complete model that allows practitioners to assess, conceptualize, and intervene in a client's specific suffering using a Buddhist framework (Lee 2022, 38–41).

Although Note, Know, Choose is a full-blown psychotherapeutic treatment model and has received some recognition as a "Buddhist psychotherapy" model along with its counterpart, Dharma therapy (Kelly 2023, 72), there have not been published empirical studies to evaluate the efficacy of Note, Know, Choose. We see this as a major weakness, so studies should be conducted to evaluate this model.

Four Noble Truths based problem solving model. Uthayaratana, Tanaphong, Nattasuda Taephant, and Kullaya Pisitsungkagarn (2019, 119) proposed a Four Noble Truths based problem solving (FNTBPS) model based on Theravāda Buddhism. Applying Buddhist concepts to the Western framework of problem solving, FNTBPS aims to help clients increase their understanding of their current psychological suffering and interventions to liberate form such suffering with a focus on the Four Noble Truths. The distinguishing feature of

5. Yim, Jennifer. "Dharma Therapy: Buddhist Spiritual Counselling: a healing journey from suffering to happiness" (Powerpoint Presentation, MaMa Charitable Foundation Symposium: Buddhist Counselling Instigating Insight into the Healing Process, Hong Kong, China, December 8 and 9, 2018).

FNTBPS, aside from mindfulness practices, is observation and investigation into how craving, clinging, and ignorance contribute to the current state of suffering. However, there have not been any case discussions or empirical studies to examine its effectiveness so far.

Dhamma therapy. Not to be confused with Dharma therapy, Wasantha Priyadarshana developed a Buddhist psychotherapy model based on Pāli literature, Theravāda Buddhist resources, and Ayurvedic medical therapy for mental illness (Priyadarshana 2017, 35). Employing psychological terms such as psychopathology, mental disorders, therapist, and treatments, Priyadarshana proposed Buddhist answers to these categories in order to guide treatment progress primarily based on meditation. In particular, he proposed the application of *sīla* (morality) for behavioral modification, the fostering of *samādhi* (concentration) to control behavioral and emotional problems, and *vipassanā* (insight) meditation to treat every kind of human predicament (Priyadarshana 2017, 38–40). However, as with FNTBPS, there have yet to be any case discussions or empirical studies to examine its effectiveness.

Both FNTBPS and Dhamma therapy present clear examples of the development of a theoretical foundation in its use of Buddhist teachings and practices. However, we believe the present lack of information about FNTBPS and Dhamma therapy make it difficult to evaluate the quality of its theoretical framework as well as its empirical efficacy. More scientific studies are therefore needed to evaluate these interventions.

The Rise of Buddhist Counseling

In the literature review and in our previous publications on this topic (Lee and Ong, 2019; Lee, 2019; Lee and Oh, 2018; Lee, 2018; Lee et al., 2017), the field of professional psychology has generally acknowledged potential shortcomings of MBIs while showing a growing interest in further integrating Buddhism into psychology, with some psychologists even taking Buddhism as the core guiding principle for a new treatment approach. Indeed, Buddhism could become a standalone theoretical orientation for counseling instead of being just one component of a treatment model. With its epistemological assumptions about human nature, psychopathology, healthy ideals, and relevant curative factors, Buddhism offers a comprehensive system of psychology to understand the human mind and associated behaviors. Due to this belief, some scholars such as de Silva (2014, 9), Srichannil and Prior (2014, 243), Jonutytė (2020, 261), Rungreangkulkij, Somporn, and Wiwat Wongtakee (2008, 127), and one of this book's authors has called for the founding of a new field called "Buddhist counseling."

Several scholars have already attempted to develop their own definition and parameters for this field to varying degrees. According to Srichannil and Prior

(2014, 244), scholars in counseling and applied psychology, Buddhist counseling is defined as a counseling process that is based on Buddhist teachings. The key element in this definition pinpoints the importance of its theoretical foundation for the practice of counseling instead of merely offering interventions or techniques. Rungreangkulkij and Wongtakee (2008, 127) applied Buddhist mindfulness training in their treatment of anxiety symptoms, yielding positive results. Although they called their intervention "Buddhist counseling," they did not articulate a definition of this term or describe their intervention as a complete model of treatment. Instead, they emphasized that Buddhist counseling has a strong focus on the "mindfulness practice" of meditation instead of using meditation as an isolated relaxation technique. This emphasis implied the importance of using mindfulness within the context of Buddhist teaching. Similarly, Padmasiri De Silva has discussed Buddhist psychotherapy and counseling extensively, comparing it with traditional Western psychology in his pivotal book, *An Introduction to Buddhist Psychology and Counselling: Pathways of Mindfulness-Based Therapies* (De Silva 2014). Nevertheless, despite thorough discussion in this book, he did not define explicitly what Buddhist psychotherapy or Buddhist counseling actually are.

What Is Buddhist Counseling?

The definition of Buddhist counseling used in this work is comprehensive in nature. One of the benefits of this all-encompassing approach is that practitioners and scholars in Buddhist counseling can integrate their own interpretations of Buddhism into their treatment model, such as developing a Zen or Tibetan Buddhist approach to counseling.

In a conceptual paper written by this book's first author and his research team (Lee et al. 2017, 1), Buddhist counseling is defined as a process of reducing suffering in individuals using wisdom and interventions from Buddhism, which aims to train the human mind to attain a state of equanimity, joy, and liberation. In a later publication by the same author, Buddhist counseling is defined as "a holistic counseling approach that helps clients use each therapeutic encounter to open a gateway to cultivating the mind for the purpose of gaining understanding of human nature in accord with the Buddhist view of reality" (Lee and Tang, 2021, 2). From these working definitions, it seems that "Buddhist counseling" is an integrative term that applies Buddhist teachings to the framework of professional counseling, thereby providing a contemporary psychological method to reduce suffering in others.

To resolve the question of defining Buddhist counseling, it would be useful to go back to the origin of the concept of counseling. Counseling is a western construct rooted in psychoanalysis, also known as "talk therapy" as developed by Sigmund Freud (Paris 2013, 99). In the early 1900s, counseling emerged as a form of advice and information-giving in school and hospital settings. After more than a hundred years of development and diversification, counseling has become a popular choice for treating socioemotional problems (Crago 2000, 73). Given its origins in psychoanalysis, counseling usually involves the development of a counselor-client relationship, helping clients accept and express their feelings, and providing guidance to help clients to cope with and solve problems (Crago 2000, 74–76). In such a situation, the role of the counselor is to build a safe, somewhat egalitarian environment that is also defined by professional boundaries. One of the largest and most recognized institutions of counseling, the American Counseling Association, has provided the following definition: "Counseling is a professional relationship that empowers diverse individuals, families, and groups to accomplish mental health, wellness, education, and career goals" (American Counseling Association 2014, 1). On top of this standardized definition, and throughout the development of psychotherapy, many different theories and practices have emerged as new ways to conceptualize and treat mental illnesses or empower clients in their particular situations. Depending on the theoretical orientation and personality of the counselor, they may use the counseling process to help clients search for meaning in life, resolve childhood conflicts, develop more realistic and helpful ways of thinking, or provide other ways of helping (Poznanski and McLennan 2003, 223). Moreover, while the terms "counseling" and "psychotherapy" are often used in a loosely interchangeable manner, counseling is usually targeted toward less severe psychological problems than psychotherapy (Crago, 2000, 73). In sum, counseling is a framework signified by a professional counseling relationship in which counselors employ a variety of microskills (e.g., paraphrasing, active listening, summarizing, etc.) to reach certain goals while the content and approaches can vary across counselors and their theoretical orientations.

Buddhism has a long history of providing psychological help to individuals across the world, but it has a different cultural nuance when compared to Western models of counseling. Instead of empowering suffering individuals through a professional relationship, Buddhist helpers are usually Buddhist or meditation teachers and monastic members who guide suffering individuals to practice the Buddhist path (Lee et al. 2017, 2). As a result, many individuals who sought guidance from Buddhist helpers have become their students and formed spiritual and therapeutic relationships with them. To reduce suffering, the students usually engage in personal practices while also cultivating relationships and regularly seeking advice and guidance. In other words, the teacher-student relationship is somewhat different from a counselor-client relationship. For example, a counselor-client relationship is a professional relationship with several features, including a client-centered approach with the client's benefit as the top priority;

a specifically goal-oriented relationship to address presenting problems in the client; a limited number of planned sessions; and ethical principles to protect the client (Nupponen 1998, 62–65). However, a teacher-student or a master-disciple relationship is usually not considered a professional relationship, does not have to be goal oriented, does not have a requirement to treat students' or disciples' benefit as the top priority, and may not have dedicated ethical principles to protect students or disciples. Furthermore, traditional Buddhist culture requires students to pay homage to and take care of one's master as much as they can, such as preparing food for the teacher and bowing to them on a daily basis (Mookerji 1989, 543). Therefore, using Buddhism as a counseling framework is a very novel endeavor.

In our perspective, counseling is a culturally accepted mode of healing in contemporary society, with such a framework being used by different theoretical orientations. Since the emergence of mindfulness in professional psychology, the field of mental health has gradually moved towards integrating Buddhism into existing models of counseling and psychotherapy over the last 30 years. The forefront of this trend is to move beyond integration by developing treatment models employing Buddhist teachings as their core theoretical foundation for counseling. As the metaphor "old wine in new bottles" implies, the aim of this book is to take the bottle as the basic framework of counseling while substituting the wine with the tea of the Buddhist *Dhamma*. In other words, Buddhist counseling can be considered as "new tea in an old bottle", integrating the contents of *Buddhadhamma* within the structure of Western-based counseling. The next section will discuss three aspects of Buddhist counseling in order to establish a foundation for later discussion.

Who Are Buddhist Counselors?

Another important assumption to address is the identity of a Buddhist counselor. Although the literature suggests that mental health professionals have utilized mindfulness and other Buddhist practices their work, there is no official term to describe such individuals yet. One obvious reason for such a limitation is because the field of Buddhist counseling is still in its infancy. In response, this book proposes one key criterion to signify the status of a Buddhist counselor: recognizable training in the professional practice of Buddhist counseling. Based on this assumption, two types of individuals can be categorized as "Buddhist counselors."

First, mental health professionals who practice a Buddhist counseling approach as their primary theoretical orientation may be referred to as Buddhist counselors. Essentially, this is similar to how practitioners of CBT can be referred to as CBT therapists, and practitioners of psychoanalysis can be referred to as psychoanalysts, as long as such mental health professionals have completed the required training and reached an expected competency in their chosen approach. In other words, qualified professionals who have received training in Buddhist counseling can be regarded as Buddhist counselors and are therefore competent to practice a Buddhist counseling approach. However, their previous professional training can be gained in various fields including counseling, social work, clinical psychology, counseling psychology, educational psychology, marriage and family therapy, or other related disciplines in mental health.

Second, individuals who have completed their professional training in Buddhist counseling can be referred to as Buddhist counselors. For example, the Centre of Buddhist Studies of the University of Hong Kong offers a Master of Buddhist Counselling program (MBC) as well as a Postgraduate Diploma in Professional Practice of Buddhist Counselling (PDBC) in collaboration with HKU SPACE. The successful completion of both programs qualifies an individual to practice Buddhist counseling and hence these individuals can be referred to as "Buddhist counselors." Moreover, graduates of comparable professional training programs may also fall into the category of Buddhist counselors.

Who Are Not Buddhist Counselors?

While Buddhist counseling is rooted in Buddhism, several related subject areas must also be considered, as these disciplines have unique features setting them apart from Buddhist counseling. First and foremost, a core question is whether the service of Buddhist chaplaincy can be considered as Buddhist counseling. Although Buddhist chaplains can be monastic members or laypeople, they are all trained professionals who can use an interfaith approach while also focusing on a particular Buddhist tradition (Lee 2022, 57–58). In the US, several recognized chaplaincy-training programs exist, such as at the Harvard School of Divinity[6], the University of the West,[7] Naropa University[8], and Emmanuel College of the University of Toronto [9]. In these programs, students receive rigorous training in contemplative practices, enhancing their capacity to provide spiritual services in usually non-religious settings (e.g., hospitals, hospice, correctional facilities, military units, etc.). In Asian countries such as Taiwan and Japan, Buddhist chaplains primarily provide spiritual care in palliative care using a faith-inspired

---

6. "Master of Divinity (MDiv) Program," Harvard University. Accessed January 21, 2023, https://hds.harvard.edu/academics/degree-programs/mdiv-program.
7. "Master of Divinity in Buddhist Chaplaincy," University of the West. Accessed January 21, 2023, https://www.uwest.edu/master-of-divinity-in-buddhist-chaplaincy-graduate-program/.
8. "Master of Divinity (MDiv) Divinity," Naropa University. Accessed January 21, 2023, https://www.naropa.edu/programs/graduate-academics/divinity/#:~:text=If%20you've%20been%20searching,of%20spiritual%20and%20religious%20backgrounds.
9. "Master of Pastoral Studies," University of Toronto. Accessed January 21, 2023, https://www.emmanuel.utoronto.ca/current-students/academics/master-of-pastoral-studies/.

worldview to help patients accept the dying process and cope with the fear of death (Chen 2014, 117). The roles of Buddhist counselors and Buddhist chaplains overlap in that they both provide care for clients or patients by utilizing certain interpretations of Buddhist teachings in their practice. However, there are several noticeable differences. First, most of the training in Buddhist chaplaincy has an interfaith component and provides basic knowledge and training in many world religions, even though such instruction may not be essential in the professional training of Buddhist counselors (Gauthier 2016, 33). Second, Buddhist chaplains provide spiritual care to address individuals' spiritual needs based on the *Buddha-dhamma* instead of providing counseling. For example, Buddhist chaplaincy training programs in America generally provide training to provide Buddhist services and rituals, such as officiating Buddhist wedding ceremonies and conducting funerary rites (Sanford and Michon 2019), although such services are not an expected or appropriate practice for Buddhist counselors according to the traditional counseling framework. Third, Buddhist chaplains usually work in field settings, such as hospitals and hospices, while Buddhist counselors work in more traditional counseling settings, including counseling centers and schools. In essence, while Buddhist chaplains can and do use skills and techniques from Buddhist counseling, the nature of such spiritual care and counseling is the key distinction between the two professions.

Moreover, Buddhist teachers or spiritual guides who do not have professional training in Buddhist counseling do not fall into the category of Buddhist counselors. Buddhist counselors do not preach the *Dhamma,* nor do they have a pastoral role; instead, Buddhist counselors are counselors who focus on listening and understanding clients and then using different skills to help them achieve liberation from their particular suffering (which will be discussed further in later chapters). In this process, the teaching of Buddhism can be a part of the counseling process, albeit in a parallel fashion, like the provision of psychoeducation in CBT. However, the "teaching" needs to be carried out skillfully and flexibly to address the specific needs of clients, and such "teaching" should not involve imposing values on clients or converting them to Buddhism. One final implication is that both monastic members and lay people can receive training to become Buddhist counselors according to the definition given in this book.

Potential Limitations to Buddhist Counseling

One common question regarding theoretical orientation is whether it is comprehensive enough to understand, explain, and treat severe mental health disorders, including psychotic disorders, bipolar disorders, borderline personality disorders, and other more complicated clinical conditions. On one hand, it would be safe to assume that Buddhist counseling is designed for mild to moderate mental health disturbances, while clients who have lost touch with reality (for example, clients suffering from delusions and hallucinations) may not benefit as much through Buddhist counseling because the understanding of Buddhist teachings and the capacity to practice them requires a certain clarity and stability of mind. On the other hand, one may argue that the Buddha claims that Buddhist training can end all forms of suffering. For example, the Buddha stated in the *Pahārāda-sutta* (AN 8.19): "Just as the great ocean has but one taste, the taste of salt, so too, this Dhamma and discipline has but one taste, the taste of liberation" (Bodhi 2012, 1144).[10]

On this ground alone, it sounds reasonable to claim that a counseling model based on Early Buddhist teachings may not limit the successful treatment of any type of suffering or mental illness. On this basis, it can be argued that Buddhist counseling should be theoretically applicable to a range of mental health issues. Because, after all, Buddhist counseling is none other than utilizing the *Buddha-dhamma* in a in a specific context of counseling services which are designed for people suffering from a variety of problems.

This book does not aim to find answers to the question of whether Buddhist counseling is incapable of treating individuals suffering from severe mental illnesses. Instead, we believe it is more important to begin exploring its application for various individuals and to adapt the Buddhist counseling approach as we address different mental health disorders. For example, mindfulness emerged as a stress reduction technique, while recent studies have shown the efficacy of mindfulness in alleviating symptoms of psychosis in different patient groups (Böge 2021, 134) which is a far more complex mental health disturbance than stress. With reference to the developmental trajectory of mindfulness, Buddhist counseling, as defined in this book, is applicable to moderate and mild mental health disturbances, while it is important for further studies to evaluate the efficacy of Buddhist counseling approaches for more severe mental health disturbances.

1.3 Statement of the Problem

An examination of research into Buddhist counseling thus far reveals several gaps in the current application of Buddhism to counseling. First, regardless of the advancement in MBIs, almost all of the current models emphasize applied techniques and skills based on Buddhist teachings. But to date, no model has discussed what a Buddhist theoretical orientation in counseling would look like. It is of no small concern that practitioners who employ Buddhist-inspired interventions may not have a sufficiently rigorous framework to conceptualize and understand their

10. AN IV, 203: *Seyyathā pi Pahārāda mahāsamuddo ekaraso loṇaraso, evam eva kho Pahārada ayam dhammavinayo ekaraso vimuttiraso.*

clients' presenting problems, thereby limiting the efficacy of theory-driven practices. Second, the trend of integrating relevant Buddhist teachings amongst mental health practitioners indicates strong interest in learning Buddhism. As Shonin and Van Gordon pointed out, the trend of MBIs is moving towards a more comprehensive integration of Buddhist teachings into mental health treatment models (Shonin and Van Gordon 2019, 1–2). So far, only a few treatment models are able to do this (e.g., MAT and CBCT). Furthermore, many important indicators of successful counseling outcomes in existing treatment models, such as human development and ideal mental health, have not received attention in Buddhist counseling or MBI models. Without a more comprehensive understanding of Buddhist principles regarding human cognition, behaviors, and other domains, mental health practitioners may not have enough guidance and references to understand the multiple dimensions of suffering in their clients. Lastly, different schools of Buddhism have given rise to disparate treatment models. For example, CBCT grew out of Tibetan Buddhism, ATP originated from Mahāyāna Buddhism, and DBT integrates the essence of Zen Buddhism, and Dharma therapy adopts Early Buddhism. Among all the approaches, Dhamma therapy is the only one that claims to be based on Early Buddhist teachings (Sik 2010, 353–54). Regarding this latter point, while many later schools, traditions, and interpretations of Buddhist teachings are well received by Buddhist and psychological communities, we see Early Buddhist teachings, which contain the pre-sectarian materials documented in the Pāli *Nikāya*s, Chinese *Āgama*s, and *Gandhāran* manuscripts, as the most accepted source for all Buddhist schools and lineages. Therefore, we argue that using Early Buddhist texts as primary sources of information can probably maximize the acceptability of a Buddhist theoretical model of counseling. As a result, this book project proposes a theoretical orientation model for counseling as based on our understanding of the Early Buddhist teachings and insights of the Buddha documented in the Pāli *Nikāya*s.

1.4 Research Questions

Despite the blossoming of MBIs, which are primarily group-based intervention tools, little is known about the applicability of Early Buddhist teachings to the development of a theoretical framework in counseling, and in particular how they allow counselors to conduct assessment, conceptualization, and specific interventions tailor-made for a client's unique background and presenting problems. Therefore, the major research questions in this book are as follows:

Primary research question:

What would a theoretical orientation for counseling based on Early Buddhist teachings look like?

In our view, a theoretical orientation is a comprehensive treatment model which integrates a theory and transforms it into practical tools for counseling, thereby allowing a counselor to assess, conceptualize, and intervene presenting problems in a client. More will be discussed in Chapter 2.

Secondary research questions:

(1) What is a theoretical orientation in professional counseling?
(2) Why is it important to develop a theoretical orientation based on Early Buddhist teachings?
(3) What are the characteristics and dimensions of a practical theoretical orientation based on Early Buddhist teachings for counseling?

The significance of this investigation may offer new insights into the application of relevant Early Buddhist teachings in mental health treatments, providing a theoretical orientation for numerous mental health professionals, while also describing a culturally-congruent treatment approach for millions of potential clients who are open to such Buddhist teachings.

1.5 Methodology

This book is an interdisciplinary study using the respected Pāli *Nikāya*s (PTS edition) as the main source of information. Occasionally, we also consulted *Abhidhamma* texts, such as the *Vibhaṅga*, *Dhammasaṅginī*, and Pāli commentaries. It should be mentioned that there are several English translations available for the *Nikāya*s, all of which were consulted. We felt that the translated works of Bhikkhu Bodhi were simple to understand and provided a standardized model of translation. Almost all of the translations used in this book are his translations; for the most part, we found no need to change his translations and quoted them directly, with several minor exceptions. In cases where Bhikkhu Bodhi's translation was not available for certain texts, or other translations were better, we utilized them in the same way that we utilized Bodhi's works. These include translations from Bhikkhu Thanissaro, Maurice Walshe, G. A. Somaratne, and Bhikkhu Anālayo. There were also instances where we believed the ideas in the Pāli passages could be conveyed in a clearer way, in which case we used our own translations. It should be emphasized that we took care in utilizing other translations, making sure that they were scrutinized well before being quoted.

It is important to note that the nature of an interdisciplinary study is different from that of a textual study. Instead of trying to study and interpret Buddhist scriptures, this project aims to establish a new field for future researchers to apply Early Buddhist teachings as a theoretical orientation for counseling. Based on this goal, the study takes several steps. First, theoretical orientations are commonly used as technical constructs to describe professional counseling models based on a particular theory, or a combination of theories. Regardless of long-term usage in the field, the definition and components of a theoretical orientation are not standardized. Thus, the primary step is to examine what is and what constitutes a theoretical orientation. We explore the different ways scholars have attempted to define and describe a theoretical orientation in counseling. Second, using the framework identified in the first step, we will review, examine, and apply Early Buddhist teachings in an attempt to develop a cogent theoretical orientation of Buddhist counseling. In particular, we take each dimension of a theoretical orientation, such as human nature, causes of psychopathology, and therapeutic interventions, and suggest appropriate Early Buddhist teachings to be integrated as the core materials for that dimension. For example, we propose that the Early Buddhist assumption of causes of suffering can fit into the dimension of psychopathology. The discussion introduces the nature of the dimension, explores the relevant Buddhist Teachings, and proposes a way to interpret and integrate such Buddhist teachings into the dimension. This theoretical orientation allows counselors to conduct assessment to collect important information of clients, use conceptualization to make sense of the client's causes of suffering, and use an appropriate intervention to liberate the client from their immediate suffering. The scope of Early Buddhist teachings primarily includes the Pāli *Nikāya*s as a primary source. Secondary sources such as academic books and peer-reviewed journals articles related to Early Buddhist teachings, Buddhist counseling, theoretical orientation, and relevant topics were also employed. The data collected from the primary sources and the secondary sources were critically, analytically, and comparatively examined, with scholarly opinions and suggestions used to adapt Early Buddhist teachings into a theoretical orientation for counseling.

The process of integration has three steps. First, we review the foundational Early Buddhist teachings from the *sutta*s, such as the Four Noble Truths, the Law of Dependent Co-arising, the five aggregates etc. Second, we decide on appropriate materials to be integrated in each specific dimension of a theoretical orientation based on the first author's training as a US licensed clinical psychologist with over ten years of professional experience, as a California Board of Psychology recognized clinical supervisor, as well as an academician in psychology. Third, in each chapter covering a specific dimension of the theoretical orientation, the authors (1) introduce the selected key concepts in Early Buddhist teachings for the particular dimension of the orientation using psychological nomenclature, (2) discuss the selected concepts in Early Buddhist teachings in the lens of traditional counseling and psychology perspectives and then drawing insights to inform practical integration for clients in contemporary society, and (3) propose potential applications to Buddhist counseling and related considerations with discussions on ways to apply an integrated approach in counseling settings. In essence, the integration will illustrate the use of Early Buddhist teachings as a conceptual guide for a counselor's personal cultivation, assessment of the client's progression in mind cultivation, conceptualization of the causes of suffering, and the interventions to liberate the client from suffering.

1.6 Scope of the Study

The focus of this book project can be clarified according to five considerations. First, the term "Early Buddhist teachings" refers to the Buddha's teachings as documented in the Pāli *Nikāyas*, which are adopted as core theoretical materials to craft our approach to professional counseling. In other words, Buddhist teachings are appropriated to fit the needs of the development of a contemporary counseling framework using technical language from psychology.

Second, this contemporary development of a theoretical orientation makes use of the Early Buddhist teachings as its source information instead of other schools or lineages. We acknowledge the psychological insights, values, and applicability of many other Buddhist traditions, such as Chinese Buddhism, Zen Buddhism, Tibetan Buddhism; Theravāda tradition based on different cultural background, such as Thai tradition and Sri Lankan tradition; and different philosophical schools, such as Sarvāstivāda, Sautrāntika, and Yogācāra. Nevertheless, such diverse Buddhist schools, traditions, and interpretations since the time of the historical Buddha arefar too broad for this study. In response, our solution is to develop a model potentially acceptable to most of the schools and lineages by using the earliest teachings of the historical Buddha as documented in the Pāli *Nikāyas*. From our perspective, since Early Buddhist teachings provide a common foundation, it should be least contradictory with other traditions, thereby potentially increasing its applicability for most other traditions and lineages.

Third, this book only focuses on the conceptual development of a theoretical orientation, while the scientific workability of the model is outside the scope of this book. To narrow its scope, we focus on developing a theoretical model in congruence with Early Buddhist teachings. Further research, both in the humanities and the social sciences, is necessary to examine the practicality of the proposed theoretical orientation. Specifically, we recommend future evaluative studies of this new model in case conceptualizations and case studies.

Fourth, Buddhist counseling does not equate to Buddhist teachings or Buddhist practices for several reasons. The counseling of clients is drastically different in terms of motivation when compared with Buddhist practitioners who practice Buddhism to reach the point of enlightenment and personal emancipation from suffering. When the Buddha disseminated his teachings, he aimed to teach the direct path to liberation and a complete cessation of suffering (Somaratne 2021, 320). In contrast, most clients in counseling are concerned with their immediate and specific suffering and hope to receive guidance on dealing with such difficult experiences. In particular, most clients come to counseling seeking help for certain mental disorders, emotional disturbances, relational problems, work stress, loss, or other challenges in life, and may not want to stay in counseling when their problems are solved. Counseling is different from teaching because clients may not be ready to renounce and fully commit to diligent practice that leads to the complete liberation of suffering. For this reason, Buddhist counseling may aim for liberation (*vimutti*) from the specific suffering motivating clients to seek treatment (i.e., the mental health problems).

Most clients are more comparable to the householders portrayed in the scriptures that hope to live a mundanely happy and functional life. Indeed, two key considerations in counseling are to meet clients in their present state of awareness and to respect their needs and goals. It may not be reasonable for clients or Buddhist counselors to expect Buddhist counseling to be a path to ultimate and full liberation. However, Buddhist counseling can still be an effective way to help clients with the primary task, which is to be liberated from their primary concerns and psychological disturbances using Buddhist means. Clients who are interested in moving forward on the path for further mental cultivation, leading to ultimate liberation from suffering (*dukkha*) as taught in Buddhism, can seek advanced guidance from Buddhist counselors or other Buddhist teachers. Based on these two reasons, this book develops a counseling model involving a gradual path. The *Pahārāda-sutta* stated, "Just as, *Pahārāda*, the great ocean slants, slopes, and inclines gradually, not dropping off abruptly, so too, in this *Dhamma* and discipline penetration to final knowledge occurs by gradual training, gradual activity, and gradual practice, not abruptly" (Bodhi 2012, 1142).

In this gradual process, the Buddhist counselor patiently and compassionately walks with a client step-by-step on the Buddhist path by gradually understanding their suffering, guiding their practice, and fostering insights into the causes and cessation of their specific suffering. This approach may take the client's advancements as a goal in itself instead of aiming for complete liberation from suffering. Clients are free to either end counseling or commit to a spiritual path at any time according to their will. Spiritual guidance towards liberation is outside the scope of this book, however; rather, the goal is to develop an academic counseling model.

Last but not least, this model should be suitable for both Buddhists and non-Buddhists. The historical Buddha taught the *Dhamma* out of compassion to all beings. Based on this aim, the theoretical model based on Early Buddhist teachings should be available to people of different faiths and religious affiliations who are nevertheless open to Buddhist Teachings. Specifically, counselors using this orientation should neither preach Buddhism as a minister nor teach Buddhist doctrine as an instructor; instead, they should respect clients' diverse religious and cultural backgrounds and tailor-make the approach to address clients' specific causes of suffering in the present moment. In other words, the theoretical orientation is non-faith based in nature in that it does not require conversion to Buddhism. The aim is to understand the human condition based on what the historical Buddha taught, such as teaching the deconstruction of greed, hatred, and delusion, the extinction of craving, and skillful means. However, counselors who use this model should be required to embody the necessary Buddhist teachings, apply them using counseling skills, and flexibly use techniques and interventions to reduce clients' suffering in personal interactions.

1.7 Significance of the Study

It is important to emphasize that the Buddhist concepts in this book may seem too introductory for Buddhist scholars because it is an interdisciplinary work written for mental health professionals who may not have a fundamental knowledge of Buddhist studies. The content of this book lays a strong enough foundation for readers to learn Buddhism as a beginner. For the same reason, this book does not break any new ground in the textual or traditional field of Buddhist studies; instead, it is one of the very first efforts to integrate Early Buddhist teachings into a theoretical orientation to support the practice of mental health professionals. In other words, the significance of this study is to provide a theory-driven framework for mental health professionals to practice Buddhist counseling.

Academically, this book makes contributions in three domains. First, since the emergence of psychoanalysis as the first model of treatment, almost all prominent theoretical orientations are based on Western theories in the history of psychotherapy (Murguia and Díaz 2015, 41). The proposed theoretical orientation is one of the very first to form its basis in Early Buddhist teachings, which goes against the common and customary practices to develop a culturally congruent treatment model for non-Western clients. According to our literature review, this book may be the first and only project to propose a theoretical orientation based on Buddhism, which is a milestone in the field of counseling and psychology. Second, the theoretical orientation presented here will provide academicians in clinical psychology, counseling psychology, social work, counseling, and Buddhist chaplaincy with a theoretical basis for their work in different mental health settings. Scientists can apply the theoretical orientation in Buddhist counseling and conduct qualitative, quantitative, and even neuroscientific studies to evaluate its efficacy for different populations. Finally, our view is that the debate on whether to secularize mindfulness, or whether it is appropriate to extract mindfulness from Buddhism, leads to a dead end. The proposal of a theoretical orientation based on Buddhism addresses the debate on whether to secularize mindfulness by proposing a more progressive possibility: instead of extracting mindfulness or other components from Buddhism, let's try to use all the keys of the Buddhist teachings as the counselor finds appropriate. In other words, perhaps it is time to move beyond the debate on mindfulness and shift attention to whether Buddhism can offer a holistic model of treatment. This book is one of the first steps to explore this theoretical possibility in developing such a treatment model. In particular, the approach of this book is to acknowledge the Buddhist Teachings as the root, but to be flexible about whether to secularize Buddhist teachings to meet clients from different backgrounds, and then skillfully integrate Buddhist Teachings with counseling techniques for the benefits of clients. There will be more discussion on these points in the coming sections.

1.8 Summary of the Chapters

Chapter 2 discusses the meaning and importance of a theoretical orientation to counseling. It includes the history of theoretical orientations with examples of their common theoretical dimensions. In essence, the difference between a lay person and a professional counselor is the counselor's ability to transform theory into effective practical means to help clients resolve their presenting problems (Gehart 2015, 3). In other words, theoretical orientation is a backbone, structuring and guiding the treatment process. Based on the reviewed definitions and dimensions, this book defines a theoretical orientation as a practical framework to conceptualize clients' experiences, which then helps in the course design and treatment, inspiring and informing appropriate interventions according to relevant counseling theories. The foci of the most common dimensions of a theoretical orientation, include dimension I: basic philosophy; dimension II: central theoretical constructs of human nature and human motivation; dimension, III: theory of human development; dimension IV: psychological dysfunction; and dimension V: interventions and techniques. Subsequently, Chapters 3 to 7 address each dimension of the theoretical orientation in detail, with each chapter including three sections: (1) introduction to associated key concepts in Early Buddhist teachings suitable for the dimension addressed, (2) a commentary according to a counseling and psychology perspective, and (3) potential applications to Buddhist counseling and related considerations.

Chapter 3 begins the discussion of the theoretical orientation underpinning Buddhist counseling by introducing a core assumption in the Buddhist worldview known as the Law of Dependent Co-arising. As a significant principle differentiating Buddhism from other schools of thought, dependent co-arising lays the theoretical foundation for non-self, impermanence, interconnectedness, and other key Buddhist concepts. An in-depth understanding of dependent co-arising is one way to realize the law of actuality, which is one of the means to liberate a person from suffering. This chapter explains the concept using Buddhist scriptures and provides a description of the twelve factors of dependent co-arising. In counseling and psychology commentary, various attempts to explain and apply dependent co-arising according to psychological nomenclature by interdisciplinary scholars of psychology and Buddhism, as well as certain explanations of the concept of dependent co-arising as used in professional counseling, will be reviewed. These attempts are noteworthy as references of practical applications to counseling, though there are two areas of concern: there is still no theoretical orientation using dependent co-arising as the backbone of treatment, and the Buddhist idea of non-self may not be as widely accepted in most models of psychological treatment. Therefore, the application and implication section proposes certain practical applications of dependent co-arising in counseling using a case study to illustrate a dependent co-arising exercise. The exercise aims to help a client deconstruct the phenomenon of suffering and cultivate an awareness of various causes and conditions contributing to such a phenomenon. Using visual and cognitive media to explore and reflect on different causes and conditions can foster a more detached perspective of one's immediate suffering, thereby fostering wisdom. This section also integrates and applies the twelve factors of dependent co-arising into a model of cognitive analysis, pinpointing potential entry points in the cycle of cognitive processes perpetuating the suffering (e.g., intervening in the gap between feeling and craving). The chapter ends with possible interventions a Buddhist counselor can make while also encouraging further applications of dependent co-arising.

Chapter 4 addresses the basic philosophy of human nature including foundational assumptions about what makes, drives, and changes a human being, which are essential assumptions in every theoretical orientation. A central theoretical construct of human nature in Buddhism is the concept of non-self; that is, the experience of "self" being just a product of logical abstractions or reifications that animate and concretize impersonal objects in order to mediate between the "outside" world and a delusional "personal identity." One significant feature of human motivation, as well as the core cause of suffering, is the clinging onto this notion of self and thereby convincing oneself of one's existence. To explain the reality of non-self (*anattā*) and liberation from suffering, the Buddha taught several models to analyze the experience of self. Among the several models, this section focuses primarily on the discussion of the five aggregates and the model of cognitive processes. The commentary under the psychology section briefly reviews the relevant literature to illustrate the central position of self in most treatment models. For instance, traditional psychotherapy models, such as psychoanalysis and humanistic/existential approaches, assume the inherent existence of a self. Recent developments in counseling psychology, such as ACT, move toward helping client develop a more transcendent and flexible sense of self while they continue to assume an immovable and stable dimension to a self at the core. No school in psychology to date has put non-self as a primary emphasis in their treatment focus. As Buddhist counseling integrates core Buddhist teachings in its treatment modality, we suggest that non-self can be a treatment objective as well as a psychotherapeutic intervention. A treatment focus based on non-self can emphasize raising a client's awareness of clinging to the notion of self and then gradually fostering non-attachment through different contemplative techniques.

Chapter 5 discusses the process of human development. A lens from traditional Western psychology views human development as the growth and development of different abilities throughout the lifespan, with major changes in cognitive, physical, social, and linguistic capacities occurring in childhood. This chapter then pinpoints one key distinction between the views of human development in Buddhism and psychology: these aspects of human development emphasized in psychology are not necessarily important to Buddhism if such changes do not relate to liberation from suffering. In fact, some Early Buddhist *sutta*s (e.g. the *Mahātaṇhāsaṅkhaya-sutta*) state that normal childhood development is simply a process of growth in unskilled qualities that only enhance dwelling in sensuality. Only with proper guidance and practice can young people walk on the path towards liberation from suffering. In contrast, this section proposes an alternative view of human development in accordance with a Buddhist counseling model, that is, as the holistic development of an individual towards liberation from suffering. After reviewing the ideal developmental models of the attainment of arahatship, the chapter reviews commentaries from contemporary scholars in psychology on how to apply the Buddhist holistic development model when evaluating the progress of a client, using such measures as that of nonattachment (Feliu-Soler et al. 2016), the assessment of spiritual growth using the Ten Ox-herding pictures (Canda and Gomi 2019), or the measurement of un-clinging (Ng 2017). In the implications section, this book proposes three core ideas: (1) that the theoretical orientation dimension of human development can take the Buddhist perspective of mental development as its conceptual framework. Such a framework considers human development as mental cultivation towards liberation from suffering, that is, as skillfulness of mind in choosing wholesome thoughts, speech, and behaviors; (2) that a Buddhist counseling orientation can also integrate insights from a psychological view of human development when it is germane to a client's cultivation of mind, and (3) that a Buddhist counseling orientation focusing on client's cultivation of mind can become an assessment scale to measure holistic development for householders and mindfulness cultivation based on particular *sutta*s.

Chapter 6 discusses psychological dysfunction and its causes, which constitute a key domain of a theoretical orientation as it defines what is problematic and informs how to cure such problems. In Buddhism, the core psychological dysfunction can be considered as pervasive suffering (*dukkha*), a universal human experience in *Saṃsāra*. In the Buddhist paradigm, the ultimate goal of practice is to end such suffering; to achieve that end, the Buddhist scriptures offer various analyses and categorizations of suffering to facilitate the process of cultivation. In this regard, suffering is an inevitable experience until one attains a very high level of cultivation to liberate oneself from it. In psychology, dysfunction generally refers to certain clinical symptoms and psychological disorders. Under this assumption of psychopathology, healthy and functional individuals in the mundane world are those free of psychological symptoms. The causes of suffering are also different in psychology and Buddhism. In the former, the causes of suffering differ according to the school of thought, such as unresolved conflicts in childhood, incongruence with intrinsic values and potentials, irrational and unhelpful beliefs, or psychological rigidity; in the latter, the core causes of suffering are ignorance and craving. Such differences give rise to a key question in Buddhist counseling: What should be the overarching treatment goal? The next section proposes that Buddhist counseling can focus on the felt-suffering of clients instead of the reckoned or pervasive suffering, since most clients seek respite from their daily woes rather than complete liberation. Accordingly, the overarching treatment goal is to apply Buddhist teachings to reduce a client's suffering by moving in the direction of non-self, or at the very least by exploring a less rigid clinging to the notion of self. The implication section then discusses a Buddhist counseling model of conceptualization (Lee and Tang 2021) to analyze clients' suffering. This model explains suffering as a discrepancy between expectations and reality, with expectations arising from one's clinging—a manifestation of craving.

Chapter 7 discusses the last dimension of the theoretical orientation as a practical approach for intervening in a client's suffering. Based on conceptualization in understanding the causes of a client's suffering, the interventions and techniques integrate counseling methods with Buddhist teachings in order to help the clients achieve their treatment goals. In Buddhism, the Noble Eightfold Path is the backbone of any intervention aiming to end suffering. The chapter introduces each one of the eight paths, putting a special emphasis on Right View (*sammā diṭṭhi*) due to its crucial and interrelated position to other paths. There are several definitions of Right View in the Buddhist scriptures, such as the ability to discern what is skillful and what is unskillful; seeing non-self, *dukkha*, and impermanence; appraisals of phenomena with the lens of dependent co-arising; and the three levels of Right View (realization of Wrong View, intellectual understanding of mundane Right View, and experiential cultivation of Right View). In essence, Right View can be considered a core intervention in Buddhist practice. Psychological treatment models also take the development of a healthier and more functional view as an important intervention, while the path of Right View is different. Similar to the discussion of psychological dysfunction, each school of thought in psychology has a different assumption of what is Right View. Among all schools, ACT has some similarities to Buddhism. Assuming that psychological dysfunction is caused by psychological inflexibility, a treatment goal of ACT is to help clients develop a more flexible view of events while easing their cognitive rigidity. Perhaps where ACT and Buddhism mainly diverge is in the assumption of personal identity and the sense of self; ACT assumes a transcendent sense of self which has no limitations and is susceptible to change, even while there is also a stable, unchangeable, and immutable "I" in the present moment. In contrast, Buddhism believes in non-self: the self is non-existent. In view of such a difference, the theoretical orientation of counseling adopts the Right View of non-self as its unique intervention goal. In the ensuing implication section, a detailed discussion follows that makes use of Right View as the core intervention involving five components: (1) cultivation of the Buddhist counselor, (2) raising awareness of Wrong Views and its suffering in clients, (3) intellectual learning, (4) reflection and contemplation, and (5) experiential practice. Each component is supplemented with sample dialogues and suggested techniques with a pseudo client in order to illustrate the practicality of this intervention.

Chapter 8 employs a hypothetical case to link all dimensions of the proposed theoretical orientation into a congruent picture. It includes: (1) an assessment process with a description of the client's suffering as well as sample assessment questions to evaluate the causes and conditions contributing to a client's suffering, (2) an application of the conceptualization model to analyze the client's expectations, clinging to a notion of self, and innermost yearnings, and (3) application of the five components to cultivate Right View together with sample dialogues and suggested techniques. This section also includes two Buddhist counseling techniques: the "Two Arrows Exercise," and "A Little Emptiness Exercise," which help clients raise awareness of the causes and conditions contributing to their suffering while noticing their clinging onto the notion of a fabricated self.

1.9 Conclusion

The first and second authors of this book came from a psychology background and were trained in traditional Western models of counseling and psychotherapy. An important part of the training was to read and be familiar with writings from founders of different theoretical orientations, such as Sigmund Freud, Carl Rogers, and Aaron Beck, to understand how these great founders apply particular philosophies and theories in practical models of treatment. From what we understand from the tradition of psychology, the theories often take the assumption of the existence of self (the root of the term psychology is *psyche,* which comes from the Greek *psykhe*, meaning "the soul") as a foundation while the treatment approach generally gravitates towards the advancement, revelation, or healing of the self. Such a purported existence of self is different from the Early Buddhist concept that states that suffering arises from clinging to the notion of self and hence liberation from suffering occurs in liberation from clinging, or simply put—the realization of non-self. We believe that the value of this book is to provide an alternative view to the traditional practice of working on the self; by adopting Early Buddhist teachings, this book develops a theoretical orientation based on non-self. We believe that this approach will resonate with thousands of individuals affiliated with Buddhism and provide a viable method to ease suffering in our contemporary world.

2

The Idea of a Theoretical Orientation

2.1 Introduction to Theoretical Orientation

For over sixty years in professional psychology, a vital step in the research process has been to develop a theoretical orientation, which for mental health professionals serves to describe their unique approach to treatment. A theoretical orientation includes a set of principles based on chosen theories to guide the counseling process and the therapeutic decisions of practitioners. There are a number of different theory-driven approaches in professional psychology that rely on specific philosophical assumptions about human nature, psychopathology, and human development, such as the psychodynamic, cognitive-behavioral, humanistic, and systemic frameworks (Poznanski and McLennan 2003, 223).

The idea of theoretical orientation has a long history in psychology. As early as the 1950s, Fiedler conducted a classic study on the relationship between therapists' theoretical orientations and their views on what constitutes an ideal therapeutic relationship (Fiedler 1950, 239). He found that even practitioners informed by differing theoretical views agree on what an ideal therapeutic relationship is (Fiedler 1950, 245). In our view, many researchers and practitioners assume and use a theoretical orientation unquestioningly without studying its nature or origin. Fiedler is one exception; although he did not focus on the nature of a theoretical orientation, he did describe the idea of theoretical orientation using the following terms: "theoretical view" (Fiedler 1950, 239), "theory semantic" (Fiedler 1950, 239), "subscribed theory" (Fiedler 1950, 240), and "schools" (Fiedler 1950, 245). These descriptive terms shed light on early therapists' views on why they subscribed to a theoretical orientation.

Even in other later studies, the definition of a theoretical orientation remains unclear. Poznanski and McLennan acknowledged that counselors' differing theoretical orientations influence the counseling and psychotherapy processes (Poznanski and McLennan 1995, 441). Even so, regardless of this influence, they noted that the concept of theoretical orientation does not have a standardized definition and is based on inconsistent means of measurement (Poznanski and McLennan 1995, 412). In support of this view, Wolff and Auckenthaler noted that while some mental health professionals subscribe to the same approach, this did not necessarily mean that they had the same understanding or application of the same theoretical orientation (Wolff and Auckenthaler 2014, 230). They pointed out that therapists who conduct research on theoretical orientations usually use a checklist approach to categorize them (e.g., "psychoanalytic," "cognitive," "behavioral," "systemic," "person-centered"), whereas many therapists apply more than one theory and use an integrative approach that cannot be captured by one discrete category (2014, 231). Based on interviews with twenty German psychologists on their theoretical orientations, Wolff and Auckenthaler concluded that the development of a theoretical orientation for a therapist is a complex, dynamic, and ongoing process associated with a therapist's identity development as well as their personal integration of concepts and skills from various counseling theories (2014, 232). These researchers also discovered an interesting insight into links between therapists' self-identity and their choice of theoretical orientation. However, while Wolff and Auckenthaler pointed out the problem of lacking a standard definition of theoretical orientation, they did not suggest any definition or remedy. We think one reason is that their description of a theoretical orientation as a dynamic and ongoing process indirectly suggests an answer: that the definition of a theoretical orientation is subjectively related to the therapist.

From these studies it can be seen that the definition of a theoretical orientation is unclear. All we can be sure about is that having a theoretical orientation is important for the process of counseling. In interviewing 103 psychologists about their theoretical orientations, Poznanski and McLennan found that numerous personal characteristics of psychologists influence their choice of a theoretical orientation (2003, 223). Such characteristics include the psychologist's age, university training, beliefs in human nature, experiences with family of origin, and other factors. Regardless of the variety of theoretical orientations and the reasons for choosing one, Poznanski and McLennan agreed with the commonly acknowledged importance of having a sound theoretical orientation in order to be effective in one's counseling practice. Therefore, this chapter will discuss the importance of a theoretical orientation in counseling and review the available definitions and dimensions of such in order to formulate a framework for analysis.

2.2 Theoretical Orientation: The Backbone of Counseling Practice

In professional psychology, a theoretical orientation, or theoretical approach, is the common term used to describe the driving theory for a psychotherapeutic practice. With the assumption that counseling or psychotherapy is a theory-driven practice, a practitioner employs a particular theoretical lens to conceptualize a client's presenting problems, analyze the reasons for suffering, intervene to reduce or eliminate the presenting problems, and make decisions on any clinical matters or activities. Because different theories encapsulate different worldviews and values, the choice of theoretical orientation often matches the attitudes, beliefs, and preferences of the mental health professional. To understand this paradigm, it is helpful to briefly review the history of psychotherapy.

Sigmund Freud, the founder of psychoanalysis, is often known as the father of psychotherapy due to his pioneering success in using therapeutic dialogues to cure mental illnesses (Shamdasani 2018, 4). The Freudian school of psychoanalysis established a foundation for talk therapies and many of his followers, including Carl Jung, Alfred Adler, Melanie Klein, and others gradually developed their own approaches based on the essential principles of psychoanalysis, commonly known as psychodynamic approaches. As the majority of mental health professionals at that time were practicing a model germane to psychoanalysis, the idea of a theoretical orientation did not emerge until different schools of thought arose (2018, 5). In the 1960s, several scholars proposed new models of psychotherapy that did not align with the fundamental principles of psychodynamic approaches. These innovative approaches included behavioral therapy by B. F. Skinner, cognitive behavioral therapy (CBT) by Aaron Beck, rational emotive behavioral therapy (REBT) by Albert Ellis, humanistic client-centered therapy by Carl Rogers, and Gestalt therapy by Fritz Perls. This diversity of psychotherapeutic models led practitioners to characterize their therapeutic approaches in terms of allegiance to one of the above schools of thought, resulting in the idea of a "theoretical orientation."

The term "theoretical orientation" signifies a theory behind a particular practice. Most of the above psychotherapeutic models were driven by different schools of philosophy. For example, CBT—the most common psychotherapy model—has roots in various ancient philosophical traditions, particularly Stoicism (Murguia and Díaz 2015, 41–42). According to Epictetus, Stoicism's founder, human beings are disturbed by their perception of events instead of the events themselves. This philosophical assumption regarding the perception or interpretation of events shaped the central idea of CBT, which sees human suffering as rooted in inaccurate, dysfunctional, or unhelpful beliefs about self, others, and the world. Guided by this principle, the intervention of a CBT practitioner helps clients evaluate self, others, and the world in accurate, functional, and helpful ways using various techniques, such as challenging irrational thoughts, focusing on neglected positivity, or practicing helpful and accurate thinking.

We believe the example of CBT demonstrates the importance of a theoretical orientation in helping a counselor understand human nature, uncover causes for psychological problems, and provide therapeutic directions in order to intervene in a client's issue. Such an important theoretical basis serves as the backbone to guide the clinical practice of mental health professionals. Given its importance, it is indeed surprising that there is no standardized operational definition of a theoretical orientation (Poznanski and Mclennan 2003, 225). The next section will explore several definitions of the concept of a theoretical orientation in order to elucidate it adequately for the purpose of this book.

2.3 Review of Definitions and Dimensions of a Theoretical Orientation

To address this research gap, the first part of this section will review the relevant literature on the definitions and common components of a theoretical orientation in order to provide a framework for the textual study. This review includes major articles related to the definition of "theoretical orientation" as well as the most commonly used textbooks for counseling and psychotherapy in order to understand how scholars and practitioners typically describe a theoretical orientation. It is important to note that many academic works did not provide a clear definition of a theoretical orientation, assuming that the reader would take "theoretical orientation" as a research feature that is ubiquitously understood. In an early text that explored whether psychologists can integrate different schools of thought into a treatment model, Richard Husband shared his observation on how the field of psychotherapy began, with psychologists first being immersed in a single school of thought, a feature that changed with the emergence of behaviorism[1] (1934, 368). In his core argument, Husband proposed that each school of thought has its own unique fundamental assumptions, many of which are incompatible with each other, suggesting that their integration may not be an effective approach to psychotherapy (Husband 1934, 369). However, throughout his arguments, Husband did not provide a clear definition of what a theoretical orientation is or what makes a school of thought, only implying it was a school of thought with some fundamental assumptions about therapy.

In another example, Ivey, Ivey, and Simek-Downing (1980), who published one of the most influential counseling and psychotherapy textbooks to date, did not clearly define what a theoretical orientation is. Instead, the authors discussed the importance of counselors developing their own theoretical orientation, again assuming that their readers would already be familiar with the concept of "theoretical orientation."

---

1. Behaviorism is a prominent school of thought in psychology that emphasizes the use of a systematic and empirical way to study human and animal behaviors (Husband 1934, 368).

Yet another example concerns Diane Gehart, a world-recognized expert in family therapy, who published several professional training textbooks for counseling and marriage and family therapy trainees. In one of her bestselling textbooks for graduate students, *Mastering Competencies in Family Therapy: A Practical Approach to Theories and Clinical Case Documentation*, she only mentioned the term theoretical orientation without any definition or description (2014, 41, 166). In a later book, *Theory and Treatment Planning in Counseling and Psychotherapy*, she described the importance of using theory as the backbone for counseling practice for three reasons (Gehart 2016, 3):

> (a) developing a specific form of helping relationship, (b) articulating a more useful understanding of clients' situations, and (c) identifying effective means to resolve clients' presenting problems.

Again, while this description articulates the function of a theory or a theoretical orientation, she did not directly explicate what a theoretical orientation actually is.

Similarly, scholars on theoretical orientations in different time periods, such as Fiedler (1950), and Poznanski and McLennan (1995), did not define what a theoretical orientation is in their studies. In our point of view, the fact that none of these scholars defined what a theoretical orientation is for entry level students may mean that this concept was assumed to be basic and common knowledge that students should have learned already. However, for the sake of this study, it is important to elucidate the definitions and descriptions of "theoretical orientation" in order to prepare the ground for a theoretical orientation based on Early Buddhist teachings. For this reason, this section will focus on several scholarly works that do provide clear and specific definitions and descriptions of the key term "theoretical orientation."

In one of the earliest books on the theory and practice of counseling and psychotherapy, Richard Nelson-Jones (2015, 23) briefly defined the scope of a theoretical orientation as a single position of theoretical concepts and practical interventions for mental health treatment. In this discussion, each theoretical framework systematically addressed four dimensions: (1) basic concepts or assumptions about human nature; (2) an explanation of the acquisition of helpful and unhelpful behaviors; (3) an explanation of the maintenance of helpful and unhelpful behaviors, and (4) an explanation of how to help clients change their behaviors and consolidate gains from treatment. Nelson-Jones (2015, 24) further asserted that theoretical orientation works as a form of guidance to help counselors make hypotheses of clients' presenting problems and then postulate how to best address these problems.

Nelson-Jones (2015, 42) provided a more comprehensive description of the dimensions of a theoretical orientation compared to his counterparts. In particular, he specified the counselor's need to understand the causes and reasons to maintain helpful and unhelpful behaviors. However, as we discovered, he did not explicate the definition of helpfulness, nor did he address whether psychopathology can be captured solely in a behavioral definition. Indeed, many schools in psychology, including person-centered and psychodynamic approaches, tend to go beyond observable behaviors in their conceptualization of psychological problems, such as the consideration of human values, meaning of life, relationships, and emotionality. For example, Viktor Frankl's (March 26, 1905–September 2, 1997) logotherapy criticized the scientific approach as focusing on behaviors while neglecting the importance of meanings (Soggie 2016, 39). He believed that the therapist's job is to honor a client's meaning because meaning is an essential dimension defining what it means to be human. In another example, the increasingly popular counseling approach of ACT emphasizes the role of core values that provide individuals with an overarching direction in life as well as providing a deeper sense of meaning to help them cope with challenges and struggles (Hayes 2002, 64). Due to these limitations in Nelson-Jones' proposed definition, we will continue to explore other definitions.

In another traditional textbook on theory and practice in counseling, Hansen et al. (1986, 87) discussed the concept of theoretical orientation as a plan or model to organize information, conduct systematic analyses, and provide logical and reasonable explanations for events, thereby informing problem-solving. According to these authors, every theoretical orientation should address three domains: personality or human development, behavioral or attitudinal change, and the role of the counselor (88). The authors place personality development in a central position because of the assumption that maladaptive behaviors can be traced back to one's personality development. As they pointed out, knowing what signifies normal and abnormal development from a theoretical perspective can guide counselors to formulate ways to help with clients' current psychological problems (Hansen, Stevic, and Warner 1986, 88). Moreover, Hansen, Stevic, and Warner described the use of a theoretical orientation as a guide for counselors to determine what kind of behavioral or attitudinal changes need to be nurtured in clients (1986, 89). In this process, counselors decide different goals for clients according to the theory and then systematically help clients move toward these goals. Last but not least, a theoretical orientation should provide clear guidance on the role of the counselor (Hansen, Stevic, and Warner 1986, 89). For example, the theory should address whether a counselor should use a diagnostic or a more directive (or nondirective) technique to promote therapeutic change. In effect, a good counselor should develop a solid foundation in the chosen theoretical orientation and have a clear understanding of these three domains in order to effectively put theory into practice (Hansen, Stevic, and Warner 1986, 89).

As we see it, the three domains outlined by Hansen, Stevic, and Warner (1986, 88–89) were groundbreaking in understanding and analyzing theoretical orientations. These proposed domains covered fundamental concepts in teaching the concept of "theoretical orientation" and successfully pinpointed the important position of the role of counselors when practicing the approaches. However, in our view, these three domains did not seem to directly address the nature and causes of psychopathology, which is crucial information for understanding and treating clients.

Poznanski and McLennan (1995, 229) were the first to review definitions of "theoretical orientation" and summarize essential components. In their review, a theoretical orientation is a structured set of assumptions that provide a treatment framework for counseling practice in the mental health profession. A theoretical orientation, according to Poznanski and McLennan, encompasses at least three components: (a) theoretical knowledge to generate hypotheses of clients' presenting problems and behaviors; (b) theory-driven treatment interventions specifically for the presenting problems; and (c) evaluation of the ongoing therapeutic process (1995, 229). In other words, a theoretical orientation is a translation of theory into action to guide therapeutic practices.

Poznanski and McLennan's (1995, 229) definition and explanation provided a concise framework with which to focus on clients' presenting problems. However, in our view, they did not address particular aspects of the structured sets of assumptions within the theoretical orientation, such as the understanding of human nature and causes of psychopathology. It is also possible to develop the definition into more specific categories to provide counselors with more references in their analyses of clients' suffering.

In addition to the development of counseling and psychotherapy, there has been an increasing call to practice an integrative theoretical orientation involving a tailor-made approach that synthesizes a variety of therapeutic concepts and techniques from other orientations. In this regard, Jones-Smith published a textbook to specifically address an integrative theoretical orientation for counseling, although she did not define what a theoretical orientation is. However, in this work, she discussed major components of a theoretical framework for counselors to consider when developing their own integrative approach. To summarize the components: (1) human nature: beliefs and values of human nature, associated influences of heredity and environment, and the role of past and present; (2) human development: critical periods in personal and behavioral development, the development of mental disorders, and human motivation for change; (3) the therapist as a person: the counselor's personal values, beliefs, biases, and personality; (4) the client's world: an understanding of a client's worldview, insight into their problems, and strengths, and; (5) the process of psychotherapy: the goals of treatment, the role of the counselor and client, the nature of the therapeutic relationship, and interventions (2016, 10–12).

These categories are more comprehensive than those of earlier scholars, such as the four dimensions proposed by Nelson-Jones (2015) and the three components proposed by Poznanski and McLennan (1995), allowing for more room to discuss a theoretical orientation. However, we argue that a theoretical orientation should use theory as a framework to conceptualize clients' presenting problems from a theoretical perspective and then determine appropriate interventions. In other words, the philosophical component of a theory is also important for facilitating the conceptual understanding of a client's experiences and suffering, something not emphasized by Jones-Smith (2016).

Yet another contemporary textbook on counseling and psychotherapy by Murdock (2017) did not provide a clear definition of "theoretical orientation," although she formulated concise and specific categories for each theoretical orientation, such as basic philosophy, human motivation, central theoretical constructs, theory of human development, health and dysfunction, the nature and process of therapy, and interventions (Murdock 2017, 32). In this book, Murdock (2017, 34) stated that a theoretical orientation is an effective tool for fostering an understanding of a client and she proceeds to offer insights as to what a counselor can do. In effect, as she pointed out, it is the counselor's job to self-reflect on their assumptions about human nature, personal values, and preferred techniques of counseling in order to choose a suitable theoretical orientation and develop their personal approach based on existing orientations (2017, 35). Overall, although Murdock has provided valuable dimensions of a theoretical orientation as well as an explanation of its importance to counseling, a definition is still required.

Because the term "theoretical orientation" is ambiguous and lacks a definition, the next step will be to respond to the research gap by proposing a definition based on the literature review and then using such a definition to develop a theoretical orientation for Buddhist counseling.

2.4 Proposed Definition and Dimensions of a Theoretical Orientation

In summarizing the literature reviewed, a good definition of a theoretical orientation should include a theory as a guiding framework as well as its implications for professional counseling. Therefore, we define a theoretical orientation as a practical framework to conceptualize clients' experiences, design a course of treatment, and intervene according to relevant counseling theories. Regarding the dimensions of a theoretical orientation, Murdock (2017) provided the most comprehensive list of such, covering components from theory to practice. For this reason, this book will adopt the components delineated by Murdock (2017,

34–35), namely: (1) basic philosophy, (2) central theoretical constructs of human nature and human motivation, (3) theory of human development, (4) psychological dysfunction, and (5) interventions. Let us examine each of these components in more detail.

1. Basic philosophy. A basic philosophy describes the overarching core assumptions about reality, the world, and human nature.

2. Central theoretical constructs of human nature and human motivation. Central theoretical constructs describe the specifics of theoretical concepts germane to mental health treatment. In particular, this section describes how the theorist views human existence. It also includes human motivation, the primary motive behind human choices being thoughts and behaviors.

3. Theory of human development. Human development describes the theory's assumptions regarding a normative and healthy developmental sequence in individuals.

4. Health and dysfunction. This section discusses the definition of dysfunction, or psychopathology, and its etiology.

5. Interventions and techniques. Interventions and techniques are actions that counselors take in order to promote therapeutic change in clients.

In order to illustrate the effectiveness of the proposed dimensions in capturing a theoretical orientation, Table 2.1 uses the most commonly used theoretical orientation of CBT to discuss each dimension using materials from *Cognitive Behavior Therapy: Basics and Beyond*, a textbook written by one of CBT's founders, Judith Beck (2011).

The coming chapters will proceed according to the following structure: (1) a review of specific Early Buddhist concepts, (2) a commentary that integrates such concepts into a theoretical orientation according to a conventional psychological perspective, and (3) a discussion of the implications of the above steps for the practice of Buddhist counseling.

Table 2.1: Proposed Dimensions of a Theoretical Orientation with Examples

Dimension	Example of Dimension According to a Cognitive Behavioral Therapy (CBT) Perspective
Basic Philosophy	The human mind has three levels of cognition: core beliefs, underlying assumptions, and automatic thoughts. Core beliefs are the most central and fundamental cognitive schemas involving self-identity because the human mind tends to see the world based on this construct and filters out information that does not go along with this belief (Beck 2011, 3).
Central Theoretical Constructs of Human Nature and Human Motivation	Thoughts, behaviors, physicality, and emotions are interrelated and interdependent. In particular, a person's thoughts directly influence one's behaviors and emotions. Negative thoughts, such as irrational and unhelpful ways of thinking, will result in dysfunctional behaviors and aversive emotions. Human beings have the potential to develop rational and helpful thinking, thereby reducing behavioral and emotional problems (Beck 2011, 30–31).
Theory of Human Development	Since birth, human beings start to formulate beliefs of self, others, and the world through interactions with their environment. To function adaptively in the environment, human beings tend to organize experiences in a coherent way to learn how to meet social demands and thus survive (Beck 2011, 32–33).
Psychological Dysfunction	A psychologically healthy person tends to be objective and realistic in his or her appraisals of events, beliefs in self, and view of others and the world. If environmental factors, such as parents, teachers, and friends, do not reflect a person's characteristics objectively and realistically, they may not be able to develop objective and realistic thinking to evaluate self, others, and the world. When a person has an irrational core belief, one usually suffers from emotional problems. For example, a person who has a core belief of "I'm incompetent" tends to selectively focus on feedback and input that confirms his incompetency while neglecting information assuring them of competency, resulting in low self-esteem and a depressed mood (Beck 2011, 33–34).

(continued on p. 53)

Table 2.1: (*continued*)

Dimension	Example of Dimension According to a Cognitive Behavioral Therapy (CBT) Perspective
Interventions and Techniques	The major goal of CBT is to reduce clients' psychological distress through cognitive and behavioral techniques, plus problem-solving skills. Intermediate goals may include forming a therapeutic alliance, learning relaxation skills and behavioral activation, or cognitive restructuring of a client's cognitive processing to develop a more objective and realistic thinking style. The counselor usually starts with building a working relationship with a client, assessing his or her presenting problems and making a diagnosis, designing a course of treatment with attainable goals, identifying their irrational thoughts and beliefs, providing behavioral and cognitive interventions, and reviewing and consolidating the gains before the end of the treatment (Beck 2011, 101–118). There are a number of behavioral and cognitive interventions, such as controlled breathing, journaling, automatic thought log, activity scheduling, homework assignments, psychoeducation, visual imagery, role-plays, thought evaluation sheets, thought-stopping, and other techniques (Beck 2011, 137–315)

3

Theoretical Orientation Dimension I: Basic Philosophy

A theoretical orientation usually begins with an all-embracing philosophical framework that lays the academic groundwork for the theory. The core foundation of the Buddhist teachings is considered to be the law of dependent arising, sometimes referred to as dependent co-arising. This introduction will briefly review several respected scholarly works on the position of dependent arising in the Buddhist teachings.

Bhikkhu Bodhi described dependent arising as the "radical insight at the heart of the Buddha's teaching" (Bodhi 1995, 1). In fact, the Buddha saw his realization of dependent arising as leading towards *Nibbāna* (1995, 1). In the *Nagara-sutta*, the Buddha shared how he discovered the ancient path traveled by previous enlightened ones and how he realized the Four Noble Truths and the law of dependent arising, thereby liberating himself from suffering. Similarly, in the *Paccaya-sutta*, the Buddha proclaimed that dependent arising is the correct path of wisdom to enlightenment. In a discussion of the *Paccaya-sutta*, Bhikkhu Bodhi made the following comment: "Once enlightened, the mission of a *Tathāgata*, a "Perfect One," is to proclaim dependent arising to the world" (Bodhi 1995, 1). To explain the importance of dependent arising, Bodhi cited two reasons: (1) dependent arising is a primary ontological principle that explains the nature of being, and (2) it provides a systemic framework for the teaching of *Dhamma*, especially the explanation of the origination and cessation of suffering.

Other prominent scholars in Early Buddhism have also pointed out the importance of dependent arising in Buddhist teachings. Karunadasa concisely described dependent arising as "the most fundamental teaching in Buddhism" (2013, 1). Meanwhile, Somaratne explained the significance of dependent arising as its capacity to allow practitioners to see the true nature of things:

> The knowledge of the Dhamma provides the skill to see the true nature of things functioning in one's own experiential structure. With such knowledge, one

> begins to see the fact that one's whole experiential structure is constituted by a multitude of impersonal systems, parts, and relationships, that operate following the patterns and laws of nature; that is that these impersonal systems arise, persist while changing, and cease—in line with nature's law, which is not other than the law of dependent co-arising. (2021, 39)

In addition to these two reasons, some scholars have pointed out ways in which dependent arising offers a new perspective to the debate on the view of eternalism and annihilationism. For instance, Karunadasa stated that dependent arising is the doctrine of the middle way, which transcends the binary opposite extremes of spiritual eternalism and materialist annihilationism (Karunadasa 2013, 23). In support of this view, Somaratne described dependent co-arising as a unique and central theory in the Buddha's teaching because dependent co-arising provides "the alternative way that not only excludes both eternalism and annihilationism, but also replaces skepticism (*saṃsaya-vāda*) for understanding the true state of affairs in our life's journey" (2021, 56).

3.1 An Explanation of Dependent Co-arising

Recognized scholars in Early Buddhism have defined dependent arising. Here we will now review the works of three major scholars, including Bodhi, Karunadasa, and Somaratne.

Bodhi (1995, 25) began his discussion of dependent arising by describing how this idea provides a "middle way" between eternalist and annihilationist views, and between dualistic and extreme views, both of which polarize human understanding and its way of being. However, Bodhi remarked that the Buddha neither offered a formal definition of dependent arising, nor provided the specific conditions of the two factors of dependent arising in the *sutta* (1995, 3). According to his interpretation of the *sutta*, Bodhi explained dependent arising as a "specific conditionality, the arising of phenomena in dependence on specific conditions". He further explained dependent arising as dealing primarily with structures and recurrent patterns of specific conditions. Instead of exploring dependent arising on philosophical grounds, Bodhi asserted that the Buddha's teaching is concerned with the problem of suffering (*dukkha*) and that dependent arising is an essential framework to address this concern. Therefore, Bodhi concluded that dependent arising was not taught as an abstract formula, but was a teaching to end existential suffering, which is the suffering of being tied to repetitive cycles of birth and death. To understand the process of ending suffering, Bodhi provided a detailed account of the twelve factors of dependent arising based on the *Mahānidāna-sutta*.

Karunadasa started his discussion of dependent arising by referring to the *Dasabala-sutta,* in which the Buddha summarized the principle of dependent co-arising as follows: "When this exists, that comes to be; with the arising of this, that arises. When this does not exist, that does not come to be; with the cessation of this, that ceases" (Bodhi 2000, 552).

Dependent arising explains the nature of the relationship between cause and effect (Karunadasa 2013, 23). Karunadasa emphasized that this causal effect does not refer to the linear relationship of B coming from A; instead, the cause can be considered to exist even when there is no substance passing from the cause to the effect. This idea of dependent arising was a groundbreaking view during the Buddha's time.

In ancient history, the prevalent explanation of reality was either spiritual eternalism or materialistic annihilationism (Karunadasa 2013, 13). Spiritual eternalism holds that while the physical body is transient and perishable, the metaphysical self or soul is eternal and immortal. In contrast, materialistic annihilationism tends to see the physical body as the only and actual existing entity, one that undergoes no consequences for its actions, has no previous life, and does not return in an afterlife. The doctrine of the Middle way of the Buddha offers a third perspective that challenges both absolutist views, asserting that every phenomenon is a product of causes and conditions.[1] Based on this perspective, Buddhism illustrates the causes and conditions of suffering and teaches a way for its complete cessation. Karunadasa (2013, 28) also applied the "middle-position" to explain human experiences. In particular, he asserted that human experiences are neither due to self-causation or external causation; instead, all human experiences are of dependent arising. While dependent arising can explain the phenomena of the world, including the evolution of society and social orders, Karunadasa put most emphasis on the implication of dependent arising to "individual existence". In particular, he discussed how the concept of dependent arising helps to analyze and break down individual existence into a number of factors using different models of understanding, such as the five aggregates, twelve sense-bases, and the eighteen elements of cognition. In his discussion, Karunadasa raised several key observations on dependent arising. First, what is dependently arisen, such as the grasping onto the five aggregates, cannot be defined as an "existence" or "non-existence," but only a continuum of arising and ceasing. Second, dependent arising refers to the arising of evenly measured effects depending on a conjunction of conditions. Third, arising refers to the phenomenon of arising together and equally instead of arising step-by-step in a successive manner. Last but not least, when the *sutta* mentions one factor as the condition for another, the goal is to

---

1. This is well stated in the *Kaccānagotta-sutta* (SN II, 17): "'All exists': Kaccāna, this is one extreme. "All does not exist' this is the second extreme. Without veering towards either of these extremes, the *Tathāgata* teaches the Dhamma by the middle" (Bodhi 2000, 544).

pinpoint the primary condition among many conditions as well as its relationship to the most conditioned factor among many others (Karunadasa 2013, 30).

Somaratne (2021) used the term "dependent co-arising" instead of "dependent arising" to emphasize "coming into existence together" (2021, 71) and explained this teaching as how "things arise codependently, as aggregates, groups, things, events, or phenomena" and that what "we experience in the world in terms of sights, sounds, and ideas are things that have dependently arisen". As he also explained, the essence of dependent arising is a "cluster of configurations" moving forward and giving rise to a new "cluster of configurations". From this perspective, Somaratne stated that every single thing is considered as conditioned by a network of factors, and hence everything is shaped according to a specific set of configurations.

Somaratne also extensively discussed the Middle Theory based on dependent co-arising (2021, 55–90). In addition to the theories of eternalism and annihilationism in ancient India, he also pointed out the belief in skepticism, which is the third alternative philosophical school that expresses doubts about eternalism and annihilationism while also refusing to commit to any point of view (2021, 56). While eternalism seeks its ultimate happiness beyond life in a freeing of the soul and annihilationism finds happiness in self-indulgence in the present life to satisfy the body, Somaratne described the Buddha's ideology of dependent arising as a way to view life and its continuation as a causal pattern of multiple factors such that ultimate happiness comes from the pacification of all subjective configurations of factors and conditions, including craving and clinging (2021, 65–66). This view does not veer off into either of the extreme views of eternalism or annihilationism while still offering a Middle Theory to explain the true nature of the inner and outside worlds (2021, 65–67). Summarizing the explanations and descriptions from the above three prominent scholars, we will try to describe the essence of dependent arising with a view to its application to counseling. We see dependent co-arising as having a core theoretical basis with a particular focus on the liberation from suffering, thereby providing a ground for the Middle Theory, non-self (*anattā*), clinging to the five aggregates, and other important teachings. The implication of dependent arising is that every phenomenon exists conditionally and interdependently because everything is mutually dependent on everything else for its existence. When the specific conditions required for its existence no longer exist, the phenomenon simultaneously discontinues. Before even the simplest of phenomena occur, numerous factors have contributed to their existence, and each phenomenon will subside when the interdependent factors that support it are no longer present. The Law of Dependent Co-arising applies to both worldly phenomena as well as subjective psychological experiences. Following Somaratne's emphasis on "coming into existence together" (2021, 71), this book will also employ the term "dependent co-arising."

The next section will further discuss the twelve factors of dependent co-arising.

3.2 The Twelve Factors of Dependent Co-arising

In the Pāli *Nikāyas*, the most significant analysis is of dependent co-arising is the twelve factors of dependent origination or dependent co-arising:

> And what, bhikkhus, is dependent co-arising? With (1) ignorance as condition, (2) volitional formations come to be; with volitional formations as condition, (3) consciousness; with consciousness as condition, (4) name-and-form; with name-and-form as condition, (5) the six sense bases; with the six sense bases as condition, (6) contact; with contact as condition, (7) feeling; with feeling as condition, (8) craving; with craving as condition, (9) clinging; with clinging as condition, (10) existence; with existence as condition, (11) birth; with birth as condition, (12) aging-and-death, sorrow, lamentation, pain, displeasure, and despair come to be. Such is the origin of this whole mass of suffering. This, bhikkhus, is called dependent origination. (Bodhi 2000, 534)[2]

The *suttas* present dependent co-arising as a chain of causation. However, a caveat Bodhi (1995) emphasized was that the formula of such a linear sequence should not be taken to imply that the conditions fit together as a temporally progressive chain of causes and effects (1995, 12–13). In reality, Bodhi explained that each discussed condition can be seen as a situation involving multiplicity embedded within a complex of conditions arising and sustaining a complex of dependently arisen phenomena (1995, 13). As Bodhi said, the formula aimed to point out the most prominent conditions or relevant conditions in the situation[3] (1995, 14). Similarly, Hunter (2012) explained that although the doctrine may have presented dependent co-arising as a linear sequence with a preceding factor becoming a condition for the subsequent one, it is indeed a cyclic process with no beginning or end (2012, 118). As he said, the formula pinpoints the most crucial condition preceding the next condition, while multiple levels of causation are given. Moreover, each factor is conditioned by the preceding factor, which becomes a condition for the factor that follows (2012, 119).

---

2. SN II, 1: *Katamo ca bhikkhave paṭiccasamuppādo. Avijjā bhikkhave saṅkhārā. saṇkhārā paccayā viññānaṃ. viññāṇapaccayā nāmarūpaṃ. nāmarūpapaccayā saḷāyatanaṃ. saḷāyatanapaccayā phasso. phassapaccayā vedanā. vedanāpaccayā taṇhā. taṇhāpaccayā upādānaṃ. upādānapaccayā bhavo. bhavapaccayā jāti. jātipaccayā jarāmaraṇaṃ soka-parideva-dukkha-domanassupāyasā sambhavanti. Evam etassa kevalassa dukkhakkhandhassa samudayo hoti.*
3. Bodhi (1995) also stated that the *Abhidhamma Piṭaka* gives a more detailed explanation on dependent co-arising (14). However, the current discussion focuses on Early Buddhist teachings as based on the Pāli *Nikāyas* and hence commentaries and their discussions are beyond the scope of this book. From this point on, the book will only briefly mention the commentaries if it is relevant to the literature review.

Some scholars, such as Gethin (1998, 149), observe that although dependent co-arising is considered the backbone of Buddhist teachings, there is very little explanation about each factor in Early Buddhist texts. In other words, the Early Buddhist scriptures presented the theories but not sufficient explanations. This was one of the reasons why various philosophical Buddhist schools emerged.

In order to adopt the concept of dependent co-arising for a theoretical orientation, we attempt to provide a general description of the twelve factors with reference to the *Vibhaṅga*. However, it is important to note that the goal of this section is not to elaborate on each factor one by one, as it can lead to an endless process with multiple explanations and interpretations.

Avijjā (ignorance), fundamentally, means non-knowldege of the reality (*dhamma*) or any of the teachings by the Buddha regarding reality. The *Vibhaṅga* defines this as non-knowledge of the Four Noble Truths.[4] Here, it should be noted, when "Four Noble Truths" are mentioned, all other fundamental teachings are included. Relatedly, in addition to "Four Noble Truths," the Dhs also explains *avijjā* as non-knowledge of dependent co-arising.[5]

Because of *avijjā*, *saṅkhāra* comes to be. *Saṅkhāra* is translated in many ways, such as volitional formations, mental formations, volitional, constructions, fabrications, and so on. *Saṅkhāra* in relation to the five aggregates is discussed in chapter 4. The concepts of *saṅkhāra* in both contexts must be regarded as the same and should not be understood as two different concepts.

The *Vibhaṅga* explains *saṅkhāra*, the second of twelve factors of dependent co-arising, as producing good resultants (*puññābhisaṅkhāra*), bad resultants (*apuññābhisaṅkhāra*), configurations producing unshakable resultants (*āneñjābhisaṅkhāra*), bodily configurations (*kāyasaṅkhāra*), verbal configurations (*vacīsaṅkhāra*), and mental configurations (*mano saṅkhāra*).[6] In other

4. Vibhaṅga 135: *Tattha katamā avijjā? Dukkhe aññāṇaṃ dukkhasamudaye aññāṇaṃ dukkhanirodhe aññāṇaṃ dukkhanirodhagāminiyā paṭipadāya aññānaṃ: ayaṃ vuccati avijjā.* (Therein, what is ignorance? Ignorance regarding suffering, its cause, cessation and the path leading to the cessation. This is called ignorance).

5. Dhs 1100: *...pubbante aññāṇaṃ, aparante aññāṇaṃ, pubbāntāparante aññāṇaṃ—idappaccayatā paṭiccasamuppannesu dhammesu aññāṇaṃ yaṃ evarūpaṃ aññāṇaṃ adassanaṃ anabhisamayo ananubodho asambodho appaṭivedho asaṅgāhanā apariyogāhanā asamapekkhanā apaccavekkhanā apaccakkhakammaṃ dummejjhaṃ balyaṃ asampajaññānaṃ moho pamoho sammoho avijjā avijjhogo avijjāyogo avijjānusayo avijjāpariyuṭṭhānaṃ avijjālaṅgī moho akusalamūlaṃ—ayaṃ vuccati avijjāsavo.* (As non-knowledge of beginning, end and both; non-knowledge of specific conditionality of dependently originated phenomena; thus, non-seeing of the unwholesome root—non-penetration, non-realization, non-awakening, non-attainment, non-restrain, non-plunging, non-consideration, non-reflection, impure, foolishness, non-discrimination, delusion, bewilderment, non-knowledge, the flood of non-knowledge, bond of non-knowledge, dormant disposition of non-knowledge, outburst of non-knowledge, obstruction of non-knowledge—this is called the outflow of ignorance).

6. Vibhaṅga 135: *puññābhisaṅkhāro apuññābhisaṅkhāro āneñjābhisaṃkhāro kāyasaṃkhāro vacīsaṃkhāro cittasaṃkhāro.*

words, the *Vibhaṅga* explains the wholesome volition of giving (*dāna*), morality (*sīla*), and cultivation (*bhāvanā*), in the planes of desire (*kāmāvacara*) and form (*rūpāvacara*) as the configurations producing good resultants.[7] Its opposite, unwholesome volition, occurs only in the plane of desire (*kāmāvacarā*), producing bad resultants (*apuññābhisaṅkhāra*).[8] Furthermore, configurations producing unshakable resultants are explained as wholesome volitions in the formless plane (*arūpāvacara*).[9] Bodily, verbal and mental configurations mean the volitional acts performed by body, speech, and mind respectively.[10]

Because of *saṅkhāra*, *viññāṇa* comes to be. *Viññāṇa* (consciousness), in Early Buddhism, is the third factor in the twelve links of dependent co-arising and the same concept as the fifth of the five aggregates. The *Vibhaṅga* explains it in the same way as is explained in the *Saṃyutta Nikāya*, which we have rendered in chapter 4.

Because of *viññāṇa*, *nāmarūpa* comes to be. *Nāmarūpa* (name and matter): Three of the five aggregates, namely feeling (*vedanā*), perception (*saññā*), and configuration (*saṃkhāra*) constitute name (*nāma*), and matter refers to the four great elements (*mahābhūtarūpaṃ*) and the objects derived from them.[11]

Because of *nāmarūpa*, *saḷāyatana* comes to be. *Saḷāyatana* (the six-fold sense-base) are the eye base, ear base, nose base, tongue base, body base, and mind base.[12]

Because of *saḷāyatana*, *phassa* comes to be. As the *Madhupiṇḍika-sutta* (MN 18) expounds, *phassa* (contact) is the meeting or conjunction of three factors: the sense base, the relevant sense object, and sense consciousness (*tiṇṇam saṅgati phasso*). Contact is six-fold: eye contact, ear contact, nose contact, tongue contact, body contact, and mind contact.[13]

Because of *phassa*, *vedanā* comes to be. *Vedanā* (feeling) is born out of the six contacts, the contact with the eye, ear, nose, tongue, body, and mind.[14] As the second of five aggregates, we have further explained this concept in chapter 4.

---

7. Vibhaṅga 135: *Kusalā cetanā kāmāvacarā rūpāvacarā dānamayā sīlamayā bhāvanāmayā: ayaṃ vuccati puññābhisaṃkhāro.*
8. Vibhaṅga 135: *Akusalā cetanā arūpāvacarā: ayaṃ vuccati apuññābhisaṃkhāro*
9. Vibhaṅga 135: *Kusalā cetanā arūpācarā: ayaṃ āneñjābhisaṃkhāro*
10. Vibhaṅga 135: *kāyasañcetanā kāyasaṃkhāro . . . vacīsaṃcetanā vacīsaṃkhāro . . . mano sañcetanā cittasaṃkhāra*
11. Vibhaṅga 136: *Vedanākkhandho saññākkhandho saṃkhārakkhandho: idaṃ vuccati nāmaṃ . . . cattāro ca mahābhūtā catunnañ ca mahābhūtānaṃ upādāya rūpaṃ; idaṃ vuccati rūpaṃ.*
12. Vibhaṅga 136: *cakkhāyatanaṃ sotāyatanaṃ ghānāyatanaṃ jivhāyatanaṃ kāyātanaṃ manāyatanam.*
13. Vibhaṅga 136: *cakkhusamphasso sotasamphasso ghānasamphasso jivhāsamphasso kāyasamphasso manosaphasso: ayam vuccati saḷāyatanapaccayā phasso.*
14. Vibhaṅga 136: *Cakkhusamphassajā vedanā sotasamphassajā vedanā ghānasamphassajā vedanā jivhāsamphassajā vedanā kāyasamphassajā vedanā manosamphassajā vedanā: ayaṃ vuccati phassapaccayā vedanā.*

Because of *vedanā*, *taṇhā* comes to be. *Taṇhā* (craving) is based on the six types of sensory objects, namely sights, sounds, smells, tastes, tactile objects, and mental phenomena.[15] The *Dhammacakkapavattana-sutta* (SN 56. 11) references three-fold craving: craving for sensual pleasure (*kāmataṇhā*), craving for becoming (*bhavataṇhā*), and craving for non-becoming (*vibhavataṇhā*).

Because of *taṇhā*, *upādāna* comes to be. *Upādāna* (clinging or attachment) is explained as four kinds: clinging to sensuality, views, precepts and religious observance, and the soul theory.[16]

Because of *upādāna*, *bhava* comes to be. *Bhava* (becoming) is explained as twofold: action becoming (*kammabhava*) and resultant becoming (*uppattibhava*).[17] The former refers to the activity that causes good resultants, bad resultants, or unshakable resultants. Furthermore, every sort of action that leads to becoming is also called action becoming.[18] The latter refers to becoming in different plane: form and formless becoming (*rūpa bhava*, *arūpabhava*), perception becoming (*saññābhavo*), non-perception becoming (*asaññābhavo*), neither perception nor non-perception becoming (*nevasaññānāsaññābhavo*), becoming with a single aggregate (*ekavokārabhavo*), becoming with four aggregates (*catuvokārabhavo*), and becoming with five aggregates (*pañcavokārabhavo*).[19] In other words, these becomings are the resultants of one's actions.

Because of *bhava*, *jāti* comes to be. *Jāti* (birth) denotes the birth of the various beings into various categories of beings: their descent, their arising, the appearance of the aggregates, and the acquiring of the sense-bases.[20] Because of *jāti*, *jarā* (ageing), *maraṇa* (death), *soka* (grief), *parideva* (lamentation), *dukkha* (pain), *domanassa* (sorrow), and *upāyāsa* (tribulation) come to be.

Besides the different interpretations of each factor, different scholars and traditions have interpreted the formulae differently, with one debate becoming most prominent: whether the twelve factors should be interpreted as (1) a description of past, present, and future causes of death and rebirth over lifetimes (Bodhi 1995, 5), or (2) a moment-to-moment description of the mind process (Jones 2009,

15. Vibhaṅga 136: *Rūpataṇhā saddataṇhā gandhataṇhā rasataṇhā phoṭṭhabbataṇhā dhammataṇhā: ayaṃ vuccati vedanā paccayā taṇhā.*
16. Vibhaṅga 136: *Kāmupādānaṃ diṭṭhupādānaṃ sīlabbatupādānaṃ attavādupādānaṃ: idaṃ vuccati tanhāpaccayā upādānaṃ.*
17. Vibhaṅga 137: *atthi kammabhavo, atthi uppattibhavo.*
18. Vibhaṅga 137: *puññābhisaṃkhāro apuññābhisaṃkhāro āneñjābhisaṃkhāro: ayaṃ vuccati kammabhavo. Sabbam pi bhavagāmikammaṃ kammabhavo.*
19. Vibhaṅga 137: *Kāmabhavo rūpabhavo arūpabhavo saññābhavo asaññābhavo neva-saññānāsaññābhavo, ekavokārabhavo catuvokārabhavo pañcavokārabhavo: ayaṃ vuccati uppattibhavo. iti ataṃ ca kammabhavo ayañ ca uppattibhavo, ayaṃ vuccati upādānapaccayā bhavo.*
20. Vibhaṅga 137: *yā tesṃ tesaṃ sattānaṃ tamhi tamhi sattanikāye jāti sañjāti okkanti abhinibbatti khandhānṃ pātubhāvo āyatanānaṃ paṭīlābho: ayaṃ vuccati bhavapaccayā jāti.*

241)? The next section will visit this debate and then articulate our position for its use in counseling.

3.3 The Three-Life Model of Dependent Co-arising and Its Rebuttals

One traditional interpretation of dependent co-arising is to understand it as a description of *saṃsāra*, a wandering cycle of death and rebirth over countless lifetimes. We will now review the position of two major scholars, namely Bhikkhu Bodhi and Nārada Mahāthera. Bodhi interpreted the formula of dependent co-arising as follows: "The prevailing interpretation regards the series as spanning three successive lives, the twelve factors representing the causal and resultant phases of these lives alternated to show the round's inherent capacity for self-regeneration" (Bodhi 1995, 5).

In this traditional interpretation by Bodhi, the twelve factors of dependent co-arising are divided into a three lives model in order to demonstrate the inner dynamics of the circle (1995, 6). Bodhi further explained that each factor succeeds one another and each past *kamma* ripens as present results, thereby eliciting a new action, followed by more results (1995, 6). He described the three lives model as follows: "The past causes include craving, clinging, and existence, the present one's ignorance and volitional formations; the present resultants begin with birth and end in death, and future birth and death will be incurred by the same resultants" (1995, 6).

Another prominent scholar in Early Buddhism and Theravada Buddhism, Nārada, has a similar position on dependent co-arising, also emphasizing the three lives model. Nārada described dependent co-arising as a discourse on the cyclical process of birth and death (2013, 47). In particular, the first two conditions—(1) ignorance and (2) activities (*saṃkhāra*)—are considered as past causes. The middle eight conditions—(3) consciousness, (4) mind and matter, (5) the six spheres of sense, (6) contact, (7) feeling, (8) craving, (9) grasping, and (10) actions—pertain to the present. We understand that in this segment, consciousness supports conditions for the developing body and mind, which involves a pattern of craving and clinging to pursue pleasant feelings and avoid unpleasant feelings. This pattern gives rise to a being, an existence, as a condition for future life. The last two conditions of (11) birth and rebirth and (12) decay, death, sorrow, lamentation, pain, grief, and despair pertain to the future, coming with the inevitable process of aging and death (Nārada 2013, 48).

These two scholars consistently used the division of the past, present, and future causes of death and rebirth to exemplify the twelve factors of dependent co-arising. Shulman (2008), who reviewed the literature on dependent co-arising, also pointed out that the traditional Theravāda tradition tends to depict the twelve factors as a process of death and rebirth unfolding over three lifetimes (2008, 304). In a similar review of traditional scriptures and classic commentaries on dependent co-arising and the three-life model of the twelve factors, Jones (2009, 242) also noted that most Early Buddhist scholars explain dependent co-arising as operating over lifetimes and as driven by *kamma*. This three-life model has a long tradition. Dessein (2014, 2), a contemporary scholar and expert on the twelve factors who used the three-life model as a starting assumption, wrote:

> conditioned origin of suffering as starting with ignorance (member 1): because one is ignorant regarding the four noble truths, one commits actions for the sake of a 'self' (*ātman*). These actions are conditioning factors (member 2) that lead to perceptual consciousness (member 3)—i.e., primary consciousness as the first element of a new life. It is the form of consciousness of a *newly born child* whose faculties are not functioning yet. . . In this way, one's present existence (member 10) is composed. Through the law of karmic retribution, this present existence will lead to *a new birth* (member 11) that, in its turn, will be subject to decay-and-dying (member 12), after which a new cycle will start.

However, the three-life model has received an increasing number of challenges from contemporary scholars.

Jones (2009, 242) reviewed and gathered criticisms from several prominent Buddhist studies scholars, such as Paul Williams, Buddhadāsa Bhikkhu, and Bhikkhu Ñāṇavīra Thera, to challenge the validity of the three-life model. Some of Jones' key arguments include the questionable and arbitrary categorization of the twelve factors into three segments, how the *Dhamma* should be timeless and not bounded by lifetimes, and that the meaning of birth (*jāti*) should be the birth of a metaphysical self instead of a physical body (Jones 2009, 244). In particular, Jones pointed out that Theravāda *Abhidhamma* texts analyze the twelve factors of dependent co-arising as occurring together in the present moment (Jones 2009, 245). However, he acknowledged that the interpretations of the three lives model or present moment model may be interpretations of discourses instead of the Buddha's direct teaching (Jones 2009, 245).

Some scholars suggest that the essence of dependent co-arising, or arguably the original intent of the formula, presents a psychological analysis of the mind and its processes (Shulman, 2008, 298). From this perspective, the twelve factors provide a moment-to-moment analysis of mental conditioning, including the formation of the subjective experience of an "I." For example, Collett Cox (1993) studied the evolution of the interpretation of dependent co-arising from the early *sutta*s to the Sarvāstivāda *Abhidharma*. She found that the later Sarvāstivāda *Abhidharma* philosophers read dependent co-arising as an abstract and independent theory of causation, while the earlier *sutta*s focus on the formation of human suffering and ways to terminate it through the understanding of the twelve factors of dependent co-arising (Cox 1993, 137). As Cox said, while the dependent co-arising perspective may be applied to external reality, the ultimate aim of Buddhism is to end suffering, which primarily concerns the experience of one's five aggregates. Once a practitioner sees the dependently co-arisen nature of the five aggregates, one can cease clinging to them, ending the suffering (Cox 1993, 138).

Perhaps the position of Shulman on dependent co-arising is the most pertinent to Buddhist counseling:

> Whether the twelve factors refer to three different lives, as the traditional view holds, or whether they relate only to one life or even to a single instance of perception, whether they were articulated in this same sequence by the Buddha or were later arranged in this way by his disciples, the different views of the twelve factors all agree on one major point: They discuss the manner in which the mind conditions the saṃsāra experience and existence. The teaching is concerned with an analysis of the workings of the mind, with identifying the different processes of mental conditioning and describing their relations. The twelve factors do not deal with how things exist, but with the processes by which the mind operates. (Shulman 2008, 305)

As Karunadasa (2013, 26) said, regardless of the diverse interpretations of dependent co-arising, it always leads to realizing the Middle way as a product of mental cultivation. However, in our view, Buddhist counseling is designed for clients seeking solutions in this life, so they may not identify as Buddhist or be committed to Buddhist practice. Therefore, the most important lesson taught by dependent co-arising is how the mind functions and how to use this understanding to gain liberation from suffering. In conclusion, the concept of dependent co-arising should be the backbone of Buddhist counseling as a psychotherapeutic model based on Buddhist teachings.

3.4 The Implications of Dependent Co-arising for the Existence of Self

One critical implication of dependent co-arising is the understanding of self as a product of causes and conditions instead of being an ultimate, existing, and single entity.

As Somaratne (2021, 65) noted, the Buddha's teaching shows how life follows the pattern of dependent co-arising in which the present state of self is configured by numerous factors in the present moment (65). The Law of Dependent Co-arising sees the experience of human suffering as a whole, including the experience of "I" or "my self," as dependently arisen in nature (Somaratne 2021, 69). Somaratne also refers to the Buddha's analysis of the five aggregates to explain how the structure of human experience depends on the Law of Dependent Co-arising (2021, 69; more detailed discussion will follow in the next chapter). Specifically, each of the five aggregates of matter, feeling, perception, configurations, and consciousness is subject to clinging, each of them being dependently arisen and serving as a condition for the experience of "I" or "my self" as well as of the experience of suffering (Somaratne 2021, 69). Realizing the five clinging-aggregates or experiential structure as "non-self" and "not myself" is the way to cease suffering (Somaratne 2021, 167).

In a similar way, Bodhi (1995, 3) described dependent co-arising as a key Buddhist teaching to end existential suffering and liberate a person from the repeated cycle of birth and death. He added that the human mind tends to establish one's sense of identity by forming conceptual designations and claiming control of the five aggregates (Bodhi 1995, 31). In other words, the designations of "mine," "I am," and "my self" are conceptual expressions of ego-consciousness that are fabricated by nature (Bodhi 1995, 31). However, an ordinary person without instruction from the Buddha sees the world from the perspective of a self and thus has a distorted lens when seeing dependent co-arising (Bodhi 1995, 32). Therefore, Bodhi (1995, 32) emphasized that there is no agent or entity behind dependent co-arising, and hence "there is no agent behind the actions, no knower behind the knowing, no transmigrating self passing through the round."

Accordingly, as we understand it, dependent co-arising forms the backbone of Buddhist theory and practice. Buddhism does not posit the existence of a permanent self or the need for the annihilation of self. Instead, it describes the self as an experience grounded in phenomena that are continuously susceptible to change. However, the human mind is inclined to form a fixed understanding of phenomena and to believe in the intrinsic, independent, and permanent nature of existence. This results in the creation of constructs or logical abstractions based on the reification of ontological events. Let us give an example. Seeing a "flower" is a phenomenon supported by the attention we pay to an object; by the way our eyes receive the sensation of light; by our previous knowledge of flowers and recognition of the present object as similar; and for the object in question that is itself supported by sunlight, soil, oxygen, nutrients, seeds, and other elements. If any of these conditions change, the phenomenon of "flower" can change or cease. A flower, in other words, does not have a self-existing nature.

Take depression as another example. Clients who suffer from major depressive episodes tend to feel trapped in a permanent state of depression in general. Using the perspective of dependent co-arising, we can interpret depression as only a mental label attached to a phenomenon constructed by its interdependent conditions at any given moment, such as physical pain in the stomach and back, unpleasant sensations in the body and mind, tiredness, recognition of a mental state called "depression," the intention and urge to resist this state, imagery and inner voices that ruminate over past events, ill-will towards oneself, and related factors. If one or several of these conditions were to cease by increasing self-compassion, which dissolves self-directed ill-will, or by soothing the strong physical discomfort, the phenomenon of depression being experienced at that moment may change or cease. Further discussion of self and non-self can be found in the next chapter.

3.5 Commentary on Dependent Co-arising According to Professional Psychology

The concept of dependent co-arising is not a common theoretical framework for traditional psychotherapeutic or counseling models. However, recent studies such as that by Bornaetxea, Gil, and Molloy (2014) have proposed ways of integrating dependent co-arising into the concept of mind or brain analysis frameworks.

In an early attempt to connect dependent co-arising and traditional theories in psychology, Bornaetxea et al. (2014, 216) reviewed the development of scientific psychotherapy, from the philosopher René Descartes to the recent development of acceptance and commitment therapy (ACT). Their purpose was to compare the idea of "construction of reality" with the dependent co-arising concept of reality. They reviewed the central ideas of prominent figures in psychology, such as Wilhelm Wundt's differentiation between physics and psychology, Burrhus Skinner's epistemology of behaviorism, and George Kelley's causal attribution model. They observed that the field of psychotherapy is moving towards an epistemological and phenomenological approach that places emphasis on how an individual constructs their reality in context: "The psychologist's goal should not be to discover the eternal laws governing the functioning of the psyche or of the human soul, but to explore the possibilities of relations between human beings. For them, psychological knowledge does not advance towards the progressive uncovering of a supposed ultimate truth, but rather towards proposing new ways of constructing reality" (Bornaetxea, Gil, and Molloy 2014, 229).

Comparing and contrasting this idea to the Buddhist view of dependent co-arising, Bornaetxea et al. (2014, 231) concluded that the formula of dependent co-arising appears to include concepts of both constructionism and constructivism, with this feature being compatible with Skinnerian behaviorism and ACT and allowing for exploration between the relationship of physical and psychological phenomena. Moreover, as they argue, dependent co-arising provides a guideline to freedom and responsibility and a practical method to become liberated from suffering.

Bornaetxea and his research team also made an insightful observation on the development of psychotherapy over the last hundred years, drawing an interesting comparison between these theories and dependent co-arising as related to personal identity (Bornaetxea, Gil, and Molloy 2014, 238). While it is an intriguing observation, it was interesting that Bornaetxea and his research colleagues did not address a key question asked by prominent psychological theories: "What is a self?" Famous theorists and practitioners, such as Sigmund Freud and Carl Rogers, had certainly described their understanding of a self, including psychic functions and the existence of an inner self (Freud and Strachey 1922, 102) and an authentic self (Rogers 1959, 223). However, these efforts seem to address the question, "What is a self like?" rather than answering the question of "What is a self?" From our reading of these early theories in psychology, the self in psychology is somewhat similar to the idea of a pre-existing soul, and this existence of self is a presupposition behind many early psychotherapy models.[21] Bornaetxea and his team explained the self as an agent with a self-modifying conscious and unconscious, with no eternal and independent self behind all the actions (Bornaetxea, Gil, and Molloy 2014, 233).

We think a limitation of Bornaetxea et al.'s research is that they did not contrast the ideas of non-self and self in psychology. Moreover, although Bornaetxea et al. (2014, 240) stated that the idea of dependent co-arising can support a helpful process of contemplation, they did not discuss the application of this concept or how it can shape a treatment modality.

An advancement in the integration of dependent co-arising in professional psychology was made by Walpola et al. (2017, 147), who used the twelve factors of dependent co-arising to map mental processes. In doing so, they made an innovative attempt to plot the function of the mind using a schematic model based on Theravāda Buddhist texts,[22] with particular reference to the *sutta*s discussing dependent co-arising. With reference to the twelve factors, Walpola and his colleagues illustrated cognitive models explaining how contact generates feeling, perception, and thoughts (Walpola et al. 2017, 146). They also explained the processes of conceptual proliferation and clinging to thoughts based on Wrong View or a distorted perception of self (Walpola et al. 2017, 157). Walpola et al.'s (2017) systematic presentation of a schematic map of the mind based on the twelve factors was an attempt, as we see it, to introduce the Buddhist understanding of cognitive functions to the social sciences and neuroscience. However, as an interdisciplinary and practice-oriented study, it lacks practical examples or

21. Detailed discussion of the concept of self in psychology can be found in the book *Self-Concept* by John Hattie. His book revisited the original concept of self by Sigmund Freud and how it develops throughout the history of psychotherapy. One important assertion is the existence of true self as first described by Freud's psychoanalytic thought. This claim appears to align with the pre-existing soul and contrasts with the Buddhist belief in non-self.
22. For the Theravāda Buddhist texts, Walpola, Walpola, Walpola, and Toneatto (2017) primarily used *sutta*s from the *Saṃyutta Nikāya*, the *Majjhima Nikāya*, and the *Aṅguttara Nikāya*, such as Setting in Motion of the Wheel of the Dharma to make their arguments (Walpola, Walpola, Walpola, and Toneatto 2017, 141).

clinical applications. Without such illustrations, it would be difficult for mental health professionals to apply the cognitive model in helping clients be aware of clinging to thoughts and letting go of their clinging. Even so, applying dependent co-arising to counseling was an encouraging starting point.

The psychotherapist, Buddhist scholar, and meditation practitioner Ellis Gabriel (2021, 1) has also presented a cognitive interpretation of the twelve factors of dependent co-arising using psychological nomenclature and adding perspectives from professional psychology. Based on our literature search, Gabriel's work is the only attempt to relate the twelve factors to traditional concepts in professional psychology and uncover new theoretical ground to inform practice. In particular, Gabriel explained each factor, reinterpreted and renamed them, and added a psychological perspective based on traditional psychotherapeutic models (Gabriel 2021). For example, he renamed "volitional formation" to "the forming unconscious field" to emphasize its role as a structuring function of the subconscious cognitive field that joins all mental elements (Gabriel 2021, 3). In another example, he described craving as "a subject of desire and fantasy" that represents the chain of preceding cognitive processes that constitute craving and linked it to the need for fulfillment as described in Freudian psychoanalysis and Carl Roger's humanistic psychology (Gabriel 2021, 11). By interpreting dependent co-arising in this new light, he hoped to bring a positive shift in psychotherapeutic techniques: "Even though psychotherapeutic techniques have developed over the last few decades and allow clients to experience relief, more satisfying approaches to everyday life and fulfilment, they typically do not touch the more fundamental levels of subject formation and thus remain limited in scope" (Gabriel 2021, 17).

We agree with his argument that many psychotherapeutic techniques are only a momentary means to help clients feel better, and that such methods may not sufficiently induce fundamental and lasting changes in a client's intrapsychic structure. We argue, though, that Buddhism reaches a deeper level to remodel the intrapsychic field by training one's mind, thereby promoting more fundamental change. We applaud Gabriel's effort and approach as he skillfully introduced the twelve factors to professional psychology and supplemented it with existing psychological ideas. However, as with Walpola et al. (2017), he presented no practical case examples to illustrate the application and treatment objectives. It is also unclear whether the end goal is to reduce or cease clinging to self.

Ho and his research colleagues (2022, 1) conducted a study on intersubjectivity in parent-child relationships and employed dependent co-arising to interpret their findings. They developed a coding system and used the theory-guided quantitative review method to evaluate thirty-five clinical trials on parenting interventions. This was to find out whether a parenting intervention can effectively reduce parenting stress if the intervention is designed to address intersubjectivity, which is defined as "one person's awareness in relation to another person's awareness"

(Ho et al. 2022, 1). Ho et al. (2022, 1) emphasized the importance of intersubjectivity in the development of human relationship as it plays an important role in accurately understanding the intentions of others, the effect of one's behaviors, and the forming of relational benevolence, especially in parent-child relationships.

In particular, Ho and his team (2022, 15) integrated the idea of intersubjectivity and dependent co-arising, leading to the idea that effective parent-child relationships require a mirror-like nature of awareness. This is itself dependent upon the interactive effects of subject (cause) and objects (conditions), as is evident in the cognitive processes of the parent and child as well as various environmental factors. In any relationship, they explain, there is no independent subject "I," as this sense of "I" is dependently arisen from the objects of "other" and hence intersubjectivity can be deemed a relational awareness of self and others (Ho et al., 16).

We think Ho and his team made a creative effort to link the traditional psychological concept of intersubjectivity with dependent co-arising to add a new perspective to effective parent-child relationships. However, they chose to address the overarching idea of dependent co-arising instead of addressing each factor and its individual implications. The paper they wrote was also theoretical and conceptual in nature, which may make it challenging for frontline counselors to apply dependent co-arising in their practice. They did mention, though briefly, the position of self according to the paradigm of dependent co-arising as follows: "An invalid belief—the belief that self or other is fixed and unchanged after any person-to-person interactions—is the root cause of entrapping one's awareness in an unhealthy state characterized by rigidity and inflexibility. The consequence of invalid beliefs in one's awareness is that one will misattribute the cause of his or her subjective experiences (qualia) to the object itself, rather than the interactive product of his or her active inference engine by the object" (Ho et al. 2022, 20). Nonetheless, they did not discuss how this idea contrasts with the assumptions of self in other schools of psychology, nor did they apply this concept in practice. In sum, we think it is a creative and insightful paper, although its applicability to counseling practice is limited due to the restricted scope of this conceptual work.

Based on the literature search we conducted, only Dharma therapy claims to use dependent co-arising as a theoretical basis for treatment, although the use of the concept of non-self (*anattā*) in their treatment repertoire is only briefly addressed (Sik and Yim 2021, 306). In Sik and Yim's (2021, 309–10) article, a hypothetical case is described in which the counselor helps a client understand the dependently originated nature of his suffering, including how the experiences of suffering can be analyzed as his clinging to the five aggregates. However, there was not a sufficiently detailed account of the application of dependent co-arising in the treatment modality, such as how to help the client reach insights, nor enough detail on the specific techniques used to achieve this end. The article also did not describe whether the hypothetical client has relinquished their clinging to the five aggregates and realized non-self as a result of treatment. Despite these weaknesses, the article did imply that the treatment had eased the patient's attachment to the notion of self, as follows: "Through the intervention process, Peter (client's name) understood that a person is made up of five aggregates . . . he should also examine the excessive attachment to self-identity" (Sik and Yim 2021, 311).

The literature search yielded very few scholarly works trying to integrate dependent co-arising with professional psychology. Among scholars and practitioners who are trying to make such an integration, there is still a lack of theoretical orientation based solely on Buddhism. The result is an unclear treatment objective. In the present context, the question we should be asking is whether the direction of treatment aims at reducing the client's clinging to self-notion and realizing non-self. Moreover, while these studies successfully addressed the integration at a theoretical level, they lack practical examples to help mental health professionals visualize its pragmatic application in the counseling room. In effect, while dependent co-arising can become a psychotherapeutic technique to promote more profound and fundamental changes in clients, this foundational theoretical work has not yet been carried out.

Whether there is a pre-existing self is a significant question in psychotherapy as it directly determines the psychotherapists' treatment direction. As Buddhist counseling shares its theoretical foundation with Buddhism, we assert that all the interventions and approaches of a Buddhist counselor should guide a client in the direction of the non-existence of an unchanging, permanent self (*anattā*), similar to the aim of Dharma therapy.

3.6 The Implications of Dependent Co-arising for Buddhist Counseling

Every theoretical orientation has a central principled framework for understanding the world. Buddhist counseling has dependent co-arising as its core theoretical principle. This theoretical construct should guide each counseling component (i.e., assessment, case conceptualization, intervention, and the therapeutic exchange). Employing dependent co-arising as the backbone for a counseling model has several implications.

Perhaps the most important implication of dependent co-arising is the view of self it proposes. As we understand it, the self is a phenomenon that provisionally exists interdependently, being interconnected with other causes and conditions. This provisional existence can be considered a first-person subjectivity driven by a web of cognitive factors. With the help of the twelve factors of dependent co-arising, we can see the psychological process of how ignorance of the true nature of self perpetuates cyclical patterns of suffering. Unfortunately, however, most individuals hold on to self-identity and the delusion that an "I" inherently exists, and such clinging to the notion of self or the five aggregates is a core cause of suffering.

Early Buddhist scriptures also documented such mistaken views of inherent existence in monastic members. For example, in the *Mahātaṇhāsaṅkhaya-sutta* (MN 38), a monk called Sāti insisted that the Buddha explained that it is the same consciousness which roams from one birth to another,[23] firmly holding on to this view regardless of contrary feedback from his peers. The Buddha admonished him for misunderstanding his teaching, holding onto and speaking of such a view of permanent consciousness instead of the dependent co-arising nature of consciousness (*paṭiccasamuppannaṁ viññāṇaṁ*). The Buddha regarded that holding onto and speaking of such a view as the Buddha's word was the same as accusing the Buddha himself (Bodhi 1995, 350).[24] In particular, the Buddha explained, "There is no origination of consciousness without a condition."[25]

From this perspective, the remedy is to understand the formula of dependent co-arising to see the process of suffering, gain insights, and practice the ceasing of unskillful mind acts. More discussion of self and non-self will be offered in the following chapters.

One common question asked by both clients and scholars about dependent co-arising when applied to Buddhist counseling concerns the meaning of the three lives model, especially in relation to past lives. We suggest that although a common interpretation of dependent co-arising in Early Buddhist teachings may not support the three-life model, discussion of this model may be a skillful means to help clients reach the therapeutic goals if it aligns with their worldview. As an example, imagine a 36-year-old client going through a divorce and feeling full of resentment against her husband, who has acted in multiple ways to ruin her career and reputation. According to the client's story, she has played a submissive role for years, conforming to her husband's demands until she could tolerate it no longer, leading to her wish for a divorce. Furthermore, regardless of how much she tried to compromise, her husband continually attacked and tortured her emotionally, such as spreading rumors of her having multiple affairs whenever the husband found her slipping out of his control. The client identifies as a Buddhist, although her practice does not stop her from ruminating over the emotional injuries and the question of why her husband keeps hurting her like this. "Why would my beloved one treat me like this?" was an emotionally charged and repeated question on

23. MN I, 256: *tathā'haṁ Bhagavatā dhammaṁ deseti ājānāmi yathā tad ev'idaṁ viññāṇaṁ sandhāvati saṁsarati, anaññan-ti.*
24. MN I, 259: *Atha ca panāyaṁ Sāti bhikkhu kevaṭṭaputto attanā duggahītena amhe c' eva abbhācikkhati.*
25. MN I, 259: *aññatra paccayā natthi viññāṇassa sambhavo ti.*

which she often ruminated, causing her much suffering. With the client's permission, the counselor brought up a discussion of her past lives:

> Counselor: "What do you understand about the influence of past lives?"
>
> Client: "I've heard about it and many Chinese Buddhist masters talked about it . . . I think they said something like 'your present life reflects your deeds in a past life.' Is it something like this?"
>
> Counselor: "The truth is that we will never know the exact answer, but we can always entertain possibilities to see if there is an alternative perspective to our suffering. Out of all the people you encountered in this present life, you met this person, you two fell in love, and both of you decided to get married, is that right?
>
> Client: "Yes."
>
> Counselor: "And of all the current relationships he has, he treats his mother well, he is pretty nice to his supervisees, but he is controlling, and perhaps the most hostile, to you. However, you have always tried to be considerate to him, so you cannot understand why he does that to you. Is that right?"
>
> Client: "That's right."
>
> Counselor: "Okay. Assuming that there was a past life you both experienced together that caused these events today, what would that past life look like?"
>
> Client: "Well, if you put it this way, it may be that we were close, but I hurt him in a certain way . . . So, in this life, he could have come back to retaliate."
>
> Counselor: "That is one possibility. Perhaps previous lives have planted certain seeds and the conditions in this life provide the environment for them to grow. If what we experience is a product of the past, things remain unresolved, and if what we do now provides the causes for the future, there is hope for change. A wise choice would be to think about what the best action might be right now to stop the damaging cycle from continuing itself."
>
> Client: ". . . So it's all about the choices I make now . . . what should I do?"
>
> Counselor: "If you step back to look at the pattern of repeated retaliation between these two people, what advice comes to your mind to end this cycle?"
>
> Client: "The ideal is forgiveness. If forgiveness is impossible, at least not causing further harm."
>
> Counselor: "That sounds like a wise choice!"

In this dialogue, the client developed an alternative perspective: "Perhaps there are unknown reasons from previous lifetimes that make him hurt me so much in this life." This perspective provides an answer to her question, which then allows her to let go of her resentment. Later in the counseling process, the client learned to set boundaries to protect herself while also choosing not to fight or take revenge, as she does not want to foster further resentment or hatred in her mind. Early Buddhism supports the practice of "letting go" and cultivating "forgiveness" (*khanti*), reflecting the understanding that one of the possible causes of the adversities one is going through is due to one's own *kamma*. For instance, in the *Aṅgulimāla-sutta*, when Ven. Aṅgulimāla was hit by a clod of earth, a stone and a shard, causing his head to bleed, his bowl to break, and his outer robe to be torn to shreds, the Buddha advised him to endure it, reflecting that it is the fruition of his own past deeds.[26] In relation to this, we can even see that reflecting on one's *kamma* is one of monks' constant practices. In the *Dasadhamma-sutta* it is stated: "One who has gone forth should often reflect: the owner of all my actions is myself. I am born of action (*kamma*). Action is my kinsman. Action is my refuge. Whatever action I perform, good or bad, I am an inheritor of its result. I am the inheritor of my own actions."[27] The main application of such reflection is to help practitioners let go of things and not harbor resentful thoughts towards those who caused them harm or treated them badly.

The second feature of dependent co-arising concerns multiple causation. Like the idea of self, every phenomenon, including suffering, is a product of causes and changes so that everything can be potentially impermanent and changeable by nature. As we see it, one must gain sufficient awareness of the causes and conditions sustaining suffering to (1) see and accept the unchangeable causes and conditions at the present moment, (2) find out the changeable causes and conditions at the present moment, and (3) make realistic changes that result in the phenomenon of suffering being extinguished. To illustrate this phenomenon, picture a Jenga tower: each condition is one block of the whole stack. A rule of the game is that we can only take away one block at a time; if we remove the most pivotal piece, the entire tower collapses.

On another note, we see that the idea of multiple causation and its implications for interconnectedness also influences our understanding of the numerous conditions that contribute to a client's suffering in the mundane world. To give an example: one common problem of clients who have psychological disorders is their experience of their conditions as permanent and unchangeable. For example, depressed clients tend to ruminate over negative thoughts and have the helpless feeling that things will not get better. This loss of sense of control and hopelessness can drag clients into the overwhelming emotional suffering of depression

26. MN II, 104: *adhivāsehi tvaṁ brāhmaṇa; adhivāsehi tvaṁ brāhmaṇa. yassa kho tvaṁ kammassa vipākena bahūni vassāni bahūni vassasatāni bahuni vassasahassāni niraye pacceyyāsi, tassa tvaṁ, brāhmaṇa kammassa vipākaṁ diṭṭhe va dhamme paṭisaṁvedesīti* (O sage, endure it, endure it. The karmic fruits, which could have burned you for hundreds of thousands of years in hell, are being experienced by you in this very life).
27. AN V, 88: *kammassako' mhi kammadāyādo kammayoni kammabandhu kammapaṭisaraṇo, yaṃ kammaṃ karissāmi kalyāṇaṃ vā pāpakaṃ vā tassa dāyā-do bhavissāmī ti pabbajitena abhiṇhaṃ paccavekkhitabbaṃ.*

without seeing any way out. Dependent co-arising, we argue, can provide a new and somewhat detached perspective of depression as a phenomenon, revealing the potential causes and conditions sustaining it. In this regard, we have created an exercise sheet to work through with clients and raise awareness of different conditions contributing to their experience of suffering, as seen in Figure 3.1.

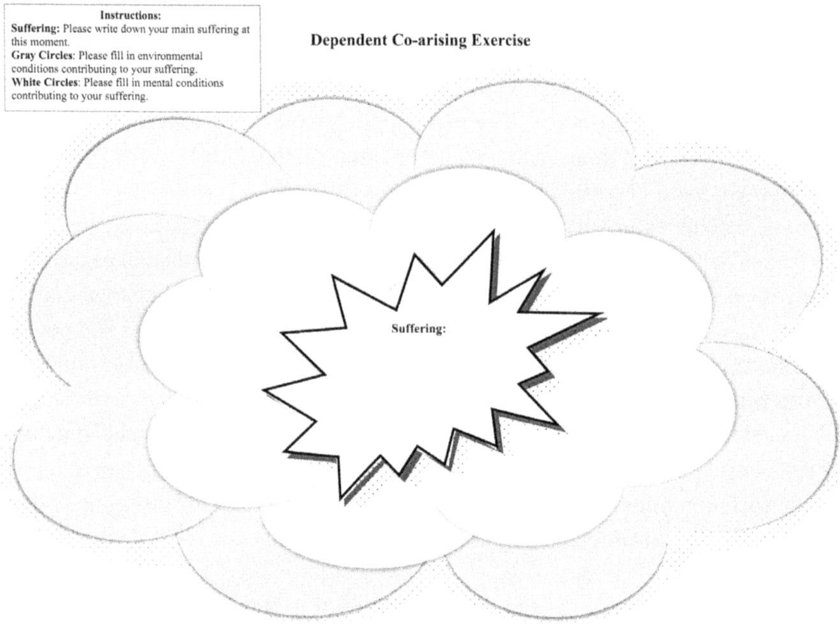

Figure 3.1: Dependent Co-arising Exercise

In this exercise, conditions are classified into four domains in order to help a client and counselor discern wholesome and unwholesome conditions. Here is an example:

- **Internal conditions.** Internal conditions refer to conditions within the five aggregates, especially mind conditions or the psychological constituents and cognitive tendencies (Lee 2022, 71). For example, one's view of self, states of mind, cognitive acts, defilements, hindrances, emotions, health condition, and so on can be considered as internal conditions. The inner circles represent internal conditions in this exercise.

- **External conditions.** External conditions refer to any condition outside of one's five aggregates, especially various conditions of the client's external environment, lived system, subsystems, and interactions between them (Lee 2022, 71). Examples include the client's social relationships, stressors at work, financial status, cultural factors of discrimination against the client's identity, politics, and other environmental factors. The outer circles represent internal conditions in this exercise.
- **Favorable conditions.** Favorable conditions are factors that reduce the client's suffering or support their cultivation to liberate themselves from suffering. These conditions can be either internal or external. For example, favorable internal conditions can be any sort of wholesome practice, such as compassion, mindfulness, loving kindness, perseverance, etc., while favorable external conditions can be supportive friends, a loving parent, availability of meditation classes in the community, and financial stability.
- **Unfavorable conditions.** Unfavorable conditions are factors that increase the client's suffering or hinder their cultivation to liberate themselves from suffering. For example, unfavorable internal conditions can be ill-will, strong sensual desires, a depressed mood, loneliness, a body with chronic illness etc., while unfavorable external conditions can be lack of friends, an emotionally abusive parent, financial hardship, and public crises such as a pandemic.

A Buddhist counselor can work with a client to identify the suffering and reveal potential causes and conditions beneath their suffering. An example will now be given of a hypothetical case based on our work with an actual client.

Daisy is a 43-year-old female suffering from depression due to the loss of her husband. Clinically, she presents with a sad mood, loss of concentration, sleep disturbance, and poor appetite. She cried several times in the session when talking about her husband. Using the dependent co-arising exercise, the counselor first helped her sort out different external environmental factors contributing to her sadness (using the gray circled areas). After a dialogue on Daisy's living situation and social network (by asking the exploratory question, "What are the things in your environment that make you depressed?"), she revealed some unfavorable environmental conditions. They included her responsibility for taking care of two young children, her work stress, lack of support from her immediate family, and financial stress. At the same time, she was able to identify support from her husband's family and support from her friends and colleagues as favorable environmental conditions in response to the counselor's question about things around her that protect her against depression.

For unfavorable mental conditions contributing to suffering (asking the exploratory question, "What thoughts and ideas usually make you depressed?"), the counselor helped her identify certain emotions and cognitive acts such as missing her husband, her doubt about her ability to manage the family, and worries about not recovering from depression (using the white circled areas). At the same time, when asked what kind of thoughts and ideas kept her going during this challenging time, she recognized her perseverance in overcoming challenges, her love for her children and her husband, and her passion for art. By explicitly discussing and writing down the related conditions on the sheet provided, Daisy gained a more objective and detached view of her depression. The counselor helped her identify the conditions that she can and cannot control. Daisy saw that she could probably take a little time to do art again as a way to soothe her emotions, mindfully immerse herself in the moment, and express how missing her husband feels.

The factors of dependent co-arising are powerful tools for a mind analysis that can provide an insightful tool for counselors to raise clients' awareness of how to notice and relinquish unskillful and unwholesome mind acts and choose more wholesome mind acts. To do so, it is necessary to apply dependent co-arising as a psychotherapeutic tool and theoretical construct in a practical setting. Let us now proceed to a second case.

Johnny is a 38-year-old Chinese man who sought counseling due to a recent breakup. He has a long history of unsuccessful relationships, although he always believed that a romantic relationship would be his best way out of his chaotic family of origin. Johnny tends to idealize romantic love and is susceptible to feeling rejected and denied when his partner fails to meet his needs. He was described as "emotionally needy" by his former girlfriend, who broke up with him.

Applying the twelve factor formula of dependent co-arising to a moment-by-moment perspective of relationship loss and grief, we can analyze how Johnny suffers in this cycle. Driven by the ignorant view (Factor 1) that love should be fulfilling and everlasting, Johnny had a volitional formation (Factor 2) for love and relationships. Aware of how his senses inform his concept of love (Factor 3), he actively predisposes his body and mind[28] (Factor 4) to get in touch with external objects, such as seeking physically attractive women, hearing soothing voices,

---

28. Mind and body (Pāli: *nāma rūpa*), also translated as "mentality and materiality" or "name and form," is a topic that has led to countless interpretations and debates in Buddhism. According to scholars, this condition refers to two concepts: (1) *Rūpa*, which can be considered as the material body as constituted by the four fundamental elements, including earth, water, fire, and wind, and (2) *nāma*, which refers to all aspects of mind, although some scholars point out that *nāma* does not include consciousness in the early scriptures (Harvey 1993, 33). The application here primarily takes mind and body as the mental and physical structure of a human being that is capable of receiving and interpreting internal and external stimuli.

smelling alluring fragrance, tasting romantic dinners, cuddling for warmth, and experiencing concepts of togetherness, connection, and love (Factor 5). The experiences of these contacts (Factor 6) give rise to pleasant feelings that trigger a strong urge to sustain and enrich such feelings (Factor 7).

This "craving" in factor 7 results in clinging (Factor 8) that gradually becomes concretized into a specific and irreplaceable concept of love for a particular woman at any given time (Factor 9). Should there be any sign of rejection, Johnny tries hard to grasp on to his partner and seek her validation (Factor 10). Then, as the couple's relationship is born (Factor 11), he believes that he will not be abandoned because the love he feels is further perpetuated. Once such a relationship is born, it goes through conflicts, unfulfilled expectations, doubts, rejection, and mistrust, which gradually dissolve the relationship. When the beloved partner can no longer stand Johnny's needs for validation and connection, Johnny falls into grief, lamentation, sorrow, and despair (Factor 12). At this stage a crystallized concept persistently affects his mind, such as "The love of my life is gone and will never come back. I am always alone, and no one loves me." In the next relationship, either in this life or subsequent lifetimes, this cycle will continue as long as he clings to the ignorant belief that true love is fulfilling and everlasting. Although Johnny is seeking counseling for the current breakup, this sequence of factors has occurred repeatedly in his previous relationships.

In the formula for dependent co-arising, a common entry point to interrupt and end the apparent endless cycle is the gap between feeling, craving, and clinging. Theoretically, if the mind can heedfully sense the feeling of pleasantness, realize exactly when the "thirst" for more pleasantness starts to arise, and make a volitional choice not to pursue this pleasantness, there will be a pause in the link between "feeling" and "craving," providing an opportunity to stop the cycle. The Buddha's succinct teaching to Bāhiya (*Udāna* 8) is, in fact, about practicing breaking the chain of dependently arisen factors at this point. The Buddha teaches this point as follows:

> Bāhiya, you should train in this way: in the seen, there will only be what is seen. In the heard, there will only be what is heard. In the sensed, there will only be what is sensed. In the known, there will only be known. When you have trained in that way, you will not be by that. When you are not by that, you will not be in that. When you are not in that, you will neither be here in this world, nor in the world beyond, or in between. This is the end of *dukkha*.[29]

29. Udāna 8: *tasmātiha te Bāhiya evaṃ sikkhitabbaṃ: diṭṭhe diṭṭhimattaṃ bhavissati, sute sutamattam bhavissati, mute mutamattaṃ bhavissati, viññāte viññātamattaṃ bhavissati. evañ hi te Bāhiya sikkhitabbaṃ: yato kho te Bāhiya diṭṭhe diṭṭamattaṃ bhavissati . . . viññāte viññātamattaṃ bhavissati, tato tvaṃ Bāhiya na tattha, yato tvaṃ Bāhiya nev'attha, tato tvaṃ Bāhiya nev'idha na huraṃ na ubhayamantarena, es'ev'anto dukkhssā ti.*

This advanced training aims at preventing the proliferation of perceptions derived from sensory experiences. This practice is powerful as it eliminates the fuel for generating craving (*taṇhā*), self-view (*diṭṭhi*), and the I-conceit (*māna*). In other words, this helps a practitioner to not get stuck in the *saṃsāric* flow. The last lines of the above passages are of great importance in understanding what is meant by "*saṃsāric* flow." It refers to present and momentary *saṃsāra*, rather than so-called "endless deaths and rebirths." What we meant by present and momentary *saṃsāra* is the cycle of proliferation of perceptions and arising of unwholesome mental states, such as craving etc. The mind proliferates due to ignorance that involves ideations of permanence, self, and the existence of permanent satisfaction. When a person does not cling to what has been seen, heard, felt, and known, he is free of the flow of the mental chain of proliferations and thus, at such moments, there will be no production of unwholesome mental states, which results in a state of peace. When an individual is at peace and free from the *samsāric* flow, he (the mind) does not belong to any time or space, and this is what it is meant by "When you have trained in that way, you will not be by that. When you are not by that, you will not be in that."

In the twelve factor model, the stage of clinging (*upādāna*) can be regarded as more noticeable and impactful than the stage of craving. This makes it relatively easier to observe and identify during daily mindfulness practice. The main point is that thoughts are natural occurrences beyond our control, but it is the act of "clinging" to those mental activities that ultimately leads to the next factor—becoming (*bhava*). In other words, to prevent the production of the chain reaction of "becoming" that leads to suffering, it is recommended to practice "letting go" or "not clinging" to the objects one has craved; when there is no clinging, there is no becoming (*upādāna nirodhā bhava nirodho*). From a doctrinal perspective, this means refraining from clinging to [any kind of] sensuality (*kāmūpādāna*), [any kind of] views (*diṭṭhupādāna*), [any sort of] precepts and religious observance (*sīlabbatupādāna*), as well as the theories of soul and self-notion (*attavādūpadāna*).

Clinging refers to feeding one's cravings. In other words, while craving can be understood as liking or wishing for something, which can be related to sensual pleasure, becoming or existence, or not becoming or non-existence, clinging refers to the act of holding tightly and not letting go of the objects of craving. It involves a more active involvement with the objects of craving (Harvey 2013, 63). Therefore, in order to avoid feeding our cravings, it is essential to be aware of them. By observing and acknowledging our cravings, we can prevent ourselves from clinging, and as a result, the cravings gradually fade away over time. In *satipaṭṭhāna* practice, this is known as practicing contemplation of the mind (*cittānupassanā*). Further, in the *Upādāna-sutta* (SN 12.52), the Buddha instructs his students to contemplate the drawback (*ādīnava*) of things to which they can cling and in doing so make the cravings cease, also leading to the cessation of clinging. Thus, there will be no opportunity to produce the chain reaction of "becoming."[30]

In the above example, the Buddhist counselor can collaborate with Johnny in the counseling session to identify his depressed mood as the core experience of suffering when breaking up with someone. Aware of how he engages in such a cycle, the Buddhist counselor can then begin to help Johnny examine his views of how exactly a love relationship can be fulfilling, as well as to reflect on his strong craving to be loved and accepted and how he adamantly clings to his perception of love relationships in an attempt to satiate his needs. It may also help to provide psychoeducation on healthy relationships in order to foster a Right View in the mundane world and help Johnny learn appropriate relationship boundaries.[31] The next level of Buddhist counseling will then examine Johnny's clinging. At this level, the Buddhist counselor may need to meticulously work with Johnny to cultivate mindfulness and see how his clinging arises. For example, it may manifest as strong bodily sensations of heat and rigidity, internal dialogues and images of how he misses and needs his loved one, or his strong urge to call or text her. Being watchful of these activities in body and mind, trying to ground attention in an object of meditation, such as his in-and-out breath, and becoming non-reactive to these responses can help Johnny create mental distance and the ability to pause from engaging in *saṃsāric* flow. Then, the Buddhist counselor can work with Johnny to help him see himself in a detached way as a vulnerable individual yearning for love while being repeatedly hurt; in particular, having never been taught appropriate ways to love, it resulted in him feeling vulnerable, weak, and lonely. Such insights, especially realizing how his previous unskillful attempts could not satisfy his clinging, can help Johnny let go, or "not cling" to his previous mental construction of love-relationships as an ideal and ultimate means for feeling secure and satisfied.

Finally, a Buddhist counselor may help Johnny learn appropriate ways to communicate his needs in relationships and set up realistic expectations. It is also essential for him to understand that loneliness is an inevitable feeling in real life, although such feelings are tolerable. With this new set of insights, Johnny is more likely to end the cycle of suffering without involving other factors in the dependent co-arising formula. For example, he may begin to recognize that his thoughts about his new girlfriends never leaving him are not realistic (intervening at the stage of ignorance), or he may control his urge to pursue inappropriate

30. SN II, 84: *Upādāniyesu bhikkhave dhammesu ādīnavānupassino viharato taṇhā nirujjhati. taṇhānirodhā upādānanirodho. upādānanirodhā bhavanirodho.*

31. "Right View" is the key component of the Noble Eightfold Path with which to see the true nature of reality. There will be a more detailed discussion in Chapter 7.

relationships despite pleasant feelings (intervening at the stage of feeling), or he may not hold on to the pleasant feelings he delights in while also being prepared to let them go (intervening at the stage of craving).

3.7 Conclusion

Dependent co-arising is the backbone and key teaching of Buddhism as well as Buddhist counseling. This chapter reviewed the basic doctrine of dependent co-arising by examining and discussing several views, presenting recent debates from professional psychology, and adding to the literature by offering practical ways to integrate dependent co-arising as both a theoretical framework for Buddhist counseling and as a psychotherapeutic technique. There are many more ways to skillfully apply this vital concept to counseling, so we hope that our preliminary attempt inspires future innovative applications.

4

Theoretical Orientation Dimension II: Central Theoretical Constructs of Human Nature and Human Motivation

Central to every theoretical orientation is the basic philosophy of human nature, as it describes the foundational assumptions about what makes, drives, and changes a human being. In psychology, different schools of thoughts use environmental, ecological, biological, subconscious, socio-political, cultural, systemic, cognitive, behavioral, humanistic, and other perspectives to explain human nature and the sense of self (Gehart 2016, 6). Driven by the Law of Dependent Co-arising discussed in the previous chapter, *self* can be regarded as a conventional and provisional existence while *non-self* is the ultimate reality. The discussion of these two aspects will elucidate the Early Buddhist understanding of human nature. This chapter will also introduce the construction of a self-notion based on the mind's clinging to the five aggregates while also utilizing the model of cognitive processes in Early Buddhist teachings in order to explain self and non-self.

4.1 Non-self

What was arguably the Buddha's first utterance after he proclaimed reaching enlightenment is documented in verses 153 and 154 of the *Dhammapada*: "This tour, this cycle of existence, has run through numerous births without encountering, looking for the builder, the creator of the world and self. For repeated birth is painful. O, you builder, the creator, you are at last seen. You will never build this house and self again. All your supports are destroyed; the structure is demolished. The mind has stopped being conditioned, the urge has ceased" (Weragoda 1993, 512–13).[1]

---

1. Dhp 153 – 154: *anekajātisaṃsāraṃ sandhāvissaṃ anibbisaṃ, gahakārakaṃ gavesanto, dukkhā jāti punappunaṃ.*
   gahakāraka diṭṭho si puna gehaṃ na kāhasi, sabbā ete phāsukā bhaggā gahakūṭaṃ visaṃkhitaṃ, visaṃkhāragataṃ cittaṃ taṇhānaṃ khayam ajjhagā.

These two verses expressed the joy the Buddha felt upon attaining full enlightenment or complete liberation from suffering. The house-builder (*gahakāraka*) appears to symbolize an unskillful mental urge to repeatedly build or fabricate the existence of self. When parts and components sustaining the house—a self—become clear and the resulting repeated sorrow and unsatisfactoriness arise, the Buddha realized an unconditioned mind state and relinquished craving. As we read it, this verse represents the Buddha's insight into the constructed and fabricated nature of the self-notion as well as the core Buddhist teaching of non-self, awareness of it being a major step towards liberation from suffering.

To understand non-self, perhaps the first concept to understand is what a *self* is. Generally speaking, in philosophy and religion, self is considered to be a permanently existing, independent, and blissful entity (Somaratne 2016, 168). In contrast, the Buddha taught that such a self does not exist in reality. Ignorance, as a cause of suffering, deludes the mundane person into believing in the existence of a self instead of realizing such a belief is only a mental creation (Somaratne 2016, 169). Echoing this idea, Karunadasa (2019, 1) described the belief in a self as similar to a belief in a soul, which is the essence of what it means to be a human being. Karunadasa wrote that "the idea of self, as we all know, assumes many forms. It appears as 'I' in ordinary discourse, as 'soul' in religion, and as 'ego' in philosophy, all such forms being considered as a 'fallacious assumption, a conception without a corresponding objective counterpart'" (Karunadasa 2019, 1). While clinging to a belief in a self is a psychological experience, it also requires ontological support to sustain it, and hence the ego-consciousness of an unenlightened person identifies with five aggregates to form the view of "I" or the view of self (Karunadasa 2019, 2–3).

To believe in a self according to the five clinging-aggregates is to consider the self as "personal, permanent, independent, and satisfactory" (Somaratne 2016, 167). The uncultivated mind (*abhāvitaṃ cittaṃ*) of a mundane person is unaware of the fact that the self is merely a mental creation so that the mundane person perceives a subject of "I" in every sensory experience (Somaratne 2016, 169). In fact, this process was termed as clinging to the five aggregates (*pañcūpādānakkhandhā)*, its meaning encompassing clinging onto matter, feeling, perception, configurations, and consciousness (Somaratne 2016, 169).

Many of the *sutta*s in the Pāli *Nikāyas*, such as the *Upādānaparipavatta-sutta* (SN 22.56), the *Nakulapitu-sutta* (SN 22.1), the *Nibbedhika-sutta* (AN 6.63), and the *Mahāhatthipadopama-sutta* (MN 28) discuss the concept of "phases" in the Buddha's teaching and how the human mind identifies with the experience of the five aggregates as self. For example, the Buddha claimed, "So long as I did not directly know as they really are the five aggregates subject to clinging in four phases, I did not claim to have awakened to the unsurpassed perfect enlightenment"

(Bodhi 2000, 895).[2] As we read it, the Buddha only claimed to have achieved perfect enlightenment when he clearly knew and saw the four phases of each aggregate: the origin (*samudayaṃ*) of the aggregate, the cessation (*nirodho*) of the aggregate, and the way leading to the cessation (*nirodhagāminiṃ paṭipadaṃ*) of the aggregate, and thereby knowing reality as it really is. In other words, seeing the nature of how the five aggregates is not self, or the realization of non-self, is a way to liberate ourselves from bondage. In the *Anattalakkhaṇa-sutta*, the Buddha stated that clinging onto the five aggregates results in afflictions, explicitly pointing out that the five aggregates are non-self (Bodhi 2000, 901), thereby instructing practitioners to cease passionately clinging on to them and developing instead the perspective "this is not mine, this I am not, this is not my self" (Bodhi 2000, 902). Moreover, many *sutta*s emphasize the importance of understanding non-self and refraining from falling into the two extremes of believing that there must be a self or non-self. In the *Vacchagotta-sutta* (SN 44.8), the Buddha remained undeclared or unexplained (*abyākataṃ*) when responding to Vacchagotta's questions of whether there is a self or not a self. When Ānanda sought clarification from the Buddha on his silence, the Buddha explained that answering either question will lead to falling into one of the two extreme views—eternalism (*sassatavāda*) and annihilationism (*ucchedavādā*)—which do not give rise to knowledge that "all phenomena are not-self."[3] In principle, we see the thrust of the Buddhist *sutta*s gravitating towards the idea that the realization of non-self is the key goal of personal cultivation, while clinging, attachment to a belief, or a notion of self is considered the core cause of suffering (Somaratne 2021, 28). Therefore, in order to apply the doctrine of non-self to any model of counseling, it is crucial to gain a deeper understanding of the five aggregates, the mind's inclination to cling on to them, and ways to see phenomena from a non-self view.

2. SN III, 59: *Yāva kīvañcāham bhikkhave ime pañcupādānakkhandhe catuparivaṭṭam yathābhūtam nābbhaññāsiṃ. neva tāvāham bhikkhave sadevake loke samārake sabrahmake sassamaṇabrāhmaṇiyā pajāya devamanussāya anuttaraṃ sammāsambodhim abhisambuddhoti paccaññāsiṃ.*
3. SN IV, 401: *Ahañ c'Ānanda Vacchagottassa paribbājakassa Atthattāti puṭṭho samāno Atthattā ti vyākareyyaṃ. api nu me tam anulomam abhavissa ñāṇassa upādāya Sabbe dhammā anattāti. No hetam bhante. Ahañ c'Ānanda Vacchagottassa paribbājakassa Natthattāti puṭṭho samāno Natthattāti vyākareyyaṃ. sammuḷhassa Ānanda Vachagotassa bhiyyo sammohāya abavissa Ahu vā me nūna pubbe attā. so etarahi natthīti.* ("If, Ānanda, when I was asked by the wanderer Vacchagota, 'Is there a self?' I had answered, 'There is a self,' would this have been consistent on my part with the arising of the knowledge that 'all phenomena are nonself?'" "No, venerable sir." "And if, when I was asked by him, 'Is there no self?' I had answered, 'There is no self,' the wanderer Vacchagotta, already confused, would have fallen into even greater confusion, thinking, 'It seems that the self I formerly had does not exist now.'") (Bodhi 2000, 1394).

In summary, the teaching of non-self (*anattā*) signifies an essential concept in Buddhism. Based on the Law Of Dependent Co-arising, Buddhists posit that "self" is a concept without an objective reality; the experience of "self" is merely the product of a process of logical abstraction or reification that animates and concretizes impersonal objects in order to mediate between the "outside" world and a delusional "personal identity." Driven by a strong desire to exist, the human mind subjectively clings to body, feelings, consciousness, experiences, values, relationships, and other conditions in order to convince itself of its own real and sustainable existence. However, such an attempt creates the bondage of self-attachment which leads to suffering. To liberate from suffering requires the realization of non-self.

Let us examine the non-self concept through the everyday example of enjoying dessert. One might think, "I am eating cheesecake and I love it!" From the viewpoint of dependent co-arising, however, "I" and "cheesecake" are not separate entities. When consciousness arises during the interaction between the taste buds and the cheesecake, there is a pleasant feeling and the mind starts to cling to this feeling by proliferating thoughts about it: "It tastes so good," "It is so comforting and soothing for my soul," and "I have to have some cheesecake every Friday night, or else I will be agitated for the whole week." Once the mind gains enough mental distance to observe how it engages in the phenomenon of eating cheesecake and understands that the experience of eating cheesecake is just the result of various conditions (the cheesecake, the restaurant, friends in the surroundings, tiredness from work, the sensation on the tongue, the feelings that arise, the mind's inner dialogue, thirst, the heat in the chest, the release of tension in the shoulders), the mind will not find a solid entity called "I." These experiences of consciousness occurring in the moment are all influenced by conditions and factors that affect one's state of mind. In other words, "self" is only a label for a provisional and transient existence experienced by the mind instead of an intrinsic and authentic being. With this realization, the mind can choose whether or not to eat the cheesecake. In layman's terms, the insight into non-self does not deny or destroy the self; instead, "I" can still accept "my" identity or personality, although I do not let such a sense of self define who I am. However, achieving this insight may require time to cultivate flexibility or skillfulness of mind to observe the sense of "I-ness" with some mental distance. To know and see that holding onto "I-ness" causes suffering, and that one can choose to let go of it, results in calmness and peace.

We have seen that non-self is the key principle to understanding human nature, and an uncultivated mind clings on to the five aggregates as ontological support to form a belief of self. The next section will discuss the nature of the five aggregates in order to establish a foundation leading to a counseling approach that works towards and with non-self.

4.2 Five Aggregates

We will begin this section with an example. As described in the *Vajirā-sutta*, the word "chariot" is used to refer to an assemblage of parts, such as the wheels, the axle, the central mainframe, reins, and so on. Similarly, the aggregates constitute the components of what we conventionally call a "being."[4] The following verse from the Buddha clearly points out that a human being is nothing more than an aggregation of conditions, in the same way that the term "chariot" is a conventional term used to refer to an apparent, inherently existing entity known as a "chariot." The reason to interpret and believe that a conditioned being is an actual existing "being" is the presence of the five aggregates. *Khandha*s, the original Pāli term for the aggregates, refers to the bulk of some entity, massive substances, or collection of things. In the *Khandha-sutta* (SN 22. 48), the Buddha summarized his teachings on the five aggregates as follows:

> And what, bhikkhus, are the five aggregates? Whatever kind of form there is, whether past, future, or present, internal or external, gross or subtle, inferior or superior, far or near: this is called the form aggregate. Whatever kind of feeling there is . . . this is called the feeling aggregate. Whatever kind of perception there is . . . this is called the perception aggregate. Whatever kind of volitional formations there are . . . these are called the volitional formations aggregate. Whatever kind of consciousness there is, whether past, future, or present, internal or external, gross or subtle, inferior or superior, far or near: this is called the consciousness aggregate. These, bhikkhus, are called the five aggregates. (Bodhi 2000, 886)[5]

In the Buddhist worldview, the function of the five aggregates describes the experience of individual existence and the operative factors of lived experience (Bodhi 2000, 840). The analysis of a person into five aggregates also describes a systematic scheme of five primary functions to explain the structure of lived experiences in contact with physical and mental objects (Bodhi 2000, 840). The *Khandhavagga*, the third book of the *Saṃyutta Nikāya*, is commonly known as the Book of the Aggregates and is a compilation of the Buddha's discourses on sentient existence using the concept of the five aggregates (Bodhi 2000, 839). As the original linguistic definition of *khandha* is "mass," using such a term to describe a person emphasizes the nature of five aggregates that always arise in groups and clusters parallel to each other (Bodhi 2000, 840).

---

4. SN I, 135: *yathā hi aṅgasambhārā – hoti saddo ratho iti.*
   evaṃ khandhesu santesu – hoti saddo ti sammuti.
5. SN III, 47: *Yaṃ kiñci bhikkhave rūpam atītānāgatapaccuppannaṃ ajjhattaṃ vā bahiddhā vā oḷārikaṃ vā sukhumaṃ vā hīnaṃ vā paṇītaṃ vā yaṃ dūre santike vā ayaṃ vuccati rūpakkhandho. yā kāci vedanā. yā kāci saññā . . . ye keci saṅkhārā . . . yaṃ kiñci viññāṇam . . . ime vuccati bhikkhave pañcūpādānakkhandhā.*

The five aggregates are a commonly used and accepted schema to describe a self. Due to its importance, the following section will discuss the nature and function of each of the aggregates.

4.2.1 Form

> And what is form? The four great elements and the form derived from them: this is called form. From the origination of nutriment (the mental defilements or unwholesome qualities of mind such as craving and ignorance) comes the origination of form. From the cessation of nutriment comes the cessation of form. This noble eight-fold path is the path leading to the cessation of form, namely Right View . . . right concentration. (Bodhi 2000, 895)[6]

The first aggregate is *rūpa*, common translations for which include corporeality, form, matter, or material quality. Among these translations, the most commonly used term for *rūpa* is matter. According to Early Buddhist *sutta*s, matter is material that can be deformed or deconstructed (Karunadasa 2010, 18), such as a body susceptible to deformation by thirst and hunger, or metal that can be deformed by heat. Matter includes the four basic elements: (1) the earth element (*pathavīdhātu*) to represent the quality of solidity; (2) the water element (*āpodhātu*) to describe the quality of fluidity and cohesiveness; (3) the fire element (*tejodhātu*) to refer to the quality of temperature, and; (4) the air element (*vāyodhātu*) signifying the quality of motion and movements (Karunadasa 2010, 163). In contrast to the popular understanding of water, fire, earth, and air, the Buddhist usage of these terms describes the characteristics of four forces in matter (Karunadasa 2010, 163). All matter consists of all four elements, while the quality of each element may differ (Karunadasa 2010, 164). Take "table" as an example: a table may have strong solidity as well as cohesiveness to sustain itself as a table, as can the temperature of a room or the table's static motion.

Rūpa also refers to the physical constituents of a person as made up of the four elements and which are commonly referred to as the physical component, usually related to the physical body (Karunadasa 2010, 17). Conditioned by volitional formations, the five material sense organs are derived from the four basic elements and manifest as the faculties of eye, ear, nose, tongue, and body (Karunadasa 2013, 32). Each faculty has its respective external object in visible, auditory, odorful, tasteful, and tangible forms. Matter is susceptible to deformation and changes, and the human body is no exception: "And why, bhikkhus, do

6. SN III, 59: *Katamañca bhikkhave rūpaṃ. Cattārī ca mahābhūtā catunnaṃ ca mahābhūtānam upādāya rūpaṃ idaṃ vuccati bhikkhave rūpaṃ. Āhārasamudayā rūpasamudayo. āhāranirodhā rūpanirodho. Ayam eva ariyo aṭṭhaṅgiko maggo rūpanirodhagāminī paṭipadā. seyyathidaṃ sammādiṭṭhi . . . sammāsamādhi.*

you call it form? 'It is deformed,' bhikkhus; therefore, it is called form. Deformed by what? Deformed by cold, deformed by heat, deformed by hunger, deformed by thirst, deformed by contact with flies, mosquitoes, wind, sun, and serpents. 'It is deformed,' bhikkhus; therefore, it is called form" (Bodhi 2000, 915).[7]

For a physical body with functional sense organs, the convergence of the sense faculties, sense objects, and sense consciousness results in sense contact (Karunadasa 2013, 68). For example, when a reader's healthy eyes (sense organ) meet this page (sense object), giving rise to eye-consciousness, the contact will initiate a sensory process and provide a requisite condition for the next aggregate, *vedanā*.

4.2.2 Feeling

> And what, bhikkhus, is feeling? There are these six classes of feeling: feeling born of eye-contact . . . feeling born of mind-contact. This is called feeling. With the arising of contact there is the arising of feeling. With the cessation of contact there is the cessation of feeling. (Bodhi 2000, 898)[8]

Vedanā is often translated as "feeling" by scholars of Buddhism and Buddhist psychology (e.g., Bhikkhu Bodhi, Y. Karunadasa, and the Pāli Text Society's Pāli-English Dictionary). It is important to note that *vedanā* is a drastically different concept from the traditional psychological understanding of feeling. *Vedanā* is a response to contacts based on the six sense bases (*āyatana*), which also includes the eye, ear, nose, tongue, body, and mind (Bodhi 2000, 841). Each of the six senses will give rise to a feeling tone, leading to a particular sense contact. In this process, there are three types of feeling: "And why do you call it feeling? It feels; that's why it's called 'feeling.' And what does it feel? It feels pleasure, pain, and neutral. It feels; that's why it's called 'feeling'" (Bodhi 2000, 915).[9]

Contact with objects generates experiences of one of three tones of feeling: pleasant, unpleasant, and neutral. In a further analysis, feeling is divided into a mental feeling tone and a bodily feeling tone, thereby resulting in a fivefold description: bodily pleasure, mental joy, bodily pain, mental pain, and neutral mental or bodily feeling. For example, one may identify the feeling from a bodily

7. SN III, 86: *Kiñca bhikkhave rūpaṃ vadetha. Ruppatīti kho bhikkhave tasmā rūpan ti vuccati. Kena ruppati. sītena ruppati uṇhena pi ruppati jigacchāya pi ruppati pipāsāya pi ruppati ḍaṃsa-makasa-vātātapa-siriṃsapa-samphassena pi ruppati. ruppatīti kho bhikkhave tasmā rūpan ti vuccati.*
8. SN III, 63: *Cha yime bhikkhave vedanākāyā. cakkhusamphassajā vedanā . . . manosamphassajā vedanā. ayaṃ vuccati bhikkhave vedanā. Phassasamudayā vedanāsamudayo.*
9. SN III, 86–7: *Kiñca bhikkhave vedanaṃ vadetha. Vediyantīti kho bhikkhave tasmā vedanā ti vuccati. kiñca vediyati. sukham pi vediyati dukkham pi vediyati adukkhamasukham pi vediyati. vediyatīti kho bhikkhave tasmā vedanā ti vuccati.*

wound as an unpleasant feeling of bodily pain, or one can identify sorrow and joy as unpleasant mental feelings (Somaratne 2021, 157). In addition, Somaratne (2021, 53) pointed out that suffering is mainly concerned with unpleasant mental feelings. In particular, he mentioned that "The categories of suffering that are found in the teachings are anxiety, despair, sorrow, disappointment, grief, doubt, agitation, worry, and fear. All these categories are about unpleasant mental feelings" (Somaratne 2021, 27).

At this point we wish to clarify the different understandings of feelings and emotions between Buddhism and Western psychology. According to the APA Dictionary of Psychology, feeling is "a self-contained phenomenal experience" which can be "subjective, evaluative, and independent of the sensations, thoughts, or images evoking them" (American Psychological Association 2018). As for emotion, this is "a complex reaction pattern, involving experiential, behavioral, and physiological elements, by which an individual attempts to deal with a personally significant matter or event" (APA 2018). In comparing the two, "feelings differ from emotions in being purely mental, whereas emotions are designed to engage with the world" (APA 2018). In other words, feelings are subjective and intrapsychic mental experiences, while emotions are multifaceted responses to the external world.

In contrast, Buddhism explains these important constructs in a different way. As mentioned before, there is "no generic term for emotions" in Buddhism; rather, *vedanā* is used to refer to "hedonic tone (feeling)" (de Silva 2014, 49) and the whole "affective dimension" (de Silva 2014, 61). It should also be noted that because of "conceptual complexities," emotions do not come as a "prototype," for example, anger, hope, remorse, compassion, or pride (de Silva 2014, 103). This complexity can be explained by noting that feelings "get converted into an emotion" when added to by a sequential amalgamation of cognitive processes, including the thoughts, appraisals, and intentions accompanied by physiological arousal, cultural, and social "filters" to interpret the experiences, and the egoistic self-assessment of emotions (de Silva 2014, 100). Therefore, in Buddhism, emotions are regarded as "constructs," an "interactive complex" (de Silva 2014, 99) emerging with the causal network of the five aggregates" (2014, 61), in this way blending cognitive, motivational, affective, and physiological arousal factors (2014, 138).

We will use de Silva's definition of emotion in our model of Buddhist counseling. When we use the term "emotion," we generally refer to the conceptual label of a particular mental state together with agitations or irritations in the mind that are linked with bodily correlations. Such emotions include anxiety, worry, jealousy, shame, excitement, or other human experiences. Like traditional counseling, emotions are an integral dimension of the therapeutic process and will be discussed further in the coming chapters.

4.2.3 Perception

> And what is perception? These six classes of perception—perception of form, perception of sound, perception of odours, perception of tastes, perception of tactile objects, perception of mental phenomena—this is called perception. (Bodhi 2000, 899)[10]

Conditioned by the feeling tone (*vedanā*), *saññā* refers to the recognition of an object appearing through the senses (Karunadasa 2013, 56). In this process of recognition, the mind draws on a past memory database to cognize the characteristics of objects and formulate concepts in naming such objects (Karunadasa 2013, 56). His understanding occurs in the *Madhupiṇḍika-sutta* (MN 18) in which the enlightened one described, "what one feels, one perceives (labels in the mind)."[11] This system of recognition has an important function in apprehending objects: "And why, bhikkhus, do you call it perception? 'It perceives,' bhikkhus; therefore, it is called perception. And what does it perceive? It perceives blue, it perceives yellow, it perceives red, it perceives white. 'It perceives,' bhikkhus; therefore, it is called perception" (Bodhi 2000, 915).[12]

Based on features and characteristics one has seen in the past, the mind cognitively labels an object with signs, symbols, or marks (Karunadasa 2013, 56). Let us provide an example. When we recognize the shapes, lines, width, depth, and height of a computer, we categorize this object as "computer" by associating the features from our previously acquired concept base of similar computers. However, if a toddler has no concept of a "computer," he will not be able to recognize it as a computer, recognizing it as something else, such as a television or toy. If this rationale stands, we believe each individual has a unique system of concepts and knowledge, and hence the same sensory inputs can generate different perceptions. In our experience in counseling situations, a child who survived physical abuse is likely to have a very different perception than a child who had never received physical abuse if both of them see an adult raising an open palm. In particular, an abused child may recognize the movement of the palm as a "spank" while the other child would perceive it as "waving."

10. SN III, 63: *Katamā ca bhikkhave saññā. Cha yime bhikkhave saññākāyā. rūpasaññā saddasaññā gandhasaññā rasasaññā phoṭṭhabbasaññā dhammasaññā ayaṃ vuccati bhikkhave saññā.*
11. MN I, 111: *Yaṁ vedeti taṁ sañjānāti.*
12. SN III, 87: *Kiñca bhikkhave saññaṃ vadetha. Sañjānātīti kho bhikkhave tasmā saññā ti vuccati. kiñca sañjānāti. nīlam pi sañjānāti pītakam pi sañjānāti lohitakam pi sañjānāti odātam pi sañjānāti sañjānāti kho bhikkhave tasmā saññā ti vuccati.*

4.2.4 Volitional formations

> And what, bhikkhus, are volitional formations? There are these six classes of volition: volition regarding forms . . . volition regarding mental phenomena. This is called volitional formations (Bodhi 2000, 899).[13]

Karunadasa translated *saṅkhāra* as both mental formation and volitional construction (Karunadasa 2013, 56). He pinpointed the complexity of this aggregate by noting that there can be different connotations and meanings of *saṅkhāra* depending on the context (Karunadasa 2013, 56). An essential aspect of this aggregate is the constructive component, which creates other aggregates, including itself (Karunadasa 2013, 57). In particular, as Karunadasa states, an important feature of volitional formation is to reify, manufacture, and amalgamate things resulting in constructed phenomena. In other words, there is a emphasis on the mind's inclination to continually fabricate things, which leads to the loss of realistic support in the act of cognition. It is considered the most dynamic human characteristic, playing an important role in constructing the phenomena of human existence (Karunadasa 2013, 59). Upon the arising of perception, volitional formations actively construct the mentally represented object in relation to the notion of self. We will provide an example: a perception of a young, small human being is "a child," while the subjective configurations, constructed and based on the notion of "I," label the object as "my beloved child." This formation or construction is based on the threefold appropriations of: this is mine, I am, and this is my self.

Somaratne (2021, 118) defined volition formation in a somewhat unique way. He stated that *saṅkhārā* refers to "configurations that function as causes and conditions for constructing a thing." In Somaratne's discussion, the meaning of *saṅkhāra* can be understood in a general sense and a specific sense (Somaratne 2021, 118). To explain this idea, Somaratne wrote that, "the general sense refers to configurations: things that function as causes and conditions for constructing a thing or other things. These configurations may include objective configurations, subjective configurations, or both. In its specific sense, it refers to subjective configurations such as intentions, desires, and wishes that serve to reconstruct or reconfigure a thing that has already been constructed or configured by a set of objective configurations" (Somaratne 2021, 118).

As we understand it, Somaratne's classification of configurations has profound meaning. First, he used dependent co-arising to explain the meaning of configuration such that all mental or physical things in the world are dependently arisen and objectively configured by different causes and conditions (Somaratne 2021, 119).

---

13. SN III, 63: *Katame ca bhikkhave saṅkhārā. Cha yime bhikkhave cetanākāyā. rūpasañcetanā . . . dhammasañcetanā. ime vuccatnti bhikkhave saṅkhārā.*

Second, he used the subjective and objective configurations to differentiate whether an individual is subjectively configuring fantasies based on personal desires or objectively configuring things as they are in reality (Somaratne 2021, 118). In his discussion, the subjective configurations are negative and superficial as they come from imagination, while the objective configurations are positive as they help to see reality (Somaratne 2021, 118). To further explain volitional formations, Somaratne pointed out that all mental and physical things in the world are dependently-arisen and objectively configured (Somaratne 2021, 118). However, when my subjective sense of "I" generates sensory experiences of the objectively configured things, the intentions, desires, or other components of subjectivity act to construct the objective configurations into subjective ones (Somaratne 2021, 119).

In applying the process of configurations to the clinging of the five aggregates, Somaratne made the following comment:

> The five aggregates—matter, feeling, perception, configurations, and consciousness—construct a life or an "individual," and the five clinging-aggregates—clinging-aggregate of matter, clinging-aggregate of feeling, clinging-aggregate of perception, clinging-aggregate of configurations, and clinging-aggregate of consciousness—construct a "person." A person is one who clings to the five aggregates as "this is mine," "this am I," or "this is my self." In other words, the mundane person considers the objectively constructed impersonal five aggregates subjectively, with his intentions, desires, cravings, and clinging, and constructs this "I" or "self" or "person" that he experiences. (Somaratne 2021, 119)

A mundane person clinging to this fourth aggregate will have the intention to transform things from what they objectively are in the world into how they are subjectively experienced in "my world" (Somaratne 2021, 123). In other words, a mundane person does not see things as they are in neutral, impersonal, and objective terms; instead, the person's intention is to appropriate neutral, impersonal, and objective things into "my" thing or the things that are for "me" (Somaratne 2021, 124).

We will summarize our understanding up to this point. The term "aggregate" is commonly translated as "formations," meaning either mental formations or volitional formations, which brings out the idea of a multiple and complex process of constructing and configuring things. The notion of "formation" indicates the creation of something beyond reality, a process that occurs in several stages. First, there are certain external things in the world. Due to the Law of Dependent Co-arising, these are objectively configured things that exist outside our five aggregates. Second, as long as the sensory experiences arise from a mundane person's contact with those things, the first configurations occur as a result of filtering, like being viewed via a lens in "my world." This sensory experience happens instantaneously, during which external objects are constructed. Subsequently, on top of the first construction, the person's subjective volitions, beliefs, values, desires, memories, and concepts take charge to further configure things in our retrospective sensory experience. This is the second construction. In applying this concept to the clinging to the five aggregates, our understanding is that: (1) the five aggregates are dependently co-arisen whether we cognize them or not, (2) our retrospective sensory experiences of the five aggregates conceptualize or configure them as an "individual" in the first configuration, and (3) clinging to the five aggregates is the second configuration when our intention, desires, and concepts personalize and grasp onto this "individual" resulting in an "I." From there, the "I" becomes the central reference point that then relates to the world subjectively, such as "this is my body," "I am sad," "I am your father," or "these properties all belong to me."

4.2.5 Consciousness

> And what is consciousness? These six classes of consciousness: eye-consciousness, ear-consciousness, nose-consciousness, tongue-consciousness, body-consciousness, mind-consciousness. This is called consciousness. (Bodhi 2000, 899)[14]

In Early Buddhist scriptures, the fifth aggregate of *viññāṇa* refers to bare attention, which must arise in conjunction with other mental factors, namely feeling, perception, configuration, sensory contact, and attention (Karunadasa 2013, 57). The primary function of *viññāṇa* is to take notice of sensory and mental data. "And why, bhikkhus, do you call it consciousness? 'It cognizes,' bhikkhus; therefore, it is called consciousness. And what does it cognize? It cognizes sour, it cognizes bitter, it cognizes pungent, it cognizes sweet, it cognizes sharp, it cognizes mild, it cognizes salty, it cognizes bland. 'It cognizes,' bhikkhus; therefore, it is called consciousness" (Bodhi 2000, 915).[15]

A basic interpretation of consciousness[16] refers to the bare attention needed to become aware of objects (Karunadasa 2013, 58). Consciousness (*viññāṇa*) is mentioned as being dependent on name (*nāma*) and form (*rūpa*)—consciousness

---

14. SN III, 64: *Katamañ ca bhikkhave viññāṇaṃ. Cha yime bhikkhave viññāṇakāyā. cakkhuviññāṇaṃ sotaviññāṇaṃ ghānaviññāṇaṃ jivhāviññāṇaṃ kāyaviññṇaṃ manoviññāṇaṃ. idaṃ vuccati bhikkhave viññāṇaṃ.*
15. SN III, 87: *Kiñca bhikkhave viññāṇaṃ vadetha. vijānātīti kho bhikkhave tasmā viññāṇan ti vuccati. Kiñca vijānāti. ambilam pi vijānāti. tittakam pi vijānāti. kaṭukam pi vijānāti madhukam pi vijānāti. khārikam pi vijānāti. akhārikam pi vijānāti loṇakam pi vijānāti. . . aloṇakam pi vijānāti. vijānātīti kho bhikkhave tasmā viññāṇan ti vuccati.*
16. In addition to Karunadasa's definition of consciousness as "bare attention," Bodhi (2003) also tells us that consciousness can explain the process of reincarnation in which a mundane person's

arises when "name" and "form" arise and ceases when they cease.[17] Here, while "name" refers to the aggregates of feeling (*vedanā*), perception (*saññā*) and formation (*saṅkhāra*), and contact (*phassa*) and attention (*manasikāra*), "form" refers to the first aggregate that is made up of the four great elements and the physical forms constituted by them.[18] From what we understand, consciousness cognizes the interdependent and co-jointed mental experience of the five aggregates. For example, regarding the eye faculty, the eye-consciousness focuses on the visual object of the ink printed on a piece of "paper," the pleasant feeling arising from sense contact, the perception of an "academic paper," and the configurations of a subjective "I" that chooses to read and think about the perceived objective of an "academic paper" (Table 4.1).

4.3 The Formation of Human Identity: Clinging to the Five Aggregates

To understand the philosophy of human nature and self-identity in Early Buddhist teachings, it is crucial to understand the difference between two related concepts: the five aggregates (*pañcakkhandhā*) and clinging to the five aggregates (*pañca-upadanakkhandhā*). According to our previous discussion on dependent co-arising, this central principle in Buddhist teaching established a framework to understand a person's reality as self-lessness or non-self (Bodhi 1995, 9). The experience of "self" in the five aggregates is dependently co-arisen; that is, it has no inherent and ultimate existence. Theoretically, one cannot cling onto the five aggregates because the five aggregates do not ultimately exist and we cannot cling onto things that are outside of existence (Somaratne 2021, 167). However, a worldly person is inclined to cling to a belief in the self by clinging to the five aggregates (Somaratne 2021, 167). Driven by craving, the mind is inclined to grasp on to the experiences of the five aggregates and form an identity of "self" (Bodhi 2000, 843). To describe this phenomenon further, Somaratne (2021, 167) pinpointed a textual term, *attavāda-upādāna*, that refers to the clinging to (*upādāna*) a belief (*vāda*) in self (*atta*). Such attachment explains the psychological state of a mundane person who believes in a self in the five aggregates, regardless of the fact that nothing exists beyond the experience of the dependently co-arisen five aggregates (Somaratne 2021, 167). Moreover, Somaratne

---

clinging to the five aggregates initiates the appearance of consciousness, which then manifests from life to life (Bodhi 2003, 842). However, this book is about Buddhist counseling, which only focuses on life in the present. The discussion of multiple lives or incarnations is not the focus here.

17. S III, 64: *Nāmarūpasamudayā viññāṇasamudayo. nāmarūpanirodhā viññāṇanirodho.*

18. SN II, 3: *Katamañca bhikkhave nāmarūpaṃ. Vedanā saññā cetanā phasso manasikāro. idam vuccati nāmaṃ. Cattāro ca mahābhūtā catunnañca mahābhūtānaṃ upādāya rūpaṃ. idam vuccati rūpaṃ.*

Table 4.1: Description of the Five Aggregates in Early Buddhist Teachings

Aggregates	Description	Example
1. Form (*Rūpa*)	All phenomena, made from the four elements, including the physical body, consisting of the six faculties—namely, eye, ear, nose, tongue, body, and mind.	A healthy eye that is capable of seeing, led by eye-consciousness to then make contact with a visual external object.
2. Feeling (*Vedanā*)	A sensational tone consisting of a pleasant feeling, unpleasant feeling, or neutral feeling arising from sense contact.	A pleasant visual feeling arising from sense contact.
3. Perception (*Saññā*)	The recognition or labeling of objects occurring through senses.	Based on past experience, the features and characteristics of the visual object give rise to the perception of a "tree."
4. Volitional Formations (*Saṅkhāra*)	The construction of the mentally represented object in relation to the notion of self.	The notion of self identifies with and fabricates "the tree" and thinks of it as "beautiful, peaceful, and enjoyable."
5. Consciousness (*Viññāṇa*)	The bare attention of cognizing physical and mental experiences.	A response to stimuli occurring via the six sense doors.

goes on to explain that the problem of human existence is due to the way human beings link the perception of self inseparably with the perception of permanence and pleasure (Somaratne 2021, 253). While this inclination reflects the human desires for pleasure and continuity, the triad perceptions of self, permanence, and pleasure will eventually result in suffering because reality is actually non-self, impermanence, and *dukkha* (Somaratne 2021, 253). The Buddha concisely summarized this teaching in the following statement: "Form is impermanent. What is impermanent is suffering. What is suffering is non-self" (Bodhi 2000, 884). This statement is the essence of the Buddha's teachings on how suffering arises from our taking of the five aggregates as self and how suffering ceases after letting go of the falsely configured self (Somaratne 2021, 253–54).

In effect, what we ordinarily refer to as "I" or "mine" is driven by a craving to cling onto the five aggregates, thereby holding onto a view or a notion of self, this clinging being the main source of suffering in human beings (Bodhi 2000, 843).

When the grasped and firmly held aggregates alter or change, the existence of self, what belongs to the self, and the meaning of self will be challenged and deconstructed. This leads the person into "sorrow, lamentation, pain, displeasure, and despair" (Bodhi 2000, 853). Therefore, as Bhikkhu Bodhi observes, while clinging to the five aggregates is initially alluring and temporarily soothing to the mind, it will always result in the burden of suffering:

> The five aggregates are truly burdens,
> The burden-carrier is the person.
> Taking up the burden is suffering in the world,
> Laying the burden down is blissful.
> Having laid the heavy burden down
> Without taking up another burden,
> Having drawn out craving with its root,
> One is free from hunger, fully quenched. (Bodhi 2000, 872)[19]

Similarly, the *Gaddula-sutta* (SN 22.99) points out that an uncultivated person is tied to one's five aggregates like a dog is tied by a leash to a stake regardless of whether the dog sits, walks, or stands (Bodhi 2000, 957). In the same way that the dog then defines its existence through its attachment to the stake and its bond to it, an uncultivated person is inclined to identify the five aggregates as self and attaches to it.[20] According to Bodhi's analysis of the five aggregates, clinging to the five aggregates occurs in two forms: appropriation and identification (Bodhi 2000, 843). Appropriation refers to how one grasps onto the five aggregates with desire and lust to assume possession; identification refers to the process of identifying with the five aggregates and using them as the central reference point or basis for conceit to form a belief that the five aggregates are one's real and existing self (Bodhi 2000, 843). Clinging to the five aggregates, as informed by the formula of dependent co-arising, is continually and ultimately sustained by ignorance, which may manifest as beliefs like "the five aggregates are permanent, a true source of happiness, and a self or accessories of a self" (Bodhi 2000, 844). In other words, ignorance fuels the appropriation and identification at a variety of cognitive levels, but it merely taints one's view of reality (Bodhi 2000, 844).

To describe the process of clinging to the five aggregates, Karunadasa (2019) used reification (*paññatti*) to discuss the dynamic of conceptualizing, reconceptualizing, and manifesting the immaterial or abstract material construct into concrete existence (Karunadasa 2019, 3). From the perspective of Early Buddhist teachings, time itself is a concept instead of an eternal and external reality (Karunadasa

19. SN III, 26: *Bhārā have pañcakkhandhā bhārahāro ca puggalo bhārādānaṃ dukkhaṃ loke bhāranikkhepanaṃ sukhaṃ. Nikkhipitvā garuṃ bhāram aññaṃ bhāram ānādiya samūlaṃ taṇham abbhuyha nicchāto parinibbuto ti.*

20. SN III, 150: *Seyyathāpi bhikkhave sā gaddulabaddho daḷhe khīle vā thambhe vā upanibaddho tam eva khīlaṃ vā thambhaṃ vā anuparidhāvati anuparivattati. evam eva kho bhikkhave assutavā puthujjano ariyānam adassāvī . . . sappurisadhamme avinīto rūpapam attato samanupassati . . . vedanā . . . saññaṃ . . . saṅkhāre . . . viññāṇam attato samanupassati.*

2019, 4). In other words, the notion of time is the mind's reification of abstract ideas, as based on events, into a concrete entity (Karunadasa 2019, 4). From our understanding of this concept, an example would be: when we see a change from darkness to brightness and experience an increase in temperature while watching the sunrise, we conceptualize these serial events as "morning," a specific label of time. According to Karunadasa, the best example of such a process would be our belief in the "self," which is a reification of the five aggregates into a psychologically concrete existence (2019, 5).

Bodhi argued that the antidote to ignorance involved in clinging to the five aggregates is wisdom, thereby seeing the five aggregates as they really are: "As impermanent, as suffering, and as non-self" (Bodhi 2000, 844). These three characteristics shed light on each aggregate to generate knowledge of how "this is not mine, this I am not, this is not my self" and realizing that the reification, appropriation, or identification of the "self" are merely fabrications and configurations driven by ignorance (Bodhi 2000, 845).

4.4 Implications of the Five Aggregates for Counseling

The first implication of clinging to the five aggregates is when a worldly person's mind selectively attends to and identifies with their mental experiences to fabricate a notion of self, with the five aggregates as building blocks to support such a concept. This is important in that the five aggregates are not in themselves the sources of suffering until they become the objects of grasping or clinging. As we have also emphasized previously, the five aggregates are nothing more than a set of dependently co-arisen experiences. Driven by craving and ignorance, believing in an independent and continuous nature of self is a highly fulfilling experience to a defiled and deluded mind, and therefore to a worldly person incapable or unwilling to see reality as it is. Only by seeing and contemplating the drawbacks (*ādīnava*) of clinging to the five aggregates, such as reflecting on how one's mind is filled with mental defilements and how clinging to the five aggregates will lead to suffering, can one penetrate through the fabricated and delusional nature of the notion of self. This insight can release one from the burden of the stress resulting from the constant construction and concoction of an illusory world.

One manifestation of this ignorance in daily life is seeing how many people devote a significant amount of time and effort to airbrushing a selfie photo, firmly believing that their image is part of the self, or even defining their self-existence. Reflecting on such egoism, such as how the selfie image is fabricated and deceptive, how physical beauty is just a notion, the physical body impermanent, and clinging to physical beauty stressful and exhausting, may help such individuals become dispassionate and able to let go of such clinging.

Taking the Buddhist teaching on clinging to the five aggregates to be a major source of suffering, one other viable implication that is applicable to counseling is to raise the client's awareness of the cognitive processes leading to this clinging, thereby liberating oneself from such clinging via a process of realization. Two subsequent treatment goals can be (1) to understand the dependently arisen nature of self, and (2) to see and know one's craving for identification with the self. Such treatment objectives can include acknowledging and recognizing craving and the true nature of self, understanding or wisely reflecting on the associated dependently arisen causes and conditions, and gradually choosing to let go of clinging through repeated mindful practices.

4.5 Commentary on Non-self in Professional Psychology

In the field of professional psychology, most schools of thought assume an inherently existing self in their psychotherapeutic models (Van Gordon, Shonin, and Griffiths 2017, 311) or are otherwise silent on the topic. William James (1890, 208), commonly known as the father of psychology, coined the term "sense of self" to articulate a philosophical exploration of what it means to be an "I" and "me." In James' definition, the sense of self comprises a subjective awareness of personal existence with a sense of agency for one's actions, a sense of continuity over time, a sense of wholeness, and a unique vitality (Basten and Touyz 2020, 161). In this definition, sense of self was divided into two parts: the self as "me," which refers to the self as an object of experience with numerous integrated aspects constituting what it means to be a whole person; and the self as "I," which reflects the self as a subjective experience with a sense of agency. Harter (2003, 612) summarized James' description of the *I-Self* as involving four criteria: (1) *self-awareness*: an understanding of subjective mental, states, needs, emotions, and cognitions, (2) *self-agency*: having authority over a person's thoughts and actions, (3) *self-continuity*: a subjective sense of self-perseverance across time, and (4) *coherence*: a self that possesses wholeness and completeness. Here, the idea of self is treated as a philosophical given such that the existence of self is a fact rather than a postulation. This initial assumption of self was highly influential to the development of later theoretical orientations.

For example, Freud (1922, 102) argued for the importance of developing a strong *ego* to meet the needs of intrinsic drives (*id*) while balancing the fulfilment of needs with social demands (*superego*). Here, ego refers to the sense of self as the thinker of a thought or subject of a sentence. Based on this assertion, his approach to psychotherapy involves a strong self-focus in terms of bringing unconscious content to awareness and inducing a cathartic process that releases suppressed negative emotions buried deep inside the self. Since the emergence of psychoanalysis, subsequent psychodynamic approaches, such as object relations and self psychology, continued to place the sense of self as a major focus of treatment involving the understanding, expression, development, and perseverance of self, together with an increasing emphasis on interpersonal relationships and environmental influences (Basten and Touyz 2020, 163). Although many founders in this school of thought acknowledged the importance of environment and relationships in formulating the sense of self, including the argument that a healthy human being has to be a social being in relation to others, the sense of self continued to be the focus of treatment. For example, Carl Rogers (1959, 197), the founder of client-centered therapy (and one of the most popular schools of psychotherapy), asserted that the most fundamental human drive is self-actualization, that is, to fulfil one's potential and achieve the highest level of humanness. Humanistic and existential therapies developed out of this idea of self, with one common treatment focus being to help clients live and behave in congruence with the intrinsic needs and ideals of the authentic self. Using a contemporary scholar's claim to conclude this section, Meares (2004, 54) contended that a general goal of psychotherapy is to help a client develop a more stable and integrated sense of self.

As many new treatment models have been influenced by Buddhism, or at least are seen as compatible with it, one may question whether such interventions have used the idea of non-self to inform any interventions. Steven Hayes, the founder of one of the most popular third wave CBT programs called Acceptance and Commitment Therapy (ACT), made the following comment about the difference between the perspectives of self in Buddhism and in ACT:

> By a transcendent self I do not mean the belief in such a self or the belief in immutability, but the experience of from-here-now and the essential continuity it provides for all verbally known events from the point of view of the knower. The claim is simply that all verbal knowing is known "from here now." That experience is an important sense of the word "I"—namely, that in one important sense "I" am from-here-now. This sense of perspective is immutable from the point of view of the knowing person. It is not immutable in the sense that it assumes a form that cannot or does not change. It is immutable in the sense that it has no form at all. It has no limits that can be known by the knower, by definition. (Hayes 2002, 65)

In this assertion, Hayes (2002, 65) described his understanding of self as having a certain flexibility that is susceptible to change. However, there is still the immutable or unchanging part of self that serves as an agent to observe and gain insight as a "knowing person." On the one hand, he does not make claims about the inherent existence of a permanent metaphysical self (Fung 2015, 568). On the other hand, ACT does not deny the existence of a self, a part of self, or a form of self that is immutable and persisting. Similarly, in a comparative study of mindfulness-based approaches, including DBT, ACT, and MBCT and

Asian philosophical traditions, Shah (2020) described the mindfulness-based approaches as focusing on helping clients separate the self from their experiences in order to foster unconditional self-acceptance. This perspective assumes the self as an existing agent or entity. In summary, although new approaches have started to acknowledge the malleability and changeability of the self, most of the psychotherapy methods generally see the self as an inherent existence and continuous entity; no traditional psychologist has claimed or agreed that the sense of self is a delusion.

According to the previous discussion, Early Buddhist teachings see the true nature of self, or the five aggregates, as subject to change and alteration instead of being a permanent, blissful, and independent entity (Somaratne 2021, 170). Distinct from the common psychological assumptions about the existence of a deeper, authentic, or permanent self, Buddhism describes a self that is the product of dependent co-arising and therefore not inherently existing. This position stands in critical opposition to theories assuming the existence of an eternal soul, a spiritual connection with a higher power, or an intrinsic and authentic "me." For novices of Buddhism, a common question is, "If there is not a 'me,' then who is behind the consciousness when reading this chapter and thinking about these ideas?"

The short answer is that the Buddhist theory of non-self does not refer to the non-existence or annihilation of a self; rather, it merely describes the mind's inclination to attribute neutral phenomena to a fantasized concrete identity. This inclination can be described as a habitual energy that leads consciousness to claim ownership of mental and bodily experiences, thereby fabricating an independent self-notion or self-identity. In other words, there is not any permanent entity called "the self" that possesses a mind. Rather, consciousness itself and its mental processes comprise the mind, and the mind becomes deluded when it becomes convinced of the notion that "this is my self." One of the most common Buddhist ways to describe this concept of the self is through clinging on to the five aggregates and believing in the five aggregates as self.

4.6 Implications of Non-self for Buddhist Counseling

In contrast to most of the theoretical orientations underpinning contemporary psychotherapy models that are based on the development of self, a Buddhist counseling model should be founded on the teaching of non-self. A theoretical orientation based on non-self, as well as the other two characteristics of existence (impermanence and suffering), should have several characteristics. Again, it is important to clarify that the teaching of non-self is not the annihilation of self, which is a common misunderstanding of this doctrine. This understanding, in fact, is just as erroneous as holding onto the notion of a permanent self. The teachings of early Buddhism reject both the concept of a permanent self (*sassatavāda*) and the annihilation of self (*ucchedavāda*), considering them as two sides of the same coin. Instead, Buddhism presents the doctrine of dependent arising as a middle-way approach, offering an alternative to these extreme views. Given that Buddhist practices focus on liberation from mental suffering, such suffering being due in part to clinging to a belief in self (Somaratne 2021, 241), a non-self treatment approach aims to intervene in the clinging on to unrealistic beliefs produced by subjective configurations.

First, then, the treatment focus should emphasize raising a client's awareness of their clinging to the notion of self. Instead of fostering a solid sense of self, Buddhist counselors will understand the delusional nature of self-notion and cultivate clients' mental capacity for nonattachment. In this approach, it is possible for Buddhist counselors to help clients get in touch with and understand their self-notion, reveal and process the craving related to it, realize the *dukkha* arising from clinging to the self-notion as well as the impermanent nature of self, and skillfully make wholesome decisions to pause or stop mental acts of clinging. The concept of impermanence, *dukkha*, and non-self are intertwined, and hence removing any one of them will extinguish all three (Somaratne 2021, 253). In the counseling process, any one of these three concepts can become the subject of an intervention. For example, a counselor can use different visualizations for a client to experiment with the view of non-self by contemplating a question such as, "What if I do not have to be George (client's name) at this moment—what would happen?" A counselor can explore and reflect on changes in life, relationships, and client's thoughts and emotions to raise their awareness of impermanence, or the counselor can reflect and help the client process the sacrifice, disappointments, emotional pain, and other forms of suffering when they hold onto who they are and what they need rigidly and adamantly. As a result, the client can consciously experience the teachings on *dukkha*. This idea will be further discussed in Chapters 7 and 8.

Furthermore, to help a client detach from clinging to a self-notion, the theory of dependent co-arising should be a guiding principle in understanding clients' presenting problems. Knowing that the self-notion is divisible and analyzable into parts and components, and that a deconstruction can challenge and dissolve clinging, Buddhist counselors can consider guiding clients to break down a mental phenomenon experientially into its various supporting factors and conditions in both body and mind. For example, when a client holds on to a particular view, every moment of emotional suffering is the product of multiple causes and conditions, with most of the conditions (such as emotions or concepts) being unknown. For example, in the case of a client who reports feeling "depressed" staying at home during the COVID-19 pandemic, the client may appear to see permanence in the impermanent (*anicce niccaṃ*), which is considered an unwise or wrong reflection or focus of attention (*ayonisomanasikāra*). This view will lead him to develop a subjective interpretation of being confined in a depressive state and lifestyle with no way out. Buddhist counselors can acknowledge a client's depression while guiding them to raise awareness of environmental factors, sociopolitical stressors, social stresses, changes in lifestyle, loss of usual coping strategies due to staying at home, bodily sensations during a depressed mood, unpleasant feelings in mind and body, perceptions of being confined, conceptual proliferations of hopelessness, and other conditions. To help clients practice the perspective of dependent co-arising, it can be effective to educate clients on the impermanent nature of things and the constantly changing nature of phenomena. For example, using the SARS outbreak as an example, a Buddhist counselor may discuss with a client how the SARS pandemic was a difficult time during which many people were depressed, while also knowing that it came to an end because everything changes. With this investigation and discernment of the multiple and interdependent conditions contributing to the depressed mood, as well as an emerging understanding of impermanence, the client is likely to become less attached to the concept of "I am depressed and I can't do anything about it" and develop new insights, such as, "There are so many factors making me feel depressed that it is actually reasonable to feel this way."

Last but not least, a non-self approach should aim to raise clients' awareness of *dukkha* in their clinging on to a self-notion. Seeing *sukha* in *dukkha* is another common reason for suffering. *Dukkha* refers to the unsatisfactoriness in life, while *sukha* refers to permanent pleasure or happiness, which are two opposite concepts. Seeing *sukha* in *dukkha* is to heedlessly and mistakenly view events and experiences of suffering as pleasurable. For example, when one is imbued with sensual pleasure during eating or sex, there is a transient feeling of gratification. In response to such gratification, the mind is inclined to crave the same or a higher level of gratification, even though the level of gratification is unsustainable, resulting in frustration, disappointment, and unsatisfactoriness. Taking a previously mentioned example from everyday life—the first bite of a chocolate cheesecake is the most fulfilling experience because it is bolstered by a novelty effect; later bites cannot match up to the first, as the mind tends to habituate sensual experiences. Moreover, the pleasurable feeling taints the mind, leading it to focus excessively on the transient pleasure, which then clouds one from noticing suffering at that moment. Such immersion in sensual pleasure instantly reduces the mind's discernment and clarity, increases distress in the body and mind, and fosters clinging. In other words, a practitioner with a heightened level of mindfulness can clearly see both the pleasurable feelings as well as the distressful feelings, thereby concluding that the distressful feelings and their consequences outweigh the transient feeling. In effect, seeing *sukha* in *dukkha* is to be ignorant about the impermanent and unsustainable nature of mundane pleasures, overlooking the distress embedded within the pleasure as well as adverse long-term effects.

Therefore, we suggest that practitioners and Buddhist counselors help their clients cultivate a more comprehensive and heedful awareness of their mind acts and resultant experiences. The goal is to help clients see the dangers and adverse consequences of mind acts, to skillfully decide not to delight in such acts, and to know the ways to stop or escape from them. For example, one maladaptive coping strategy for stress is drinking. While alcohol consumption may induce a temporary sense of pleasure, overconsumption tends to result in insomnia, depressed mood, anxiety, physical harm to organs, addiction to alcohol, and impaired judgment, which may then lead to risk-taking behaviors.[21] There are ways for Buddhist counselors to help clients perceive *dukkha* as it is, such as to collaborate with them by discussing the consequences of the volition and wish to drink, discern the pleasant feeling arising from thoughts of drinking, develop mental reminders of unpleasant consequences, explore wholesome coping strategies to replace drinking, use mindfulness techniques to refrain from engaging in alluring fabrications in drinking in the hope of soothing irritation and urges in the mind, and to thereby use mental discipline to protect oneself from such urges and other unwholesome mind acts. Among these techniques, the most important initial step is the mental reminder of the dangers associated with drinking, or the realization of *dukkha* in *dukkha*, in order to guard the mind from suffering. There will be more discussion of *dukkha* in the following chapters.

4.7 Conclusion

Diane Gehart pointed out in her counseling theories guidebook: "Theory gives counselors a system for making useful meaning of the information they get about clients so that they can say and do things that will be useful to clients" (Gehart 2016, 12). Each theoretical orientation applies a particular theory as its blueprint to guide every clinical decision of a counselor. For Buddhist counselors, dependent co-arising and non-self are the most important theoretical constructs for guiding and informing the development of a treatment plan. The current theoretical orientation adopts *non-self* as the guiding principle for treatment, and hence the goal

21. There have been years of research on alcohol as a maladaptive coping strategy and on the damage caused by alcohol consumption. For example, Skrzynski and Creswell conducted a meta-analysis and reviewed 21 published studies to examine how adolescents and young adults use alcohol as a coping mechanism and found that psychosocial problems are associated with solitary drinking as a coping mechanism (Skrzynski and Creswell 2020, 1989). Moreover, the damage of chronic drinking can be seen in numerous research studies, such as increased risk of chronic kidney damage (Li et al. 2019, 1360), structural shrinkage of cortical and subcortical gray matter (Yang et al. 2016, 92), and increased risk of unprotected sexual behaviors (Rehm et al. 2012, 51).

setting process should gravitate towards facilitating clients' realization of non-self and relinquishing one's clinging to the self-notion. In other words, no Buddhist counseling model should deviate from the core Buddhist teaching of non-self as an overarching treatment goal. This goal will guide the development of Buddhist counseling in the following chapters.

5

Theoretical Orientation Dimension III: Human Development

In traditional and secular-based professional psychology, the theoretical orientation of human development generally refers to how human beings develop different abilities over one lifetime. In Buddhism, the idea of development involves two distinct dimensions: (1) the growing of unskillful qualities in an uncultivated individual, or (2) the holistic development of liberation from suffering in an individual. This chapter will briefly review both dimensions, provide commentary from the perspective of secular psychology, and provide suggestions for applying such concepts to Buddhist counseling.

5.1 The Development of Unskillful Qualities in an Uncultivated Individual

In general, human development is a term describing how human beings grow and change throughout a lifetime. One of the assumptions of such growth is a progressive movement towards more advanced stages, thereby allowing oneself to improve in cognitive, socio-emotional, or other functioning. In the Buddhist worldview, the formula of dependent co-arising indicates that a mundane person enters a repeated cyclic existence of becoming, birth and death, and suffering due to ignorance (Bodhi 1995, 7). In this mundane developmental trajectory, a lifetime involves the process of birth, aging, illness, and death, or in other words, the "development" of a physical body from birth to death (Bodhi 1995, 7–8). However, as pointed out in the *Mahātaṇhāsaṅkhaya-sutta* (MN 38), the developmental process of a mundane life does not represent any automatic improvement or advancement in the process of liberation from suffering; instead, mundane development can simply be the development of unskillful qualities that increase a person's suffering (Bodhi 1995, 359). For example, when driven by aversion, both a young child and a cognitively and physically developed adult may not have advanced in using skillful strategies to mitigate their own suffering and that of others. Instead, they might allow their aversion to lead to physical confrontations to achieve their desires or resort to verbal abuse towards those they find undesirable. Therefore, from the standpoint of Early Buddhist teachings, we cannot assume that development necessarily involves growth towards a favorable or soteriological direction. To understand this further, we will explore the topic of human development in general, and child development in particular, as found in Buddhist scriptures, in the same way that discussion of human development in secular psychology usually starts with child development.

The literature on Buddhist psychology related to children and childhood is scarce. Of the few references, Sasson (2013, 183) noted the scholarly trend of describing Buddhism as an asocial and renunciation-focused practice in which mundane possessions, such as wealth, women, and children, can be obstructions to practice. Nakagawa (2005, 34–35) supported this view by claiming that Buddhism does not have a systematic theology on the development of children and adolescents. He also added that the Buddha named his son Rāhula, meaning "eclipse," implying that Rāhula's birth was an obstruction to Siddhartha's renunciation, as when the moon obstructs the sun during an eclipse. Other scholars, such as Crosby (2012, 99), interpreted this differently and noted the importance of Rāhula to the development of the Buddha's skillful means by using age-appropriate instruction to teach him the *Dhamma*.

This section will now briefly review these two perspectives and propose some implications of these standpoints for human development in Buddhist counseling.

First, the *Mahātaṇhāsaṅkhaya-sutta* provides a detailed discussion of the unwholesome qualities associated with children:

> The mother then carries the embryo in her womb for nine or ten months with much anxiety, as a heavy burden. Then, at the end of nine or ten months, the mother gives birth with much anxiety, as a heavy burden. Then, when the child is born, she nourishes it with her own blood; for the mother's breast-milk is called blood in the Noble One's Discipline.
>
> When he grows up and his faculties mature, the child plays at such games as toy ploughs, tipcat, somersaults, toy windmills, toy measures, toy carts, and a toy bow and arrow.
>
> When he grows up and his faculties mature still further, the youth enjoys himself provided and endowed with the five cords of sensual pleasure, with forms cognizable by the eye . . . sounds cognizable by the ear . . . odours cognizable by the nose . . . flavours cognizable by the tongue . . . tangibles cognizable by the body that are wished for, desired, agreeable and likeable, connected with sensual desire, and provocative of lust. (Bodhi 1995, 358, 359)[1]

1. MN I, 266: *Tam-enaṁ bhikkhave mātā nava vā dasa vā māse gabbhaṁ kucchinā pariharati mahatā saṃsayena garum-bhāraṁ. Tam-enaṁ bhikkhave mātā navannaṁ vā dasannaṁ vā*

In this discourse, the Buddha described child development as beginning with the pain, burden, and anxiety of the mother's pregnancy and delivery. After birth, development occurs when a child's sense faculties mature while interacting with the world; however, a child only uses this capacity for trivial games and enjoyment, which does not result in meaningful gains. The maturation of the sense faculties is a neutral process, but a child has strong inclinations to apply the sense faculties unskillfully. When a child develops, the child uses its enhanced capacity to pursue sensual pleasures to satiate sense desires.

The Buddha continued with the discussion of an uncultivated developmental trajectory as follows:

> On cognizing an idea with the intellect, he is infatuated with pleasing ideas and gets upset over unpleasing ideas. He dwells with body-mindfulness unestablished, with limited awareness. He doesn't discern, as it has come to be, the awareness-release and discernment-release where those evil, unskillful qualities cease without remainder. Engaged thus in compliance and opposition, he relishes any feeling he feels—pleasure, pain, neither-pleasure-nor-pain—welcomes it and remains fastened to it. As he relishes that feeling, welcomes it, and remains fastened to it, delight arises. Now, any delight in feeling is clinging. From his clinging as a requisite condition comes becoming. From becoming as a requisite condition comes birth. From birth as a requisite condition, then aging-and-death, sorrow, lamentation, pain, distress, and despair come into play. Such is the origination of this entire mass of stress and suffering. (Bodhi 1995, 359)[2]

As the Buddha explains, without awareness of the danger in the above process, a child continues to take joy in the pleasure of the six sense facilities and engages iteratively and actively in the cycle of suffering. In other words, the developmental trajectory evolves towards the deepening of delusion and suffering through to adulthood. Perpetuation of unskillful choices continuously binds the individual's mind to the cycle of suffering unless the child hears the *Dhamma*, realizes the burden and suffering implicit in mundane life, and decides to abandon worldly belongings and devote themselves to the path of cultivation.

Although this view of child development may be less positive when compared to conventional developmental psychology, Early Buddhist scriptures provide indications that child education can promote wholesome development, especially when youngsters have reached certain stages. Perhaps some classic examples of child or youth education in Early Buddhism are the discourses from the historical Buddha to his son, Rāhula. In the *Ambalaṭṭhika-Rāhulovāda-sutta* (MN

māsānaṁ accayena vijāyati mahatā saṃsayena . . . kāyaviññeyyehi phoṭṭhabbehi iṭṭhehi kantehi manāpehi piyarūpehi kāmūpasaṁhitehi rajanīyehi.

2. MN I, 266–267: *manasā dhammaṁ viññāya piyarūpe dhamme sārajjati. appiyarūpe dhamme byāpajjati, anupaṭṭhita kāyassati ca viharati parittacetaso . . . evametassa kevalassa dukkhakkhandhassa samudayo hoti.*

61), the Buddha taught his son the danger of deliberate lies and the importance of repeated reflection in order to purify body *kamma* (action), speech *kamma*, and mind *kamma* (Bodhi 1995, 524–26). In analyzing *sutta*s, verses, and other relevant texts on the interaction of the Buddha and Rāhula, Crosby (2013, 98) even described Rāhula as the original model for child monastics, portraying many wholesome qualities. Although the Buddha abandoned his son and family for a path leading towards liberation from suffering, he returned to share his wisdom with his son. This decision suggests that children can be taught, and that there is value in Buddhist education.[3]

Buddhist-inspired education and pedagogy is an important field of learning in Buddhist studies, such education purportedly starting in ancient India. Radhakumud Mookerji was one of the earliest scholars to publish research on ancient Indian education. His book, *Ancient Indian Education: Brahmanical and Buddhist* is one of the most cited works in this field, showing that the history of the Buddhist education system is practically the same as the sangha[4] or Buddhist monastic order. This became a learning framework for the later development of Buddhist education in different forms (Mookerji 1989, 394). The book carried out a comprehensive review and critical analysis of the significance, characteristics, and development of ancient Indian education involving Vedic culture, Brahmanism, Buddhism, and other more contemporary influences in educational

3. Among encouraging stories in commentaries related to child education in Buddhism, the story of two brothers, Cullapanthaka and Mahāpanthaka, is instructive (*Dhammapada-aṭṭhakathā* I, 239–255). The elder brother, Mahāpanthaka, often went to hear the Buddha's preaching and was later ordained as a monk, becoming an arahant in a short time. The elder brother then ordained his younger brother, Cullapanthaka, believing that he would also become a cultivated monk. He was, however, hugely disappointed by his brother's dullness, as he could not even learn a single stanza. As a result, Mahāpanthaka asked his younger brother to leave the Sangha and resume a mundane life. Cullapanthaka loved the Buddha's teaching but decided to leave, as he also believed that he was stupid and incapable of learning. When the Buddha encountered Cullapanthaka on his way out, the Buddha consoled him and taught him a basic visualization exercise with which Cullapanthaka attained arahantship. It turned out that Cullapanthaka was smart in his own way, his expertise being different from his brother. This difference of talent had been misunderstood as stupidity by his brother. The story shows that the Buddha did not give up on Cullapanthaka, patiently comforting and guiding him, revealing the Buddha's openness in training youngsters. More importantly, using an appropriate method to guide a child is the key message of the story; that is, the Buddha was able to identify the brothers' individual strengths and cultivate each of them in turn.
4. This view on the *Saṅgha* is supported by Koul, Verma, and Vanashri (2019, 21–42) who reviewed the history of scientific development in India in their book, *Science Education in India: Philosophical, Historical, and Contemporary Conversations*. A noteworthy part of the text addresses the position of Buddhist education in the development of science and other aspects of education (21–42). It also discusses the crucial role of the *Viharas*, the early forms of Buddhist monasteries in which monastic students and teachers resided together for shelter, education, and practice and which also served as the pioneers of Buddhist schools. They also define the main objective of Buddhist education, which is to teach students to be liberated from suffering, the cycle of rebirth, and to attain *Nibbāna*.

development, some of which are not as relevant to the current discussion. Here we will focus on the section of Mookerji's work germane to the Buddhist education of primary-aged children (Mookerji 1989, 246–48, 395–99, 528–29).

It was uncommon for children to join any *Saṅgha* in ancient India, except for those who had been given their parents' permission (Mookerji 1989, 397) and who showed strong intellectual capacity (1989, 175). The age restriction on admission, which was fifteen years of age, was first introduced by the Buddha because the Buddha's father had grieved over the loss of his heirs (i.e., the Buddha himself and his grandson, Rāhula) to the *Saṅgha*. However, several characteristics of Buddhist education in ancient India pointed out by Mookerji are worth mentioning, as they are generally related to Buddhist child education. First, education was primarily designed for higher caste children because the first assessment of a potential candidate concerned the student's name and lineage, followed by possession of a good memory, chaste behavior, and good character (Mookerji 1989, 180). Second, students had many duties beyond learning, including the duty to take care of one's teacher, reciting sacred texts, worshipping, and paying homage to the elders of the village (Mookerji 1989, 543). Third, the teacher-student relationship in Buddhist education always had a personal touch. The most important duty of a teacher was to select passages from the *Tipiṭaka* to teach and explain patiently to the students, while other duties involved taking care of them during illness, in effect attending to them as if they were the teachers' own children (Mookerji 1989, 542–43). In reviewing the development of Buddhist education from ancient India to contemporary India, Mookerji argued that many monasteries started to oversee higher and elementary education during the 1700s (Mookerji 1989, 528). In the education system, subjects included both secular and religious knowledge, such as grammar, science, arts and crafts, and the *Abhidharma* (Mookerji 1989, 528–29). In other words, elementary school aged children were exposed to Buddhist thought as well as other subjects during that period. Through Mookerji's analysis, we can see that the evolution of Buddhist education widened the age of entry by admitting not only teenage students into the *Saṅgha* as novice monks, but also by starting to educate young children in both secular and religious knowledge. Indeed, the Buddhist education system seems to have paved a pathway for the development of contemporary education in India.

In her book *Buddhist Education in Ancient India*, Rachita Chaudhuri discussed the education system in the *Saṅgha* during and after the Buddha's time with a particular focus on its organization and administration, its educational approach for monks and nuns, its system of punishment and discipline, and how some residential monasteries became renowned universities for Buddhist education with curriculums that included secular components (Chaudhuri 2008, 20–21). Supporting Mookerji's analysis, Chaudhuri pointed out the integration of secular education into Buddhist education curricula and argued that Buddhist monastic institutions could be pioneers in incorporating secular subjects such as mathematics, astronomy, and medicine into their curricula, bringing a broader and more profound influence to bear on the development of education in India (Chaudhuri 2008, 221–23). However, Chaudhuri did not discuss any particular application of Buddhist education to children in ancient India.

In fact, the literature on Buddhist education is concerned mainly with monastic education for adults. For example, there are intensive discussions on the investigation and analysis of the origin, development, and implications of monastic education in different countries such as Korea (e.g. Kaplan 2020), Laos and Thailand (Abeysekara 2011), and China (Borchert and Rowe 2017). Based on the above evidence that children were usually not admitted to the *Saṅgha* in ancient India, the undeveloped capacity of children to learn the *Dhamma* at a young age as indicated by the previous discussion, and the lack of literature on Buddhist education for children, it is reasonable to conclude that traditional Buddhist education was designed for adults.[5] As can also be seen so far, the concept of developmental psychology in the study of children's growth span seems to be irrelevant to the Buddhist theoretical orientation.

In conclusion, due to inborn ignorance and unskillful habits, children are born with unwholesome inclinations, and normal development tends to foster the growth of these unskillful habits. In effect, without proper guidance, a deluded mind will appear. As Early Buddhist teachings assume that the ultimate goal of practice is liberation from suffering, human development can be understood as the process that we undergo to reach this ultimate goal. In other words, Buddhism's definition of human development refers to the person or mind's developmental trajectory towards liberation from suffering. With the very specific aim of *Nibbāna*, the next section will use the Buddhist perspective to see human development as such a process of cultivation towards liberation.

5.2 Human Development on the Spiritual Path

Given that liberation from suffering is the ultimate goal of Buddhist practice, the direction of human development should align with this goal. Parallel to this understanding, the Buddhist view of human development can be seen as the holistic

5. The emergence of secularized mindfulness, which indirectly fostered the acceptance of Buddhism, has significantly impacted Buddhist education for children in contemporary society. Zen master Thích Nhất Hạnh is one major figure who promoted teaching Buddhism to children. He has published many books teaching Buddhist mindfulness to children (e.g. Thích and Chau 2011; Thích 2020). Grandmaster Hsing Yun, the founder of Fo Guang Shan, also founded a number of elementary and secondary schools based on Buddhist Teachings (Chia 2015, 143). Moreover, some community programs have incorporated Buddhist teachings into the education of youth. For example, Sue and Sue (2013) published a book describing how they incorporated Buddhist teachings to foster students' social and emotional learning in the United States.

cultivation of nonattachment to the five aggregates by walking the Buddhist path. This process uses the mind as the entry point in order to bring about well-rounded development. In the *Aṅguttara Nikāya* (AN 1.21–24), the Buddha explicitly discussed several aspects of mental development. Here are some of the assertions:

> "Bhikkhus, I do not see even one other thing that when undeveloped is so unwieldy as the mind. An undeveloped mind is unwieldy." (Bodhi 2012, 92)[6]
>
> "Bhikkhus, I do not see even one other thing that when developed is so wieldy as the mind. A developed mind is wieldy." (Bodhi 2012, 93)[7]
>
> "Bhikkhus, I do not see even one other thing that when undeveloped leads to such great harm as the mind. An undeveloped mind leads to great harm." (Bodhi 2012, 93)[8]
>
> "Bhikkhus, I do not see even one other thing that when developed leads to such great good as the mind. A developed mind leads to great good." (Bodhi 2012, 93)[9]

These statements are some of the most succinct summaries of the importance of developing or cultivating one's mind. They provide practitioners with the confidence that training the mind is highly beneficial, while not training it can have detrimental effects. They provide a Buddhist definition of development as a process of mental development. In other words, development in Buddhism may not concern progress in making physical changes, gaining mundane knowledge, or improving social skills; instead, it concerns how the mind advances towards a state of liberation from suffering. Teachings on cultivated and uncultivated minds are also beautifully presented in verse in the third chapter, the *Citta-vagga*, of the *Dhammapada*.

We can see the importance of mental development and its benefits in another famous *sutta*, the *Sallatha-sutta* (SN 36.6), which discusses how external reality, such as physical pain, does not differentiate between a cultivated and an uncultivated person. However, development of the mind in these two individuals makes a significant difference:

> Bhikkhus, the uninstructed worldling feels a pleasant feeling, a painful feeling, and a neither-painful-nor-pleasant feeling. The instructed noble disciple too feels a pleasant feeling, [208] a painful feeling, and a neither-painful-nor-pleasant

6. AN I, 5: *Nāhaṃ bhikkhave aññaṃ ekadhammam pi samanupassāmi yaṃ evaṃ abhāvitam akammanīyaṃ hoti yathayidaṃ cittaṃ.*
7. AN I, 5: *Nāhaṃ bhikkhave aññaṃ ekadhammam pi samanupassāmi yaṃ evaṃ bhāvitam kammanīyaṃ hoti yathayidaṃ cittaṃ.*
8. AN I, 5: *Nāhaṃ bhikkkhave aññaṃ ekadhammam pi samanupassāmi yaṃ evaṃ abhāvitaṃ mahato anatthāya saṃvatatti yathayidaṃ cittam.*
9. AN I, 5: *Nāhaṃ bhikkhave aññaṃ ekadhammam pi samanupassāmi yaṃ evaṃ bhāvitaṃ mahato atthāya saṃvattati yathayidaṃ cittaṃ.*

> feeling. Therein, bhikkhus, what is the distinction, the disparity, the difference between the instructed noble disciple and the uninstructed worldling? (Bodhi 2000, 1263)[10]
>
> [W]hen the uninstructed worldling is being contacted by a painful feeling, he sorrows, grieves, and laments; he weeps beating his breast and becomes distraught. He feels two feelings—a bodily one and a mental one. Suppose they were to strike a man with a dart, and then they would strike him immediately afterwards with a second dart, so that the man would feel a feeling caused by two darts. So too, when the uninstructed worldling is being contacted by a painful feeling . . . he feels two feelings—a bodily one and a mental one. (Bodhi 2000, 1264)[11]
>
> [W]hen the instructed noble disciple is contacted by a painful feeling, he does not sorrow, grieve, or lament; he does not weep beating his breast and become distraught. He feels one feeling—a bodily one, not a mental one. Suppose they were to strike a man with a dart, but they would not strike him immediately afterwards with a second dart, so that the man would feel a feeling caused by one dart only. So too, when the instructed noble disciple is contacted by a painful feeling . . . he feels one feeling—a bodily one, not a mental one. (Bodhi 2000, 1264)[12]

This *sutta* clarifies that physical experiences are the same for cultivated and uncultivated individuals. However, the subjective experience of mental suffering only applies to uncultivated individuals. We can also see that well-instructed disciples of the noble ones have made advancements in their practice to avoid mental suffering in spite of their physical suffering. As we understand it, the goal of Buddhist practice is mental development leading to liberation from suffering. As such, a cultivated mind can experience physical suffering as it is; in other words, it does not aggravate existing suffering by additional resistance, lamentation, grief,

---

10. SN IV, 207: *Assutavā bhikkhave puthujjano sukham pi vedanaṃ vediyati dukkham pi vedanam vediyati adukkhamasukham pi vedanaṃ vediyati. Sutavā bhikkhave ariyasāvako sukham pi vedanaṃ vediyati dukkham pi vedanaṃ vediyati adukkhamasukham pi vedanam vediyati. Tatra bhikkhave ko viseso ko adhippāyoso kim nānākaraṇaṃ sutavato ariyasāvakassa assutavatā puthujjanāti.*
11. SN IV, 207: *Assutavā bhikkhave puthujjano dukkhāya vedanāya puṭṭho samāno socati kilamati paridevati urattālīkandati sammoham āpajjati. so dve vedanā vidiyati kāyikañ ca cetasikañ ca. Seyyathāpi bhikkhave purisaṃ sallena vijjheyyuṃ. tam enam dutiyena sallena vijjheyyuṃ. evaṃ hi so bhikkhave puriso dve salle vedanā vediyati. evam eva kho bhikkhave assutavā puthujjano dukkhāya vedanāya puṭṭho samāno socati kilamati paridevati urattāliṃ kandati sammoham āpajjati. so dve vedanā vediyati kāyikaṃca cetasikañca.*
12. SN IV, 207: *Sutava ca kho bhikkhave ariyasāvako dukkhāya vedanāya puṭṭho samāno na socati na kilamati na paridevati na urattālīkandati na sammoham āpajjati. so ekaṃ vedanaṃ vediyati kāyikaṃ. na cetasikaṃ. Seyyathāpi bhikkhave purisaṃ sallena vijjheyyuṃ na tam enaṃ dutiyena sallena anuvijjheyyuṃ. Evaṃ hi so bhikkhave puriso ekasallena vedanaṃ vediyati. Evam eva kho bhikkhave sutavā ariyasāako dukkhāya vedanāya phuṭṭho samāno na socati na kilamati na paridevati na urattāḷīkandati na sammoham āpajjati. so ekaṃ vedanaṃ vediyati kāyikaṃ na cetasikaṃ.*

sadness, or other reactions. Because of this, the Buddha proclaimed himself as the "arrow remover" or "surgeon" (Sn 560: *sallakatto*),[13] in the sense that he removes (by doing surgery) the second arrow (the arrow of mental suffering) by helping the sufferers cultivate their uncultivated minds. In this sense, the advancement from an uncultivated person to a cultivated person signifies the essence of development in Early Buddhist teachings.[14] The emphasis on mind provides a useful ground for analysis and understanding and an access point to cultivation. Summarizing these discourses and findings, we propose to conceptualize the human development aspect of a theoretical orientation based on Early Buddhist teachings as a process of cultivation towards liberation from suffering.

5.3 Ideal Human Development in Early Buddhist Teachings

In Buddhism, the most iconic and fully developed human being is the historical Buddha, Siddhartha Gautama, who represented perfect cultivation on the path to the realization of *Nibbāna*, resulting in complete liberation from suffering. In other words, the fully developed stage is a healthy ideal that allows a person to live without suffering. The Buddha sees this cessation of suffering as the ultimate priority in life, so he only taught knowledge germane to the cessation of suffering. Such functionality is seen in the famous *Siṃsapā-sutta* (SN 56.31), in which the Buddha used a metaphor to describe his wealth of knowledge as comparable to all the leaves in the forest. However, he only taught about the few leaves in his hand, which represent the essential knowledge of liberation from suffering. As other knowledge can be unhelpful to liberation, the Buddha purposefully did not teach it (Bodhi 2000, 1857–58). In light of this goal, functionality in society, internal aspirations, resolution of internal conflicts, or absence of clinical symptoms are only meaningful if they are associated with liberation from suffering.

As a result of the Buddha's search for an answer to the ending of suffering, he successfully attained perfect enlightenment or *Nibbāna*, which is regarded as "the highest possible form of happiness" (Anālayo 2018, 264). One important note about this specific form of happiness is that the concept of happiness is not restricted to feelings or emotions, because this happiness can occur when feelings and cognitions have ceased (Anālayo 2018, 264). Linguistically, the term *Nibbāna*

13. In another instance, in the *Itivuttaka* (101), the Buddha also proclaimed the same, adding another word: *'bhisakko sallakatto'* (physician, the arrow remover/surgeon).
14. Although this discussion emphasizes the influence of mind, it acknowledges the paradigm of dependent co-arising in which mind is an interdependent experience with other conditions; that is, it cannot be developed or cultivated by itself. Instead, we can see mind as a broader category which coexists with and needs to be developed together with the other aggregates, although the present discussion pinpoints the importance of mind in the sense of cultivation as mental development.

refers to "the going out of a lamp or a fire," that is, the fires of lust, aversion, and delusion (Anālayo 2018, 257). *Nibbāna* is also described as the eradication or extinguishing of craving as well as the complete cessation of *dukkha*. From this standpoint, the Buddha was the most mentally healthy person alive, one who had successfully overcome all causes of suffering and who decided to teach others his realizations to aid their liberation from suffering as well.

The Buddha used a parable in the *Nagara-sutta* (SN 12.65) to describe his teaching as a way to share his realizations:

> So too, bhikkhus, I saw the ancient path, the ancient road travelled by the Perfectly Enlightened Ones of the past. And what is that ancient path, that ancient road? It is just this Noble Eightfold Path; that is, Right View, Right Intention, Right Speech, Right Action, Right Livelihood, Right Effort, Right Mindfulness, Right Concentration. I followed that path and by doing so I have directly known aging-and-death, its origin, its cessation, and the way leading to its cessation. I have directly known birth . . . existence . . . clinging . . . craving . . . feeling . . . contact . . . the six sense bases . . . name-and-form . . . consciousness . . . volitional formations, their origin, their cessation, and the way leading to their cessation. Having directly known them, I have explained them to the bhikkhus, the *bhikkhunīs*, the male lay followers, and the female lay followers. This holy life, bhikkhus, has become successful and prosperous, extended, popular, widespread, well proclaimed among devas and humans. (Bodhi 2000, 603–4)[15]

In this discourse, the Buddha did not claim any unique divine role in teaching such wisdom, given that it was also realized by ancient sages; rather, he humbly shared his experiences and practices with others in order to assist them in reaching this state of mind, guiding others on the same path of cultivation. The practitioners who reached *Nibbāna* are referred to as *arahats*. While it is an engaging topic, the difference between a buddha and an *arahat* is not the focus of this book, especially when both a buddha and an *arahat* have realized *Nibbāna* and are completely liberated from suffering. In other words, both a buddha and an *arahat* can be considered as having attained the same mentally healthy ideal. In fact, in Early Buddhist teachings, fully cultivated practitioners following the Buddha's path are regarded as *arahats* instead of buddhas, one reason being to signify the Buddha's pioneering position in revealing the path to enlightenment. For this reason, this book takes the *arahat* as the model of psychological health in Early Buddhist teachings.

According to several discourses in Early Buddhist teachings (SN 55.5, MN 95, SN 45.2, AN 8.54), there are four stages of enlightenment that lead to arahathood. This delineation is one of the most widely accepted ways to understand

15. SN II, 106: *Evam eva khvāham bhikkhaveadassaṃ purāṇaṃ maggaṃ purāṇañjasaṃ pubbakehi sammāsabuddhehi anuyātaṃ.*

the levels of cultivation. We will use the work of Rupert Gethin, a contemporary expert in the *Nikayas* and *Abhidhamma*, as well as the research of Y. Karunadasa, as the main reference to understand this. At each of the four stages, different fetters are abandoned, totaling ten in number when one attains arahathood (Gethin 1998, 194).

The first level is stream-attainer (*sotāpanna*) (Gethin 1998, 194). This is considered the beginning of the path, and at this stage one is endowed with the right or proper view (*sammā-diṭṭhi*). The four conditions required to reach this level are: associating with people of integrity (*sappurisasaṃsevo*), listening to the true *Dhamma* (*saddhamma-savaṇaṃ*), practicing appropriate attention (*yonisomanasikāro*), and practicing the *Dhamma* (*dhammānudhammapaṭipatti*; Bodhi 2000, 1792). At this level, the practitioner has relinquished the first three fetters, including the belief in an ego entity (*sakkāya-diṭṭhi*), skeptical doubt (*vicikicchā*), and clinging to mere rites and rituals as a means to emancipation (*sīlabbata-parāmāsa*; Karunadasa 2010, 132). One interpretation of this mental advancement is that the practitioner's mind has a residual degree of ignorance and impurity and that it causes an irreversible psychological transformation (Amaro 2019, 1953). The second level is once-returner (*sakadāgāmī*). This stage describes practitioners who have successfully diminished sense-desire (*kāma-rāga*) and ill-will (*vyāpāda*) (Gethin 1998, 194). One may still have mild hatred or greed in this mental state, but these poisons do not dominate one's thoughts. The third level is the non-returner (*anāgāmī*). At this level, the fetters of sense-desire (*kāma-rāga*) and ill-will (*vyāpāda*) are completely eliminated (Gethin 1998, 194). The fourth stage is the arahat, usually referred to as "one who has awakened as a disciple" (Gethin 1998, 32). The final fetters eliminated at this stage include craving for fine-material existence (*rūpa-rāga*), craving for immaterial existence (*arūpa-rāga*), conceit (*māna*), restlessness (*uddhacca*), and ignorance (*avijjā*; Karunadasa 2010, 132). From an Early Buddhist perspective, this is the final stage of development and is considered as being ultimately liberated from suffering (Gethin 1998, 9).

Another potential descriptor of human development in Early Buddhist teachings is the series of meditative stages known as *jhāna*,[16] which is the cultivation of concentration through absorption into an object of meditation (Anālayo, 2019, 2341). *Jhāna* is an interesting, and somewhat controversial, topic in Buddhist studies. The Buddha taught *jhāna* on various occasions and there are detailed descriptions of *jhāna* in some *suttas*, such as AN 9.36 and AN 4.41. As seen in the *Siṃsapā-sutta* (SN 56.31), the Buddha only taught knowledge that was conducive

16. The term *jhāna* is usually translated as "absorption," "mind training," or "meditative state," meaning to capture a mental state of peace and calmness by concentrating on a specific object of meditation. For example, Gethin describes the fourth *jhāna* as a perfect mental calmness and equilibrium (Gethin 1998, 22).

to liberation from suffering, so it is logical to see the *jhāna*s as an important practice on the path. At the same time, there are *sutta*s documenting the stories of individuals who did not display evidence of having experienced the stages of *jhāna* while advancing on the path to enlightenment after receiving the Buddha's discourse. Such lack of evidence raises the question of whether the *jhāna*s are actually a necessary component on the path to liberation. Whatever the answer may be, this book will not debate the instrumentality of the *jhāna*s to spiritual development, though we regard the development of *jhāna* as a possible way to view human development as the cultivation of the mind.

In the teachings on meditation in Early Buddhist scriptures, the Buddha spoke of four levels of *jhāna*. For example, in the *Bhayabherava-sutta* (MN 4), the Buddha summarized his experiences of the four *jhāna* as follows:

> Tireless energy was aroused in me and unremitting mindfulness was established, my body was tranquil and untroubled, my mind concentrated and unified. (Bodhi 1995, 104)
>
> Quite secluded from sensual pleasures, secluded from unwholesome states, I entered upon and abided in the first *jhāna*, which is accompanied by applied and sustained thought, with rapture and pleasure born of seclusion. (Bodhi 1995, 104)
>
> With the stilling of applied and sustained thought, I entered upon and abided in the second *jhāna*, which has self-confidence and singleness of mind without applied and sustained thought, with rapture and pleasure born of concentration.
>
> With the fading away as well of rapture, I abided in equanimity, and mindful and fully aware, still feeling pleasure with the body, I entered upon and abided in the third *jhāna*, on account of which noble ones announce: "He has a pleasant abiding who has equanimity and is mindful." (Bodhi 1995, 105)
>
> With the abandoning of pleasure and pain, and with the previous disappearance of joy and grief, I entered upon and abided in the fourth *jhāna*, which has neither-pain-nor-pleasure and purity of mindfulness due to equanimity. (Bodhi 1995, 105)

The Buddha recalled his experiences of *jhāna* as leading him to a state of deep calmness and equanimity (Gethin 1998, 22). The state of peace experienced in *jhāna* facilitated the Buddha in the process of awakening and helped him understand suffering and its cessation (Gethin 1998, 23). Theoretically, we can understand the development of the *jhāna*s as one progressive system that conceptualizes human development as a series of stages in attaining mental calmness. While the practice of *jhāna*s itself does not lead to the ultimate cessation of suffering, it can be a helpful practice on the path.

One further way to evaluate human development is via the attainment of Right View, which involves the progressive realization of non-attachment of the mind. Right View, also known as *samma-diṭṭhi*, is a central idea in Buddhism and a key component in all its practices. It can be defined as an accurate understanding of the fundamental truths of things, such as impermanence, non-self, and unsatisfactoriness. A root cause of suffering is clinging to self-notion, while the significance of Right View is to know and see the fabricated nature of that self-notion, thereby dissolving clinging onto fabricated identities. With reference to the previous discussion on the *jhāna*s, the practice of concentrated states of absorption can at most attain mental stillness and calmness, thereby providing a temporary cessation of defilements. Right View, however, leads to clear, still, and calm mind states that can observe the nature of things leading to liberation from suffering. The development of Right View can be seen as a gradual process involving the realizing of Wrong View and its attendant suffering, learning Right View conceptually, and realizing Right View through contemplative practices. In this process, a practitioner will see the constructed and fabricated nature of things, including one's self-notion, and then learn to become non-attached by witnessing the dependently co-arisen nature of phenomena. This cultivation of Right View can be regarded as the mind's advancement towards non-attachment. Given its importance, Right View will be a key topic of discussion in later chapters.

The next section will explore human development from a psychological perspective as well as provide commentary on the proposed Buddhist view of human development.

5.4 Commentary on Human Development According to Professional Psychology

In comparing developmental psychology and Early Buddhist scriptures, there seems to be a fundamentally different assumption in the direction of development between the two schools: psychology generally assumes child development to be a series of positive changes from birth onwards, while Early Buddhist teachings assume that child development involves the maturation of negative characteristics in uncultivated children and families.

In secular psychology, human development is considered to be a process of learning, maturation, and adaptation. Theoretical models usually examine human growth and changes over the lifespan and focus on multiple aspects, such as the physical, cognitive, social, intellectual, personality, and emotional domains. Many models categorize development throughout the lifespan into various life stages and illustrate important development milestones at each level. For example, Piaget (1964, 11) introduced a classic universal model of human development to explain the stages and characteristics of child cognitive development. In this model, the discussion of cognitive development starts from birth. There are four stages: (1) the sensorimotor stage (0 to 2 years), where infants explore and learn about the world predominantly through the five senses; (2) the operational stage (2 to 7 years), in which preschool children start to understand the world using symbolic meaning and thinking through exploration with languages and concepts, while logical thinking has yet to develop; (3) the concrete-operational stage (7 to 11 years) where children start to think logically, can classify, organize, sort objects into different categories, and understand different perspectives; and (4) the formal operational stage (11 to adulthood), where adolescents can think logically and abstractly and understand the world beyond concrete experiences. In this theoretical model, Piaget (1964, 11) emphasizes the idea of development towards a more competent and capable direction. Each stage has specific gains and limitations, and children should manifest the typical characteristics of a particular stage to be considered as undergoing normal development.

In contemporary professional psychology, many practitioners continue to use human development theories, including Piaget's model of cognitive development, to determine whether a child's development falls within a normal range and then use such theoretical references to inform interventions in counseling practice (Fond-Harmant, Laurence, and Mihaela Gavrila-Ardelean 2016, 117). For example, the commonly used *Infancy, Childhood, and Relationship Enrichment* (ICARE) assessment form focuses on evaluating developmental stages in five domains: socio-emotional, motor skills, sensory skills, language skills, and cognitive skills (Los Angeles County Department of Mental Health 2020, 1–10). In each domain, a trained mental health professional uses clinical interviews with children to determine whether they have met expected developmental milestones at their age level, thereby screening for areas of deficit for treatment purposes.[17] In our understanding of this paradigm, the application of theories of development from psychology has several characteristics: (1) development has a positive connotation and is believed to be a normal and healthy human experience; (2) development is commonly considered to occur in stages; (3) stages are applied to evaluate the wellbeing of individuals, and; (4) problems meeting expected developmental milestones may be indicative of pathology.

As shown in the previous discussion, mundane human development is not a usual topic of discussion in the Pāli *Nikāya*s; indeed, Buddhism is fundamentally and originally designed for practitioners who have reached a certain level of higher thinking. Most Buddhist *sutta*s depict the Buddha having conversations with adults, and there is minimal discussion of how children develop over time. Therefore, it was rare to see arguments integrating Early Buddhist teachings

17. I will provide an example: a normal socioemotional milestone for a 9-month-old baby is reaching out to their caregiver for social interaction, while any deficit in this behavior might be indicative of developmental delay or disorders, such as autism.

with human development in educational or counseling contexts.[18] Even so, we argue for the dimension of human development in the current Early Buddhist theoretical orientation to take mental cultivation as the developmental trajectory. To buttress this argument, we want to point out a few supporting claims. First, when the Buddha discussed his experiences of *jhāna*, he described a four-stage model in the progressive soothing of one's mind through a developmental trajectory of states of concentration (Bodhi 1995, 104–5). Gethin describes this model of *jhāna* development as a psychological hierarchy (Gethin 1998, 124). Second, Gethin described the cultivation of *jhāna* as a sequential process in which the mental qualities cultivated during *jhāna* play an important role in the attainment of *Nibbāna* (Gethin 1998, 124). Third, the realization of Right View provides a gradual path in fostering non-attachment and liberation from suffering. Parallel to the model of cognitive development proposed by Piaget, which assumes a trajectory of development towards more complex cognitions (1964, 11), it makes sense to understand the *jhāna* model of mental development towards more skillful mind states as another model of human development. Moreover, this model of mind development follows the four characteristics of developmental theories: (1) human development has a positive teleology given that the direction of development is liberation from suffering; (2) it can categorize development into stages, such as the stages of *jhāna* and arahatship; (3) these stages may be used to evaluate the level of mental cultivation in individuals, and; (4) problems at any developmental stage may indicate pathology that can appear in the form of defilements, hindrances, or other obstacles, for which certain interventions or practices can help an individual advance to the next stage. Given its practicality, therefore, we

---

18. Only recently have Chan and Zen Buddhist scholars produced more work on integrating Buddhist teachings to inform counseling practices. For example, Zen Buddhist and researcher Edward Canda produced several scholarly works integrating Zen Buddhist, psychological, and social work concepts into human and spiritual development models. For instance, Canda and Gomi (2019) compared the Ten Ox Herding Pictures with traditional human developmental theories in psychology and then used it as a reference to reflect on spiritual growth for social workers and mental health professionals (44). Similarly, Sears (2016), a clinical psychologist in the US and a Zen Buddhist scholar, published a book on the development of the brain and self-concept according to perspectives from psychology and Zen Buddhism. The book cross-referenced the Zen Buddhist concept of self and the neuroscience of brain development with the idea of no-self, providing a flexible and malleable sense of identity (Sears, 2016, 14). These are two of the most representative scholarly works on the topic. However, in their application of Buddhist concepts to developmental theories, neither scholar investigated the position of human development in Early Buddhist teachings or analyzed how the historical Buddha understood human development. We argue that the assumptions behind "human development" significantly differ between Early Buddhist teachings and psychology, a feature which has hindered scholars' investigation of concepts of human development in Early Buddhist scriptures. This difference includes assumptions about what is considered healthy. Expecting a healthy person to be liberated from suffering is very different to human development in psychology.

believe this model of mental development can serve as the dimension of human development in this theoretical orientation.

5.5 The Healthy Ideal in Professional Psychology

What is a psychologically healthy person like? The answer to what appears to be an easy question requires a sophisticated answer. Perhaps the most commonly used standard nowadays is the *Diagnostic and Statistical Manual of Mental Disorders, fifth edition* (DSM-5), which draws a fine line between normality and clinically significant mental disorders (American Psychiatric Association 2013, 21). A generic diagnostic criterion to diagnose a mental disorder is whether it has caused "clinically significant distress or impairment in social, occupational, or other important areas of functioning" (American Psychiatric Association 2013, 21). Moreover, each diagnosis of a mental disorder consists of several clinical symptoms that interfere with a person's daily functioning, such as sleep disturbance, low appetite, loss of concentration, emotional disturbance, suicidal thoughts, problematic behaviors and relationships, and other psychosocial manifestations. This definition makes several assumptions. First, being psychologically healthy means "without clinical symptoms." Second, as long as the psychological disturbance does not significantly impair a person's daily functioning, the person is considered healthy. Third, it assumes that a mental disorder is not a standard part or experience of life, and healthy people should not suffer from it.

Evolving from the traditional definition of the healthy ideal as the absence of mental illness, the field of mental health has tried to create broader definitions. In 2004, the World Health Organization (WHO) defined mental health as "a state of well-being in which the individual realizes his or her own abilities, can cope with the normal stresses of life, can work productively and fruitfully, and is able to make a contribution to his or her community" (World Health Organization 2004, 1). However, we believe this definition does not include concern about mental illness. Instead, mental health focuses on a person's capacity to cope with stress and work productively in one's community—the ideal mentally healthy person is a highly functioning person. While this definition moves away from the stigmatization of mental illness, it fails to capture a person's subjective well-being. Let us give an example: a person can experience a significant level of anger, depression, or other disturbing emotions. However, if they are capable of coping with normal stress in life while functioning effectively, this suffering person can be regarded as mentally healthy. Moreover, we think this definition seems to imply a social standard that judges whether a person contributes productively to one's community, which may have different cultural biases and assumptions.

Besides the DSM-5 and the WHO's definitions of mental health, each school of thought has unique beliefs on the ideal mentally healthy person. According to psychoanalysis, the most traditional psychotherapeutic approach, a psychologically healthy person has developed a structurally complete self (Tengland 2001, 35). In this paradigm, mental health is considered to consist of an inner balance between three personality constructs: the id, the ego, and the superego (Tengland 2001, 36). Ideally, a healthy person has a strong and containing ego that successfully manages the id and superego, meeting their inner needs within realistic constraints (Tengland 2001, 36). This healthy person has a deep self-knowledge of the unconscious, is autonomous and self-reliant, and exercises flexibility in behaviors and relationships in daily life (Tengland 2001, 36). However, most individuals are not psychologically healthy, and psychoanalytic treatment can take years to complete (Tengland 2001, 36).

Another prominent and traditional approach in psychotherapy, client-centered therapy, generally assumes that a psychologically healthy individual is a self-actualized person (Kim 2018, 201). Driven by a formative tendency, a person who fosters the natural tendency to fulfil their underlying potential and maximize personal maturation is seen to be psychologically healthy (Kim 2018, 203). Most importantly, client-centered therapy believes every person has an intrinsic inclination towards this healthy ideal (Salisbury, 2021). A self-actualized person tends to evaluate experiences and make judgments based on personal values and standards while not relying on conditions of worth from others (Kim, 2018, 205).

Lastly, one of the most popular treatment approaches, Cognitive Behavioral Therapy (CBT), assumes a psychologically healthy person is adaptive, objective, and realistic in their appraisal of events, has a belief in self, and has a positive view of others and the world (Beck 2011, 3). Psychologically healthy people can also flexibly and objectively appraise themselves in specific situations (Beck 2011, 3). Using the example of losing a football game, a less psychologically healthy person concludes that "I cannot do anything right," a strong statement that overgeneralizes failure, resulting in negative emotions and behaviors. However, a psychologically healthy person may conclude that "I am not good at football," which can generate a reasonable number of negative emotions that are less likely to result in negative behaviors. CBT assumes that psychological disorders are related mainly to the dysfunctional and irrational beliefs and perspectives that cause one to hold beliefs that are out of proportion, or even out of context, leading to emotional disturbances (Beck 2011, 27). Therefore, when one's views are realistic and reasonable, the experienced emotions and resulting behaviors will also be realistic and reasonable (Beck 2011, 136). In other words, a psychologically healthy person will still experience difficult emotions when these emotions are reasonable reflections of reality, such as feeling sad when losing significant others or feeling anxious during a presentation. However, as one's perspective is realistic and adaptive, these emotional disturbances do not escalate to a clinically significant level that impairs the person's functioning, such as major depressive disorder or phobias (Beck 2011, 53).

In general, each school of thought and diagnostic perspective in psychology has an understanding and interpretation of a healthy ideal. To summarize these views, the healthy ideal in psychology commonly requires one to have (1) functionality in one's external environment, (2) absence of clinical symptoms, or (3) a level of refinement of internal processes, such as the resolution of internal conflicts or the flourishing of aspirations. One factor common to these psychological perspectives is that no definition explicitly mentions happiness or an ideal state of freedom from suffering. In this respect, Buddhism is somewhat different in that it assumes the existence of a state of liberation. The next section will discuss how to reconcile these differences in a Buddhist counseling model.

5.6 Implications of Mind Development for Buddhist Counseling Practice

A Buddhist theoretical orientation for human development incorporates the traditional framework and assumptions of psychology as well as concepts from Early Buddhist *sutta*s. Reflecting on several possible meanings of human development in Buddhism, this section will delineate some implications and applications of Buddhist insights to Buddhist counseling.

First and foremost, the theoretical dimension of human development can take the Buddhist perspective of mental development as its conceptual framework. In particular, progress in mental development can be gauged by ascertaining the level of mind cultivation towards liberation from suffering; that is, the skillfulness of the mind in choosing wholesome thoughts, speech, and behaviors. At least two validated psychometric scales can be used to measure this mental development.

The first one is the Nonattachment Scale (NAS) proposed by Feliu-Soler et al. (2016, 1156–69). Applying the nonattachment measure as inspired by Buddhism, Feliu-Soler created this 30-item scale to measure nonattachment in several dimensions, including the ability to let go of regrets, maintain inner peace during disturbing situations, become immersed in joy in the present moment, relinquish possession of things and relationships, and be comfortable with oneself (Feliu-Soler et al. 2016, 1156). Since nonattachment is considered a sign of wisdom, as well as being the goal of Early Buddhist practice, this measurement can be used to evaluate a person's progress in achieving nonattachment.

The second scale is the Un-clinging Scale developed by Ng et al. (2017, 277). This scale goes beyond the Western definition of mindfulness and employs the core Buddhist concept of un-clinging as the primary measurement construct (Ng et al. 2017, 278). It is a 5-item scale measuring the frequency of being caught up in or dwelling on unpleasant emotions, unpleasant thoughts, unpleasant sensations, unpleasant psychological responses, and desires, and the extent to which an individual can avoid being trapped in the above states. This scale can also be used as an evaluation of personal cultivation.

Second, there is also a good reason for our Buddhist-inspired theoretical orientation to adopt insights gained from human development in psychology, since a good conceptual framework should be applicable to people of all ages. In other words, a theoretical orientation based on Early Buddhist teachings can integrate insights from psychology to extend its scope for providing treatment to children if the components do not violate Buddhist teachings. For example, both schools emphasize the importance of the environment, especially parenting and education. In particular, the Buddha's teaching of Rāhula can be seen as an example of parenting that involves a compassionate and patient father sharing wisdom with his son. With proper teaching and practice, the Buddhist stance acknowledges that humans develop in a positive direction, namely, to achieve liberation from suffering. With that said, both schools agree on fostering positive human development. Practically, and from a mundane perspective, the main conditions in psychology and human development—such as cognitive abilities, physiological changes, language capacity, and social competencies—are all important factors influencing the degree of suffering in clients. As Buddhist counselors primarily focus on lay people, it is crucial to consider these factors during assessment, conceptualization, and intervention.

Third, if one strictly transfers and applies the end goal of mind development from Buddhism to counseling, a Buddhist counselor would expect every client to reach arahatship, or complete liberation from suffering, as the end goal of treatment. However, most clients are not motivated enough to make the effort to learn and practice Buddhist teachings over a long period of time; instead, they hope to learn ways to cope with their immediate and everyday suffering. In response to such a need, Buddhist counselors can use the practice as a guide and direction for tailor-made interventions according to the client's readiness level and intensity of practice. Furthermore, since several discourses considered lay people in the teaching of the stream-entry (*sotāpatti*) stage (MN 95, AN 8.54, MN 56), it may be plausible for them to aim for this goal. For instance, the *Dutiyasāriputta-sutta* (SN 55.5) delineated and described four factors supporting the attainment of stream-entry (Bodhi 2000, 1792). Our model integrates these factors as domains for human development. The first domain is the capacity to associate with good people (*sappurisa-saṃsevo*). Befriending wise, ethical, and compassionate individuals will promote positive growth for children and adults. This factor can apply to the extent to which a person knows how to discern good friends and make an effort to connect with these individuals. The second domain is the capacity to attend to wise teachings (*saddhamma-savaṇaṃ*). This condition evaluates how a person listens to and learns the Buddha's teachings in order to acquire knowledge for mind cultivation. The third factor is the capacity for wise reflection (*yonisomanasikāro*). This development refers to one's ability to reflect on the origin of events and problems. In every momentary experience, there is opportunity to reflect on feelings, thoughts, volitions, and behaviors to sort out an event's causes, conditions, and consequences. Wise reflection means observing and contemplating the patterns, sequences, and interdependent conditions of experiences to understand how things function. The fourth factor is the capacity to practice under the *Dhamma* (*dhammānudhammapaṭipatti*). This domain gauges the extent to which a person practices meditation to purify their view of reality; in other words, the goal should be detaching from a self-view, thereby easing ill-will and hatred and fostering wisdom. This practice is likely to inform daily actions and decisions and lead to more wholesome consequences in everyday encounters in order to be liberated from the presenting psychological problem. Likewise, the whole section of the *Sotāpatti saṃyutta* (Bodhi 2000, 1788–837), as well as many other *sutta*s in the *Nikāya*s, deals with the concept of stream-entry. In short, the attainment of Right View, which eventually leads to the arising of the remaining noble paths, is the attainment of stream-entry. Although entry is revered as a difficult achievement in traditional Buddhist countries, the early *sutta*s depict it as merely the initial step towards true practice, as it is directly associated with proper understanding or view (*sammā-diṭṭhi*).

In working with a client who is interested in learning Buddhist teachings, Buddhist counselors can consider using the following chart each week or session to help clients reach their four developmental goals:

Meeting the goals involves a continuous process of striving that will require repeated effort, including association with the *Dhamma* (for example, learning the Buddhist worldview and applying it in daily life) and practicing continuously (such as developing and committing to the practice of meditation). Buddhist counselors can discuss each goal with the client and reflect on how to achieve them in daily life. For example, they can help clients identify good friends, explore suitable Buddhist books or media, teach clients ways to contemplate and reflect on distressing incidents to see their origins and conditions, and guide them through weekly meditation practice. Again, there can be many creative applications of the teachings in counseling, and there is significant room for empirical evaluation and validation. This exercise is only a trial application of the Buddhist perspective on human development.

Since mindfulness has become a standard therapeutic technique in professional psychology, a scale to measure the advancement of personal cultivation can be helpful. Although there are existing and validated scales to measure the level of mindfulness in lay practitioners (such as the Toronto Mindfulness Scale, the Philadelphia Mindfulness Scale, State Mindfulness Scale, etc.), they are designed

Table 5.1: Four Development Goals

Cultivation Goals	**Moving away from developmental goal this week**	**On track towards developmental goal this week**	**Reached developmental goal this week**	**Action plan to achieve goals or sustain development this week**
Association with good peers				
Attending to wise teachings				
Wise reflections				
Practice in accordance with the *Dhamma*				

to measure contemporary definitions of mindfulness, relying on psychological constructs such as acceptance and present-moment awareness (Cardaciotto 2008, 204). As such, they may not apply to the Buddhist ideology of mind cultivation. There is also a dearth of mindfulness or meditation scales using Buddhist scriptures as a theoretical background. For this reason, Buddhist counselors and scholars must develop and study meditation scales based on Buddhist teachings in order to track clients' progress in Buddhist meditation. For example, Table 5.2 modifies parts of the *Satipaṭṭhāna-sutta* to measure advancement in mind cultivation for beginner meditators. Buddhist counselors should work with clients in teaching a specific mindfulness practice and then help them identify an object of meditation. Moreover, clients can develop a regular mindfulness practice via the counseling process and then complete the scales consistently to evaluate their progress.

Table 5.2: Scale for Mindfulness Cultivation

Instruction: Below is a list of possible experiences during meditation practice. Please read each statement and indicate the extent to which you agree with it. Please use your experiences in your regular meditation sessions during the past week as a reference.

Experience in Meditation	1	2	3	4	5
I am able to observe changes in bodily sensations.	Not at all	A little	Moderately	Quite a bit	Very much
I am able to observe changes in feeling tones (i.e., pleasant feelings, unpleasant feelings, or neutral feelings in body and mind).	Not at all	A little	Moderately	Quite a bit	Very much
I am able to observe changes in thoughts.	Not at all	A little	Moderately	Quite a bit	Very much
I am able to observe how different factors give rise to an experience in my body and mind.	Not at all	A little	Moderately	Quite a bit	Very much
I am able to observe how a thought comes up and dissipates without interference.	Not at all	A little	Moderately	Quite a bit	Very much
I am aware of the sensations of each in- and out-breath without distraction.	Not at all	A little	Moderately	Quite a bit	Very much
I am aware of the changes in each in- and out-breath, such as the changes in rhythm, strength, and duration.	Not at all	A little	Moderately	Quite a bit	Very much
When my mind is filled with sensual desire, I can feel it.	Not at all	A little	Moderately	Quite a bit	Very much
When my mind is filled with ill-will, I can see it.	Not at all	A little	Moderately	Quite a bit	Very much
When my mind is mentally dull and lacks energy, I am aware of it.	Not at all	A little	Moderately	Quite a bit	Very much

(continued on p. 126)

Table 5.2: (*continued*)

Experience in Meditation	1	2	3	4	5
When my mind is agitated and worried, I am aware of it.	Not at all	A little	Moderately	Quite a bit	Very much
When my mind is filled with doubts, I am aware of it.	Not at all	A little	Moderately	Quite a bit	Very much
When my mind is distracted by unwholesome thoughts and emotions, I can see how they arise and cease.	Not at all	A little	Moderately	Quite a bit	Very much
I am able to note that whatever thoughts are coming, they are not "me" "mine" "myself."	Not at all	A little	Moderately	Quite a bit	Very much
I am able to note that whatever feelings are being felt, whether pleasant, unpleasant or neutral, they are not "me" "mine" "myself."	Not at all	A little	Moderately	Quite a bit	Very much
While observing the thoughts and feelings, I am able to let them come and go.	Not at all	A little	Moderately	Quite a bit	Very much
I am able to non-attach myself from the thoughts and feelings and any ensuing conflicts.	Not at all	A little	Moderately	Quite a bit	Very much
I am able to stay calm and unaffected by thoughts and feelings that arise.	Not at all	A little	Moderately	Quite a bit	Very much

5.7 Conclusion

This chapter reviewed the perspective of human development in secular psychology while investigating the potential of integrating additional views from Early Buddhist teachings, arguing that the Buddhist concept of human development is better understood as a pathway of mental development. Based on this assumption, the final section of the chapter proposed possible applications of the concept of *kamma* and the stages of meditation in Buddhist counseling. It is important to recognize that this section aims to propose a new direction for research and practice, noting that evaluating and validating these applications will require more scholarly effort. Therefore, its application remains open for further interpretation and adjustment.

6
Theoretical Orientation Dimension IV: Health and Dysfunction

The theoretical orientation used in this book for understanding psychological dysfunction addresses two topics: what is considered a dysfunction and what causes it. In general, each theoretical orientation has an assumption of psychological well-being, with dysfunction being behavior that deviates from normal functioning. This chapter explores dysfunction and its causes as presented in Early Buddhist teachings, and then adds commentary from psychology, drawing out the implications of suffering for Buddhist counseling.

6.1 *Dukkha*

In the Buddha's first sermon, also known as the First Turning of the Dhamma Wheel, the Buddha shared his realization of the Middle Way as well the Four Noble Truths in the *Dhammacakkappavattana-sutta* (SN 56.11):

> (First Noble Truth: *Dukkha*) "Now this, bhikkhus, is the noble truth of suffering: birth is suffering, aging is suffering, illness is suffering, death is suffering; union with what is displeasing is suffering; separation from what is pleasing is suffering; not to get what one wants is suffering; in brief, the five aggregates subject to clinging are suffering. (Bodhi 2000, 1844)[1]

The Buddha underwent a long and arduous journey in seeking complete cessation of suffering, although he did not claim his discovery to be a divine revelation; instead, he taught his insight and comprehension of the *Dhamma* for the benefit of others (Karunadasa 2013, 1). During this first sermon, the First Noble Truth signifies an acknowledgement of *dukkha* and lays the structural framework for

1. SN V, 421: *Idaṃ kho pana bhikkhave dukkham ariyasaccaṃ. Jāti pi dukkhā jarā pi dukkhā vyādhi pi dukkhā maraṇam pi dukkhaṃ sokaparidevadukkhadomanassupāyāsā pi dukkhā. appiyehi sampayogo dukkho piyehi vippayogo dukkho. yam picchaṃ na labhati tam pi dukkhaṃ. saṃkhittena pañcūpādānakkhandhā pi dukkhā.*

all important teachings of Early Buddhist teachings (Harvey 2014, 26). *Dukkha* is also considered to be one of the three main characteristics of all sentient existence, together with impermanence (*anicca*) and non-self[2] (*anatta*; Karunadasa 2013, 5). The Buddha also stated clearly that his purpose in teaching is to make known to the world the nature of suffering and its cessation; hence, his key teachings need to be considered as an explanation of how suffering arises, with instructions then given on how to make it cease (Somaratne 2021, 237). Taken together, it is reasonable to conclude that suffering is the only reason for Buddhism's existence and that *dukkha* is the main dysfunction in human beings.

Dukkha, translated as "suffering," "dissatisfaction," or "stress," is what Buddhist practices aim to treat (Somaratne 2021, 237). In the description of the above *sutta*, suffering is explained and categorized in a variety of ways. This section will briefly review certain characteristics of *dukkha* in Buddhism and present the most common categorization, namely, the eight forms of *dukkha*.

First, the Buddha's teaching of *dukkha* is not what we normally think about in an everyday context; instead, the message is in the details, facts, and implications, which require effortful contemplation and practice to comprehend (Somaratne 2021, 238). For example, suffering can be classified as: (1) felt suffering and (2) reckoned suffering (Somaratne 2021, 238). Felt suffering refers to unpleasant or painful feelings that are felt mentally, physically, or both, which are common mundane human experiences and easier to understand (Somaratne 2021, 238). Reckoned suffering is a type of suffering that needs to be considered, understood, or viewed, and includes any neutral or unpleasant feeling (Somaratne 2021, 238). This second type of suffering is a core teaching of the Buddha, constituting an accurate perception of the pervasiveness of suffering, including non-clinging, as a way to experience the cessation of suffering (Somaratne 2021, 239).

Second, according to the Law of Dependent Co-arising, *dukkha* is a conditioned experience dependent on impermanent causes and conditions (Karunadasa 2013, 69). One implication of this conditioned experience is that there is no true relief and peace as long as one is in the cycle of *saṃsāra* and clings to the five aggregates (Trungpa 2009, 8). But this perspective does not argue that sensual gratification is morally wrong; rather, it asserts that sensual gratification cannot lead to ultimate happiness or the cessation of suffering (Karunadasa 2013, 73).

Third, the key purpose of Buddhist practice is to cease all types of mental suffering, such as anxiety, worry, grief, and despair caused by loss, ageing, sickness, death, or physical pain (Somaratne 2021, 241). In other words, the goal of practice

2. It is important to note that we should not interpret the Buddha's teaching as "everything is suffering," as it will only lead to pessimistic and unhelpful perceptions (Somaratne 2021, 237). On the contrary, the goal of practice is to see and understand the suffering arising from clinging to the five aggregates, thereby practicing the diminishing and eventual ceasing of the subjective configurations of "I" in order to experience liberation from suffering (Somaratne 2021, 241).

is to cease the subjective conditions leading to mental suffering (Somaratne 2021, 241). In particular, two key conditions giving rise to mental suffering include the perception of self in the five aggregates and clinging to them as "This is my self" (Somaratne 2021, 241). The path that leads to liberation from suffering develops the perception of non-self by seeing the nature of impermanence and the suffering caused by the nature of the five aggregates (Somaratne 2021, 241–42). As we have mentioned in previous chapters, this goal is adopted as the treatment goal of our theoretical orientation.

After acknowledging the position of *dukkha* in lived experiences, the Buddha continued with the second Noble Truth to explicate the causes of *dukkha*: "Now this, bhikkhus, is the noble truth of the origin of suffering: it is this craving which leads to renewed existence, accompanied by delight and lust, seeking delight here and there; that is, craving for sensual pleasures, craving for existence, craving for extermination" (Bodhi 2000, 1845).[3]

As discussed in the first author's earlier publication on Buddhist counseling (Lee, 2021), the Buddha directly pinpointed the Second Noble Truth, craving (*taṇhā*) as the root cause of suffering (Lee 2021, 241) as well as the core cause of dysfunction. Fueled by ignorance, *taṇhā* emerges as a powerful lust or a strong mental or physical thirst and longing for one of three experiences: craving for sensual pleasures (*kāma-taṇhā*), craving for existence (*bhava-taṇhā*), and craving for annihilation (*vibhava-taṇhā*) (see chapter 4 for details).

Linking this discussion to the discussion on non-self in the previous chapter, Buddhism holds that all forms of mental irregularity are derived from strong identification of the five aggregates with an actual self. The five aggregates, like masses of fire (*ādittapariyāya*), are also neutral conditioned phenomena: arising, passing away, and changing constantly, subject to the law of dependent co-arising and three characteristics of the existence of sentient beings and giving rise to the experiences of human life and living. They do not necessarily cause suffering by themselves (Bodhi 2000, 1143). The cause of suffering, rather, is the mind's clinging to the five aggregates, which results in the illusory creation of a stable, autonomous, and permanent sense of self through reification and conceptualization (Lee 2022, 32). It is our deep-rooted habit to cling to the idea that these sets of ever-changing processes are equal to "me" and to wrongly think that "I should always be under 'my' control." From this attachment to a fixed but fabricated sense of self, we begin to erroneously believe that there is a separate, inherently existing personality, to define ourselves in relation to external objects, and to establish further clinging, such as clinging to sense-pleasures and clinging to Wrong Views

3. SN V, 421: *Idaṃ kho pana bhikkhave dukkhasamudayam ariyasaccaṃ. Yāyaṃ taṇhā ponobhavikā nandi rāgasahagatā tatra tatrābhinandini seyyathidaṃ. Kāmataṇhā bhava taṇhā vibhavataṇhā.*

(i.e., "this is mine" and "this is myself"; Lee 2022, 93). The problem that results from such beliefs is impaired functionality.

Human beings tend to personalize the five aggregates and take them too seriously without being aware of their nature (Lee 2022, 30). When we do this, we are unable to comprehend that all conditioned phenomena arise from external circumstances and internal mental actions that are subject to change (Lee 2022, 30). Constantly arising and ceasing thoughts and emotions are viewed as "my thoughts" and "my emotions" and grasped on to as real (Lee 2022, 27). Furthermore, whenever the five aggregates change without our expecting them to, a habitual ego defense mechanism like a "fight-flight-freeze" reaction is automatically activated to protect the illusory existence of this self-identity (Lee 2022, 31). As a result, the totality of our experience is confined to our limited perspective of ourselves, rendering us unable to accept reality as it is and present appropriate responses to the new sets of causes and conditions that meet us in the present moment (Lee 2022, 32). This is how suffering arises.

The First and Second Noble Truths provide a clear picture of what is dysfunctional and what the causes of dysfunction are, according to Early Buddhist teachings. The next chapter will discuss the Third and Fourth Noble Truths as interventions.

6.2 Commentary on *Dukkha* and Its Causes According to Psychology

From the perspective of secular psychology, there are several potential differences in the understanding of dysfunction. In psychology, psychopathology and mental health disorders are general terms to describe psychological disturbances (American Psychiatric Association 2013, 23). The most commonly used diagnostic manual, the DSM-5, employs a medical model to define human dysfunctions as categories of mental disorders impairing a person's psychological wellbeing and functioning. Similarly, the tenth edition of *The Classification of Mental and Behavioral Disorders* (ICD-10), another internationally recognized medical classification manual published by the World Health Organization (WHO), classifies and defines mental disorders according to clinically recognizable symptoms that are distress-related and which interfere with personal functioning (WHO 2003, 11). As we understand it, these two widely accepted diagnostic manuals, used by thousands of mental health professionals around the world, point out that psychological dysfunctions are basically "disorders" with "clinical symptoms." This assumption implies a social norm according to which "healthy" individuals function and are free of (or relatively free of) clinical symptoms. Counseling and psychotherapy are thus offered to individuals with clinical symptoms with the aim of symptom reduction. Buddhism, on the other hand, understands suffering as a universal phenomenon and a common human experience instead of being a psychopathology (Somaratne 2021, 239). Only highly cultivated individuals can be psychologically healthy and liberated from suffering; essentially, every individual is suffering from clinical symptoms to some degree and needs treatment (Gethin 1998, 9). Early Buddhist teachings often point out that sentient beings are suffering. For example, the *Nagara-sutta* (12.65) starts with the statement: "Alas! the world has fallen into trouble" (SN II, 104: *kicchā vatāyāṃ loko āpanno*), while the *Dhammapada* (146) states: "Why is there laughter, what joy are you having, when the world is always burning? Being in the darkness, why not seek for a lamp?" (*ko nu hāso kimānando, niccaṃ pajjalite sati, andhakārena onaddhā, padīpaṃ na gavesatha*). From the Buddhist perspective, psychological disorders are all part of *dukkha* and are an inevitable experience for every individual living in this world. Buddhism proposes that factors causing suffering—such as separation from loved ones, not getting what one wants, or association with people and things we dislike—are always present, but that the subjective experience of suffering can be reduced, and even, in the case of enlightenment, completely eliminated (Somaratne 2021, 238). In a general sense, to be liberated from suffering is to realize the laws of all things as they are (*dhammatā*) by cultivating the mind to cease subjective configuration. However, traditional professional psychology assumes that only certain individuals suffering from a clinical level of symptoms require treatment. This difference is important to consider for Buddhist counseling.

We also notice that causes of suffering are significantly different in Buddhism and professional psychology. According to research studies on mental disorders, causes of mental disorders are multidimensional and can include environmental stress, childhood experiences, maladaptive coping mechanisms, personality traits, genetics, nutrition, perinatal infections, and many other factors (Lu 2019, 28). At the same time, every theoretical orientation in professional psychology has its own assumptions in explaining the causes of suffering (Gehart 2014, 7).

To briefly illustrate the various approaches driven by disparate theoretical orientations, we will now use a hypothetical example to demonstrate how these theoretical orientations conceptualize the causes of suffering differently while also providing feedback on the differences among the theoretical orientations. In particular, Valerie's case reveals how early experiences affect later experiences in life:

> Valerie is a 29-year-old financial analyst working at a "Big Four" accounting firm and decided to seek counseling for her intense anxiety and depressed mood. She describes herself as having sleeping problems, loss of concentration, low appetite, intense worries about not being able to finish her thesis on time, feeling sad sometimes, and having averse feelings about her supervisor. She hopes to find ways to cope with her anxiety so that she can manage her work and continue

to earn more money. In addition, she has a strong interest in fashion design, but she gave up on pursuing this path because her family, especially her mother, did not see it as a proper profession.

First, psychodynamic theories generally focus on how early relationships influence the formation of a self-concept and a relationship blueprint (Bianco, Simone, Paolo Barilaro, and Palmieri 2016, 552). They assume that the cause of dysfunction is rooted in individuals' unmet needs, which are later associated with the development of negative feelings in current relationships and which replicate unhealthy relationships with primary caregivers (parents; Bianco, Simone, Paolo Barilaro, and Palmieri 2016, 553). Thus, a psychodynamic counselor may assess Valerie's relationships with and perceptions of her parents to examine whether she has been re-enacting unhealthy relational patterns in current relationships, especially in her relationship with her supervisor. For example, Valerie may subconsciously experience her supervisor as her critical and rejecting mother and thus transfer the negative relational experience with her mother to her supervisor-supervisee relationship, which provokes an overwhelming sense of anxiety in her. Moreover, while Valerie's pursuit of career and financial success may fulfill her family's expectation of being a successful professional, her own aspiration for fashion design was quashed. Her need to satisfy her family's expectations and become a child worthy of love and care created lots of anxiety, and her sadness stems from her inability to follow her aspirations. Taking this into account, a psychodynamic intervention may help Valerie contain her anxiety by putting up her defenses, leading to transference. The psychodynamic agenda emphasizes fulfilling her unmet needs and analyzing and expressing her deeper emotions.

Using our understanding of Buddhism, we do not consider this approach to be the best path liberating her from suffering The rationale is that craving is an unquenchable thirst which cannot be ultimately satisfied (Teasdale and Chaskalson 2011, 94), and hence her ultimate happiness will never be sought in the gratification of desires (Karunadasa 2013, 74). This rationale does not limit the potential for Buddhist counseling to provisionally facilitate the release of emotions and having desires met in skillful ways. However, Buddhist practice aims for the higher goal of detaching mindfully from passion and craving as well as clinging to the notion of self in order to end suffering. According to this line of thinking, a Buddhist counseling approach can guide Valerie towards realizing that she has rigidly formed and become attached to a notion of self that is characterized by achievements, and how she has been working hard based on her yearning for her mother's love and approval. Seeing and knowing the suffering induced by these attempts together with knowing the impermanent nature of self-notion may help Valerie choose to let go of clinging to such a notion. In this regard, Buddhism takes the stance that suffering or stress can be overcome not by those who do not see and know, but only by seer and knower; that is, by knowing and seeing what is unwise reflection and what is wise reflection.[4] Simply put, the latter refers to seeing things as they are while the former means being unable to grasp the reality.

As for person-centered therapy, this approach generally focuses on providing an unconditional and nurturing environment for the growth of the authentic self (Kim 2018, 201). This model assumes that the cause of dysfunction is the lack of an unconditional and nurturing environment for the growth of the authentic self, thereby leading to living under inauthentic conditions of worth (Kim 2018, 201). A counselor may therefore use person-centered therapy to explore Valerie's deeper reasons for working in her field and positioning money as a high priority in life, including the related internal needs and environmental demands, thereby understanding the incongruence between her inauthentic self and ideal self. Valerie's pursuit of career and financial success had fulfilled her family's expectation to be a perfect, successful professional, but it had masked her true desire of becoming a fashion designer. However, her need to satisfy her family's expectations to become a child worthy of love and care (i.e., conditional love) created unbearable anxiety. The sadness may come from her inability to follow her aspirations towards self-actualization. Person-centered therapy aims to create a therapeutic environment characterized by empathy, congruence (genuineness), and unconditional positive regard (Kim 2018, 202). That approach will enable Valerie to get in touch with her intrinsic values and explore her life decisions with more congruence between her needs and environmental demands.

However, in the person-centered model, the assumption of an authentic self and intrinsic values does not align with the Buddhist teaching of non-self and the suffering that arises from clinging to views. From our understanding of Buddhism, the person-centered approach can be effective in reducing a certain level of felt-suffering, but it cannot lead to the experience of liberation from pervasive suffering, because the person-centered approach of nurturing the growth of an authentic self may be considered as fostering a more mundanely functional clinging to the notion of self. Our theoretical orientation takes non-self as the ultimate goal. Hence, our comments on this approach are similar to those on the psychodynamic approach: Buddhist counselors can help a client raise their awareness of clinging to a notion of self and the subjective conditions, not for the purpose of holding onto them better, but for the sake of letting go of them.

Finally, cognitive behavioral therapy (CBT) generally focuses on adopting rational and pragmatic beliefs and thinking, as it assumes that the cause of dysfunction is irrational and unrealistic thinking patterns and attitudes (Beck

4. MN I, 7: *Jānato ahaṁ bhikkhave passato āsavānaṁ khayam, vadāmi, no ajānato no apassato. Kiñ ca bhikkhave jānato kiṁ passato āsavānaṁ khayo hoti: yoniso ca manasikāraṁ ayoniso ca manasikāraṁ.*

2011, 27). A counselor who uses a CBT approach will explore Valerie's thoughts, assumptions, and beliefs contributing to her symptoms of anxiety. For example, Valerie may have frequent, negative, and irrational thoughts like "I am not good enough for this job" when she needs to perform expertly in the company, resulting in worry, anxiety, rumination, and physiological problems. Cognitive-behavioral interventions may focus on teaching Valerie behavioral techniques to cope with her anxiety symptoms, raising Valerie's awareness of her thought processes, and fostering more helpful and rational thoughts and beliefs.

In a way, irrational thoughts and beliefs overlap in part with the Buddhist teaching of Wrong View and subsequent suffering. However, the understanding of what is "Right View" is a moot point. In CBT, reality corresponds to an objective and observable world, while dysfunction comes from the mismatch between one's assumptions, beliefs, and thoughts and external reality (Segal, Williams, and Teasdale 2013, 189). However, CBT does not provide a clear definition of what reality is. In the Buddhist paradigm, the original root of suffering is ignorance (*avijjā*), which can be understood as the misunderstanding or distortion of reality (Lee 2022, 90). It should be noted that the idea of ignorance in Buddhism never refers to a lack of knowledge or intelligence in worldly matters such as science, mathematics, or economics; rather, it refers to a lack of understanding and acceptance of the Law of Dependent Co-arising. Therefore, the assumptions of reality characterizing the two schools of thought—CBT and Buddhism—differ to a potentially significant degree. In our understanding, the Buddhist theoretical orientation can guide Valerie to cultivate awareness of her cognitive acts through mental cultivation. When her mind gains more clarity and stability, the Buddhist counselor can guide her to observe the arising and ceasing of cognitive acts without identification. If disturbing cognitive acts persist, such as "I am such a failure" or "no cares about what I really want," and Valerie cannot refrain from identifying with and proliferating on them, Buddhist counseling can guide Valerie to examine and investigate her thoughts in order to understand the causes and conditions sustaining them, such as embedded yearnings, desires, and other defilements. Such continual awareness and contemplation are likely to help Valerie let go of the desire to resist the suffering-induced cognitive acts.

To summarize general assumptions as well as specific assumptions of psychopathology and its root causes in psychology—it is clear that the fundamental assumptions are more significant than those in Early Buddhist teachings. In particular, reckoned suffering does not have any correlates in psychology, while clinging to self-notion would not be deemed as a cause of suffering in psychological models. To develop a theoretical orientation, it is necessary to construct a model of case conceptualization or case formulation (that is, an in-depth analysis on why clients suffer in order to shed light on treatment planning) of the cause of suffering, which needs to be practical enough to understand the suffering of most clients and accessible enough for mental health professionals with different Buddhist backgrounds to understand. While no systematic conceptualization model in Buddhism exists, the next section will bring one into focus. It is also important to note that a case conceptualization is a continual and iterative analysis that can guide the clinical decisions of counselors. With that said, a good counselor should not rigidly grasp onto a conceptualized understanding of a client; instead, a good counselor should exercise mental flexibility to revise one's understanding of a client and advance the analysis along with the progression of counseling.

6.3 Implications of *Dukkha* and Its Causes for Buddhist Counseling

First and foremost, we argue that a theoretical orientation concerning psychological functioning can be based on the Buddhist understanding of suffering and its causes. By realizing non-self as the overarching treatment goal, the reduction of suffering is the main treatment objective. Similar to previous discussions on the focus of Buddhist counseling for secular-minded individuals who may not be ready to devote themselves to walking the Buddhist path, such people may only be motivated to deal with their emotional suffering or other felt suffering. However, it does not stop Buddhist counselors from applying Buddhist teachings to reduce a client's suffering by moving in the direction of non-self, or at the very least by exploring a less rigid clinging to the notion of self.

In a recent publication, the first author and his colleague proposed a Buddhist counseling model of conceptualization based on the Buddhist teachings (Lee and Tang 2021, 6). This model integrated some essential teachings based on the Four Noble Truths and the twelve-factor formula of dependent co-arising into a simple but coherent framework. The following section presents an updated description of the model.

To explain *dukkha* in layman's terms, we suffer because "what should be" does not align with "what is" in the world. As simple as it may sound, most of us are driven by an ignorant nature that fails to see and accept what is actually happening; instead, we are prone to becoming addicted to our cravings and desires, expecting our needs to be satisfied, and consequently we tend to distort or deny actual happenings when reality fails to satisfy us. This distortion may bring about temporary satisfaction, but it will eventually result in greater suffering. Ignorance describes our lack of insight into the process of resisting reality and perpetuating suffering through our own re-conceptualizations of what reality actually is. From a Buddhist perspective, ignorance manifests in many ways. In this model (Figure 6.1), we use the concepts of craving, clinging, and expectations to illustrate the major causes of suffering.

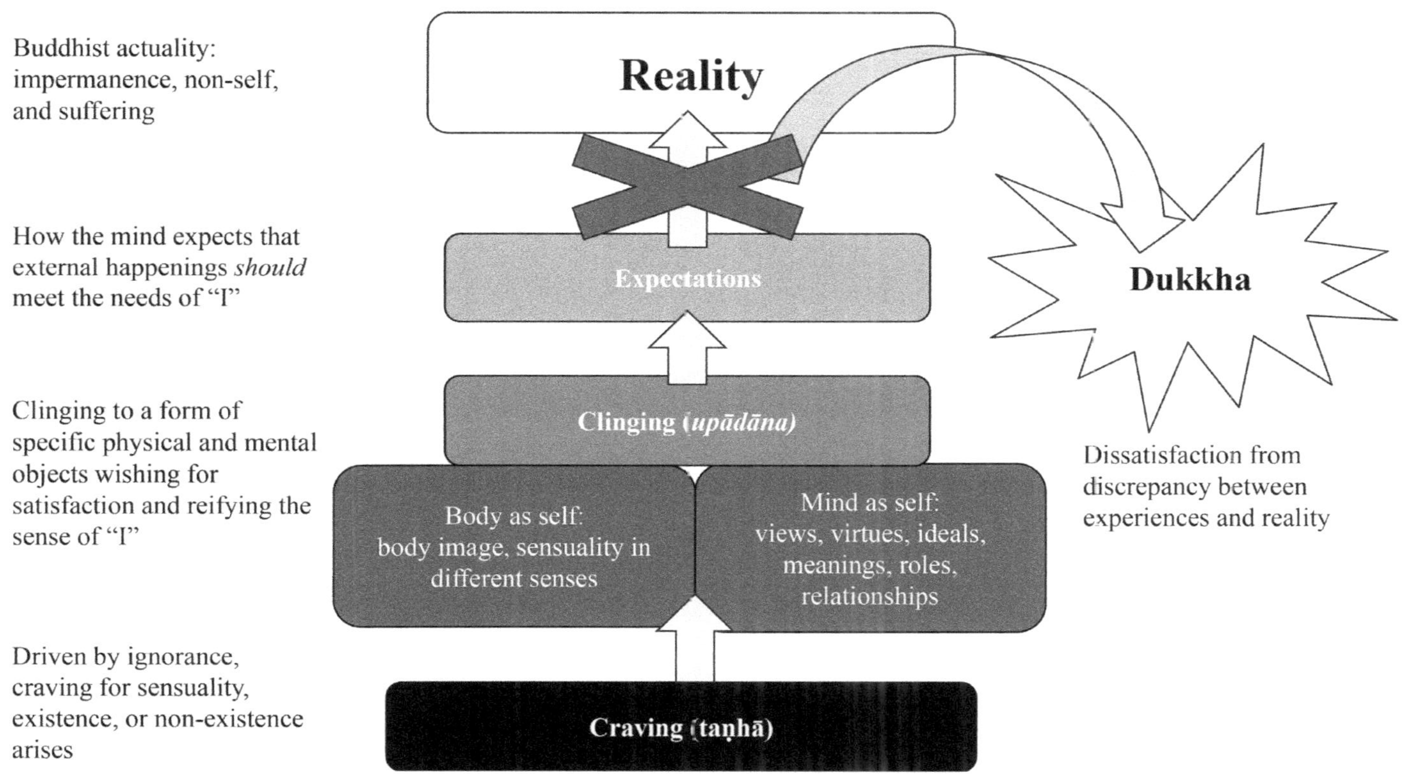

Figure 6.1: Buddhist Psychological Conceptualization of Human Suffering

Craving. As discussed in the previous section, craving is a strong and unquenchable thirst that makes the mind feel compelled to have its needs met. It is a preceding condition as well as a driving force for clinging.

Clinging. Driven by craving, human minds tend to grasp on to the external world and fabricate a solid relationship between mind and objects. This attempt to satiate desire is a process called clinging (*upādāna*), which is commonly translated as "attachment." The three types of craving lead one's mind to grasp on to environmental factors. This grasping, or clinging, helps the mind to concretize and materialize its habitual drive for permanence, which in turn fuels further craving. Clinging is a strong psychological attachment to, identification with, and immersion in mental or physical objects, coupled with the delusion that possessing those objects can satisfy craving. For example, a woman born and raised in a family culture of rigidly defined gender roles may naturally develop a belief that being a mother is the only way to be recognized and valued. Her craving for existence drives her to meet this social expectation, and consequently she clings to her role as a mother. After becoming a "mother," a self-concept to which she clings, she then becomes overly attached to her relationship with her child, which further feeds her craving to sustain the identity of being a good mother. This mother may then ignore the emerging independence of her 3-year-old child by infantilizing him, which serves to make her feel needed. From the perspective of dependent co-arising, the conditions for the child are constantly changing because he experiences continuous physical, socioemotional, cognitive, and motor development; her child of today has grown up to be different from her child of yesterday. However, the mother may fixate on the previous concept of "my child" who is highly dependent on her, thereby ignoring his developmental changes and grasping on to an unrealistic concept that fulfills her need for existence. In short, clinging to the notion of self is a key factor in suffering and understanding how clients view, sustain, and hold onto the notion of self, which can then elucidate why they suffer so much.

Expectations. Driven by craving and solidified by clinging, the mind tends to form assumptions about the world and place expectations onto the self, others, relationships, and the nature of things in order to satiate the mind with the idea that those expectations will be met. In other words, the mind comes to expect external happenings that meet our needs (Figure 6.1). This conceptualization of expectations is derived from the Buddhist concept of clinging and inspired by the idea of expectations in CBT and Reality Therapy; it describes the mind's insistence on what should happen, instead of what actually is happening. Returning to the aforementioned example, the mother's clinging to her role may produce expectations that her son should continuously depend on her despite his increasing maturity. However, reality is characterized by impermanence, which manifests as continually changing roles and relationships. Even so, the mother may come to expect her son to live close to home, talk to her regularly, seek emotional comfort from her, and ask her to do his chores. When her son finally starts to strike out on his own and become autonomous, this support for her identity collapses, which challenges her definition of self. Such discrepancies between expectations and reality result in suffering.

It is essential to further explain the relationship between clinging and pleasure. Driven by craving, the nature of the mind is such that it is inclined to feed on what feels pleasurable and rewarding, and it may gradually cling to physical or mental objects of satisfaction. Misunderstanding this concept may lead to the inaccurate conclusion that pleasure is wrong and that one needs to refrain from pleasure to avoid suffering. In Buddhism, however, pleasure is a phenomenon of both body and mind. Mindfully experiencing pleasure in the present moment, like tasting, appreciating the taste, and enjoying a delicious piece of chocolate, does not necessarily result in suffering. Nonetheless, when one lets craving for sensuality take charge, and when the mind dwells on thoughts and emotions to continue or expand the feeling of pleasure, attachment to the taste—in other words, suffering—will arise when chocolate is not available. Alternatively, the same piece of chocolate may become less satisfying, as one small piece is never enough when one becomes attached to getting more and more. This example illustrates that attaining satisfaction lies in the practice of training oneself in non-attachment or non-clinging.

Meanwhile, different levels of experience may trigger different intensities of clinging. Using the same example of the mother above, fully immersing in the pleasant experiences of connecting with her son or eating a piece of fine chocolate is not problematic in the moment during which it occurs. It may, however, be easy for her to let go of the chocolate but challenging for her to let go of the notion of a son who needs her, especially when her self-notion is being a "good mother." Suffering comes into play when her craving and clinging drives her to resist changes in her roles and relationships, struggling to maintain the same role with her son even when reality challenges her expectations. In other words, it is comparatively easier to enjoy pleasant feelings without clinging to neutral daily activities, such as drinking tea, eating chocolate, or chatting with acquaintances. The same may be much more challenging when the object of clinging resonates with how we construct the notion of self, such as our self-identity, love relationships, and core values.

Finally, this Buddhist counseling model and its attendant method of conceptualization can be used to understand the causes of suffering in clients in order to generate insights for interventions. In doing so, this model is not meant to discourage Buddhist counselors from employing psychological assumptions and knowledge in Buddhist counseling to conceptualize human suffering. Indeed, Buddhist counselors should also gain sufficient knowledge about the conceptualization of psychological problems and disorders in Western psychology in order to facilitate their understanding of the nature and causes of suffering in the mundane world, therefore allowing cross-disciplinary discussions to support and help a client. In this regard, the final chapter will use a case study that makes use of psychological concepts while also illustrating the viability of the above model.

6.4 Conclusion

With its unique theoretical orientation, Buddhism offers a clear understanding of dysfunction: suffering is the main disorder, and craving is the main driving factor. By integrating ideas of dysfunction from both professional psychology and Buddhist teachings on suffering, the treatment objective of Buddhist counseling can be to reduce clients' subjective experience of suffering. As counseling goals always need to match a client's readiness and motivation, it may not be realistic or possible to expect clients to liberate themselves from suffering during counseling. However, the integration of Buddhist teachings with knowledge and practice from secular psychology can provide very helpful techniques and tools to conceptualize clients' causes of suffering and shed light on ways to reduce it.

7

Theoretical Orientation Dimension V: Interventions and Techniques

A key dimension of any theoretical orientation in counseling is that of interventions which are methods that are intended to promote therapeutic change in clients (Gehart 2016, 19). In other words, a set of interventions applies the theoretical assumptions of a paradigm to healing actions, thereby bridging the gap of conceptual understanding of a client's presenting problems into concrete ways to address their suffering (Gehart 2016, 28). In the field of Buddhist-inspired counseling, an intervention translates understanding of a client's suffering into an action that reduces or eradicates their suffering (Lee 2022, 18). In this regard, healing techniques are the specific therapeutic tools that a counselor implements to help a client. Taking CBT as an example (Spalek and Spalek 2019, 32), dysfunction is assumed to be due to irrational beliefs, and therefore the standard intervention is to help clients restructure their beliefs into a more rational, objective, and functional state (the goal). The specific technique for doing this is to keep a thought log to note and record automatic thoughts for examination and discussion (the tool). In Buddhism, there are a number of effective interventions and techniques to eliminate suffering which this chapter attempts to collate and present. We will start with reviewing the relevant *sutta*s.

7.1 Intervention in Buddhism

Early Buddhist teachings aim for liberation from suffering, so it can be argued that all teachings of the Buddha constitute an intervention. One of the most fundamental interventions that encapsulates the entire body of Buddhist teachings is that of the Four Noble Truths,[1] which is composed of: suffering (*dukkhaṃ ariya*

1. As the *Mahāhatthipadopama-sutta* (MN I, 184) remarks, all the wholesome practices of *Dhamma* come under the teaching of the Four Noble Truths: "*seyyathāpi, āvuso, yāni kānici jaṅgalānaṃ pānānaṃ padajātāni sabbāni tāni hatthipade samodhānaṃ gacchanti, hatthipadaṃ tesaṃ aggamakkhāyāti yadidaṃ mahantattena, evameva kho āvuso ye keci kusalā dhammā sabbe te*

saccaṃ); the arising of suffering (*dukkhasamudayaṃ ariyasaccaṃ*); the cessation of suffering (*dukkhadirodhaṃ ariyasaccaṃ*); and the path to practice for the cessation of suffering (*dukkhanirodhagāminī paṭipadā ariyasaccaṃ*). In particular, the Fourth Noble Truth, which directly refers to the Noble Eightfold Path leading to the cessation of suffering, is the most important for our discussion. The *Dhammacakkappavattana-sutta* (SN 56.11) renders the Noble Eightfold Path as follows:

> O, Bhikkhus, what is the middle-way path that awakened to by the Tathāgata, which gives vision, knowledge . . . and leads to Nibbāna? It is the noble eightfold paths, namely: right view, right intention, right speech, right action, right livelihood, right effort, right mindfulness and right concentration.[2]

As an intervention designated to ameliorate or end suffering, the Buddha elucidated a system to cultivate the cessation of suffering, namely the Noble Eightfold Path of eight practices, and categorized them as a threefold system of training:

> the Noble Eightfold Path is included by the three aggregates. Right speech, right action, and right livelihood are included in the aggregate of virtue (*sīla*). Right effort, right mindfulness, and right concentration are included in the aggregate of concentration (*samādhi*). Right view and right intention are included in the aggregate of wisdom (*paññā*) (trans. Bodhi 1995, 398).[3]

Since the root of suffering is ignorance (*avijjā*), the remedy is to raise awareness of the true nature of phenomena through this threefold training, to cultivate a stable, clear, and discerning mind through meditation to cease subjective configurations, and reflecting and contemplating on the true nature of all phenomena to understand reality as it truly is (Somaratne 2021, 6).

---

catūsu ariyasaccesu saṅgahaṁ gacchanti." (The footprints of all the animals that walk can fit into the footprint of an elephant, and for this reason, it is said, the elephant's footprint is the largest of all. Similarly, all the wholesome practices are included in the teaching of four noble truths.)

2. SN V 421: *Katamā ca sā bhikkhave majjhimā paṭipadā Tathāgatena abhisambuddhā cakkhukaraṇī ñāṇakaraṇī . . . ayam eva ariyo aṭṭhaṅgiko maggo, seyyathidaṃ sammādiṭṭhi.*
3. MN I, 301: *Yā c'āvuso Visākha sammāvācā yo ca sammākammanto yo ca sammāājīvo, ime dhammā sīlakkhandhe saṅgahitā; yo ca sammāvāyāmo yā ca sammāsati yo ca sammāsamādhi, ime dhammā samādhikkhandhe saṅgahitā; yā ca sammādiṭṭhi yo ca sammāsaṅkappo, ime dhammā paññākkhandhe saṅgahītā ti.*

7.2 The Noble Eightfold Path as a Threefold Training Intervention

7.2.1 Wisdom (*paññā*)

Right View and Right Intention are classified as wisdom training.

Right View (*Sammā diṭṭhi*).[4] In general, Right View is defined as the understanding of the four noble truths. In the list, it comes first because it is the starting point for the practice of the seven other practices—it is the forerunner of all other practices and a guiding principle for all other components among the eight (Figure 7.1). In other words, Right View is the key element of the Noble Eightfold Path. Moreover, Right View leads the way in five areas including view, thought, speech, action, and livelihood (Somaratne 2021, 347). The reason is that Right View establishes the attitude for one to know and differentiate rightness and wrongness in view, thought, speech, action, and livelihood (Somaratne 2021, 347). The practice of each of the noble paths reciprocally fosters an experiential development of Right View, which will be discussed in depth in the coming section due to its importance.

Right Intention (*Sammā Saṅkappa*). According to the *Magga-saṃyutta*, for one with Right View, Right Intention comes to be.[5] Right Intention can be seen as the intentional or conative aspect of mental activity associated with Right View;[6] this can also be regarded as the mind's commitment to following the path of cultivation (Karunadasa 2013, 96). According to the *Magga-vibhaṅga-sutta* (SN 45.8), there are three types of Right Intention: (1) the intention of renunciation (to refrain from self-centered desires and egocentric drives); (2) the intention of non-hatred (to refrain from aversion), and (3) the intention of nonmaleficence (to refrain from harmful or cruel thoughts about self or others) (Karunadasa 2013, 96).[7] In sum, Right Intention can be seen as the mind's intention to follow the

4. Although we are using the most common translation of *sammā diṭṭhi*—"Right View" here, we must note that the term *sammā* refers to something more than just "right." In fact, we believe that the English term "right" can even be misleading, given that the term is subjective and therefore tends to an extreme position. Rather, *sammā diṭṭhi* is a middle view which avoids all extremes. It also gives the sense of what is proper, appropriate, perfect, and so on. Hence, it is to be noted, that although we are using the common term "Right View" throughout the chapter, the meaning of *sammā diṭṭhi* is broader in meaning. It denotes proper view that avoids being biased towards any extreme views, being visionary in that it is beneficial to oneself as well as others, and wholesome in that it leads to one's liberation.

5. SN V, 2: *Sammādiṭṭhissa sammāsaṇkappo pahoti.*

6. Bodhi, Bhikkhu. "The Noble Eightfold Path the Way to the End of Suffering." *Access to Insight (BCBS Edition)*, 30 November 2013, http://www.accesstoinsight.org/lib/authors/bodhi/waytoend.html.

7. SN V, 221: *Katamo ca, bhikkhave, sammāsaṅkappo? Yo kho, bhikkhave, nekkhammasaṅkappo, abyāpādasaṅkappo, avihiṁsāsaṅkappo—ayaṁ vuccati, bhikkhave, sammāsaṅkappo.*

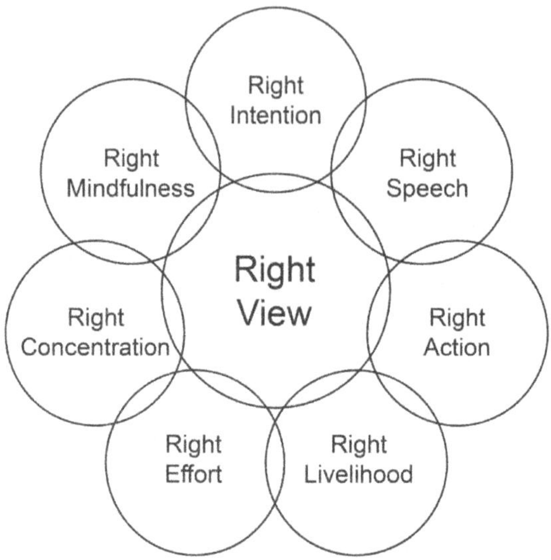

Figure 7.1: A Diagram of the Noble Eightfold Path

correct path by making decisions congruent with Buddhist teachings (Lee 2022, 45).

7.2.2 Concentration (*samādhi*)

Right Effort, Right Mindfulness, and Right Concentration are classified as concentration training.

Right Effort (*Sammā vāyāma*). According to the *Magga-saṃyutta*, for one who has Right Livelihood, Right Effort comes to be.[8] In the Pāli canon, we find many synonymous terms for *sammā vāyāma*, such as *viriya*, *ātāpi*, *sammappadhāna*, *dhiti* etc. Right Effort consists in using mindfulness and effort itself to convert one's thought, speech, and action from wrong to right (Somaratne 2021, 345). In other words, the principle of Right Effort refers to the practitioner's[9] devoted energy to support one's cultivation towards liberation from suffering.[10] In sum, Right Effort signifies exertion, commitment, patience, and repeated practice in continuously shaping and upgrading the mind (Lee 2022, 42).

8. SN V, 2: *Sammāājīvassa sammāvāyāmo pahoti.*
9. "Practitioner" here refers to an individual who practices the teachings of the Buddha rather than as a clinical or counseling practitioner.
10. Bodhi, Bhikkhu. "The Noble Eightfold Path the Way to the End of Suffering." *Access to Insight (BCBS Edition)*, 30 November 2013, http://www.accesstoinsight.org/lib/authors/bodhi/waytoend.html.

Sammā vāyāma, in general, is defined as four types of striving in Early Buddhist teachings. As the *Sammappadhāna-saṃyutta* (SN 49.24) states:

1. He aspires for the non-arising of unarisen faulty unwholesome [mental] states; he makes effort, arouses energy, applies his mind, and exerts himself.[11]
2. He aspires for abandoning arisen faulty and unwholesome [mental] states; he makes effort, arouses energy, applies his mind, and exerts himself.[12]
3. He aspires for the arising of unarisen wholesome [mental] states; he makes effort, arouses energy, applies his mind, and exerts himself.[13]
4. He aspires for the maintenance of arisen wholesome [mental] states, for their non-disappearance, for their increasing, for their full development, for the accomplishment of mental cultivation; he makes effort, arouses energy, applies his mind, and exerts himself.[14]

Right Mindfulness (*Sammā sati*). According to the *Magga-saṃyutta*, for one with Right Effort, Right Mindfulness comes to be.[15] According to the *Satipaṭṭhāna sutta* (MN 10), Right Mindfulness contemplates four foundations: body (*kāya*), feelings (*vedanā*), mind (*citta*), and realities of phenomena (*dhamma*s). As the *sutta* describes the practice of Right Mindfulness is to dwell observing body in the body (*kāye kāyānupassī viharati*), observing feeling in the feelings (*vedanāsu vedanānupassī viharati*), observing mind in the mind (*citte cittānupassī viharati)*, and watching phenomena in the phenomena (*dhamme dhammānupassī viharati*), ardently (*ātāpi*), and clearly comprehending (*sampajāno*) each of these foundations, being mindful (*satimā*) of any objects of meditation, and overcoming discontent and covetousness (*vineyya loke abhijjhādomanassaṃ*) (MN I 55–63). Practicing mindfulness in the right manner will allow a practitioner to see the four foundations as they are, thereby abandoning Wrong View and cultivating Right View (Anālayo 2003, 20).

One significant difference between Right Mindfulness and the common concept of modern mindfulness is the "right" (*sammā*) component (Lee 2022, 43). Modern mindfulness emphasizes awareness in the present moment without judgment to soothe the mind, while traditional Buddhist mindfulness emphasizes the rightness of a calmed mind that analyzes the true nature of things, such as

11. SN IV, 244: *anuppannānam pāpakānam akusalānaṃ dhammānam anuppādāya chandaṃ janeti vāyamati viriyam ārabhati cittam paggaṇhāti padahati.*
12. SN IV, 244: *uppannānam pāpakānam akusalānaṃ dhammānam pahānāya chandaṃ janeti vāyamati viriyam ārabhati cittam paggaṇhāti padahati.*
13. SN IV, 244: *anuppannānaṃ kusalānaṃ dhammānam uppādāya chandaṃ janeti vāyamati viriyam ārabhati cittam paggaṇhāti.*
14. SN IV, 244: *Uppannānaṃ kusalānaṃ dhammānaṃ ṭhitiyā asammosāya bhiyyobhāvāya vepullāya bhāvanāya pāripūriyā chandaṃ janeti vāyamati viriyam ārabhati cittam paggaṇhāti padahati*
15. SN V, 2: *sammāvāyāmassa sammāsati pahoti*

non-self, *dukkha*, and impermanence (Lee 2022, 43). Moreover, it must be pointed out that Right Mindfulness is only one of eight steps of the Noble Eightfold Path. As described by the progressive threefold classification of the eight steps, mindfulness must be supported by virtuous conduct (*sīla*) and wisdom (*paññā*) to reduce suffering effectively (Lee 2022, 43). In Buddhist meditation, mindfulness is necessarily associated with *vipassanā* (insight); that is, to see the true nature of all phenomena, though modern-day practitioners of mindfulness can easily divorce it from insight. When mindfulness is only defined as a state of awareness and attentiveness without any discernment, one can simply engage mindfully in unwholesome actions, such as violence, using harmful speech against others, or pursuing evil thoughts (Lee 2022, 43). For example, Sun, in her article examines the development of mindfulness from its historical forms to contemporary applications, a case in point being the use of mindfulness skills by the US Marine Corps to optimize combat performance (Sun 2014, 402). But Right Mindfulness should be a practitioner's constant companion to help them realize and embody the Buddhist teachings (Lee 2022, 43).

Right Concentration (*Sammā samādhi*). As the *Magga-saṃyutta* remarks, for one of Right Mindfulness, Right Concentration comes to be.[16] Generally, in the *Nikāya*s, Right Concentration is defined as a path culminating in Right Mindfulness.

> What, bhikkhus, is noble right concentration with its supports and its requisites; that is, right view, right intention, right speech, right action, right livelihood, right effort, and right mindfulness? Unification of mind equipped with these seven factors is called noble right concentration with its support and its requisites. (Bodhi 1995, 934)[17]

Right Concentration is the unification of mind with an object of meditation, resulting in a calm, clear, and pure state (Karunadasa 2013, 98). Right Mindfulness and Right Effort are effective in helping practitioners transform their views, thoughts, speech, actions, and livelihood from wrong to right at a beginning stage (Somaratne 2021, 345). At a higher state of cultivation, such transformation requires the support of Right Concentration to penetrate the true nature of things and see things as they truly are (Somaratne 2021, 345). In other words, it can be regarded as an advanced state of mind that is essential for the attainment of wisdom (Karunadasa 2013, 98). However, it is also important not to confuse Right Concentration with the four-fold absorptions (*jhāna*s). In ancient

16. SN V, 2: *sammāsatissa sammāsamādhi pahoti*
17. MN III, 71; SN V, 21; AN IV, 40: *Katamo ca bhikkhave, ariyo sammāsamādhi sa-upaniso saparikkhāro? Seyyathīdaṁ: sammādiṭṭhi sammāsaṁkappo . . . Yā kho, bhikkhave, imehi sattaṅgehi cittassa ekaggatā parikkhatā, ayaṁ vuccati, bhikkhave, ariyo sammāsamādhi sa-upaniso iti pi, saparikkhāro iti pi.*

India, before the Buddha was enlightened, there were yogis who attained deep concentration, including the Buddha's former teachers Ālārakālāma and Uddaka Rāmaputta. Yet their attainments were not considered "right" concentration, so the Buddha left them. Another clear example of this stance would be Devadatta, who was said to have attained a high degree of *jhāna* and even performed miracles, impressing King Ajātasattu so much that he gave his support to the former's desire to assassinate the Buddha. This is to say that the attainment of *jhāna* is not the attainment of "right" concentration. So now, whether *jhāna* is important in the attainment of Right Concentration is the subject of heated debate. As Anālayo (2010, 73) observes, several discourses allow full awakening based only on the ability to attain the first *jhāna*, while there are other discourses, including the *Mahācattārīsaka-sutta*, which do not mention the attainment of *jhāna* at all in their definitions of Right Concentration. This leads to two conclusions: (1) achieving only the first *jhāna*, the least advanced level of absorption, is sufficient for the attainment of ultimate liberation; or (2) in this context, *jhāna*s are unnecessary for the attainment of ultimate liberation. What is important, according to Early Buddhist *sutta*s, is the unification (*cittassa ekaggatā*) of seven of the eight noble paths (*ariya maggāni*) that begin with Right View (*sammā diṭṭhi*). This is well explained by the Buddha in the *sutta*s, including the *Mahācattārīsaka-sutta* (117), as shown in the quotation above defining Right Concentration. In other words, for the unification of the mind to become "right" concentration, it needs to be contextualized within the scheme of the Noble Eightfold Path (Analayo 2010, 73). The *jhāna*s are necessary only for attaining liberation by way of the threefold higher knowledge (*tevijjā*) (Analayo 2010, 73). According to the *Dvedhāvitakka-sutta* (MN 19), the Buddha's experience of enlightenment occurred gradually through the attainment of the four *jhāna*s. This led to the acquisition of the threefold higher knowledge, ultimately culminating in the realization of the destruction of cankers or outflows (*āsavakkhayañāṇa*).

7.2.3 Virtuous Conduct

Right Speech, Right Action, and Right Livelihood are classified as virtuous conduct training.

Right Speech (*Sammā vācā*). According to the *Magga-saṃyutta*, for one of Right Intention, Right Speech comes to be.[18] In other words, Right Speech is the verbal manifestation of Right Intention, in which one speaks in a truthful, meaningful, and timely way that is unharmful and beneficial both to oneself

18. SN V, 2: *Sammāsaṅkappassa sammāvācā pahoti.*

and others.[19] Right Speech is to speak in devotion to truth to make the speaker trustworthy and reliable, dissociating with any falsehood (Karunadasa 2013, 97). In essence, Right Speech is the vocal aspect of Buddhist practice and the vocal actions that result in social effects (Lee 2022, 46).

Right Action (*Sammā kammanta*). According to the *Magga-saṃyutta*, for one of Right Speech, Right Action comes to be.[20] Right Action refers to bodily acts or behavioral choices based on Right Views (Lee 2022, 46). As stated in the *Maggavibhaṅga-sutta*, Right Action refers to the prevention of any harm to life, taking what is not given, and sexual misconduct (Somaratne 2021, 346).[21] In other words, Right Action means to cultivate love and compassion for all beings and to practice the purity of heart in all interpersonal relationships (Karunadasa 2013, 97). Moreover, Right Action requires the practitioner to abandon actions leading to unwholesome gratification of desire and to act in accord with Right View (Karunadasa 2013, 97).

Right Livelihood (*Sammā ājīva*). According to the *Magga-saṃyutta*, for one of Right Action, Right Livelihood comes to be.[22] Livelihood is the way to secure the necessities of life, such as financial or vocational choices supporting one's life (Karunadasa 2013, 98). As stated in the *Maggavibhaṅga-sutta*, Right Livelihood is to make a living by way of a right mode of livelihood while abandoning all wrong modes of livelihood, such as trading in weapons, human beings, living beings, poisons, and intoxicating substances.[23] In other words, Right Livelihood means living a life in congruence with the moral expectations of Buddhism (Lee 2022, 47).

The Noble Eightfold Path, as can be seen above, provides the proper guidance for a healthy life as well as for spiritual development. A healthy life here refers to a lifestyle which avoids all possible disturbances, both external (environmental) and internal (mental). Following such a guideline is considered necessary for a dedicated practice for spiritual development and inner peace. While such a practice helps greatly in promoting a healthy lifestyle for people in general, it will also help the spiritual development of any dedicated Buddhist practitioner. The first point, as seen above, is the cultivation of Right View. When carefully observed, the seven paths, from the second to the eighth, gradually arise (are practiced) once the first path of Right View is cultivated. Hence, as the *Mahācattārīsaka-sutta*

19. This statement is based on the *Abhayarājakumāra-sutta* (MN 58), which refers to the type of speech that the Buddha uttered.
20. MN 58, 498: *Sammā vācassa sammākammanto pahoti.*
21. SN V, 9: *Katamo ca bhikkhave sammākammanto. Yā kho bhikkhave pānātipātā veramaṇī adinnādānā veramaṇī abrahmacariyā veramaṇī. Ayaṃ vuccati bhikkhave sammākammanto.*
22. SN V, 9: *Sammākammantassa sammā ājīvo pahoti*
23. SN V, 9: *Katamo ca bhikkhave sammāājīvo. Idha bhikkhave ariyasāvako micchāājīvaṃ pahāya sammāājīvena jīvitaṃ kappeti. Ayaṃ vuccati sammāājīvo.*

states, Right View is the forerunner (*pubbaṅgama*) of all other paths. In other words, Right View is the foundation of all other practices.[24] However, it should also be noted that true understanding and knowledge are important in order to have a sense of what Right View is. In such a case, as the Buddha pointed out (such as in the *Magga-saṃyutta*), this knowledge is the prerequisite for entering wholesome *dhammas*,[25] followed by shame and fear (of wrongdoing). For a person with knowledge, Right View comes to be,[26] and so the other paths then arise.

7.3 Right View as the Core Intervention

Ignorance of reality and the Buddha's teachings on reality, such as the four noble truths, dependent arising, etc., is the main factor contributing to the experience of suffering. The *Magga-saṃyutta* remarks that ignorance (*avijjā*) is the forerunner (*pubbaṅgamā*) of unwholesome *dhammas*—the opposite or wrong (*micchā*) practices of the Noble Eightfold Path; when there is ignorance, wrong view comes to be, and so on for the other wrong paths, along with shamelessness and fearlessness (in wrongdoing).[27] Since the root of suffering is ignorance (*avijjā*), replacing ignorance with knowledge (*vijjā*) is a natural therapeutic ingredient for eradicating suffering (Somaratne 2021, 29). There are many angles from which one can discuss Right View. We will start by discussing the content of Right View using three relevant and major *suttas*: the *Sammadiṭṭhi-sutta* (MN 9), the *Kaccānagotta-sutta* (SN 12.15), and the *Mahācattārīsaka-sutta* (MN 117) in a later discussion.

In the *Sammādiṭṭhi-sutta*, Sāriputta (MN 9) describes sixteen aspects of Right View, starting with discernment for skillfulness, the four nutriments, *dukkha*, each of the twelve factors of dependent co-arising, and defilements (see Table 7.1; Bodhi 1995, 132). The *Sammādiṭṭhi-sutta* defines Right view as such: "Right view is the ability to discern what is skillful (*kusala*), what is unskillful (*akusala*), and their roots (*mūla*); thus a person becomes endowed with Right View, his view has become firm, he is endowed with unwavering faith in the *Dhamma*, and he has arrived at this true *Dhamma*."[28] In discussing unskillfulness, Sāriputta described

24. The *Mahācattārīsaka-sutta* (MN III, 71–78) highlights this fact clearly in the statement *tatra bhikkhave, sammādiṭṭhipubbaṅgamā hoti* (therein, *bhikkhus*, right view is the forerunner).
25. Here in this context, *dhammas* refers to the Noble Eightfold Path.
26. SN V, 2: *Vijjā ca kho bhikkhave pubbaṅgamā kusalānaṃ dhammānaṃ samāpattiyā anudeva hirottappaṃ samāpattiyā anudeva hirottappaṃ. Vijjāgatassa bhikkhave viddasuno sammādiṭṭhi pahoti. Sammādiṭṭhassa.*
27. SN V, 2: *Avijjā bhikkhave pubbaṅgamā akusalānaṃ dhammānam samāpattiyā anudeva ahirikam anottappaṃ. Avijjāgatassa bhikkhave aviddasuno micchādiṭṭhi pahot. Micchādiṭṭhassa micchāsaṅkappo.*
28. MN I, 46, 47: *Yato kho āvuso ariyasāvako akusalañ-ca pajānāti akusalamūlañ-ca pajānāti, kusalañ-ca pajānāti kusalamūlañ-ca pajānāti, ettāvatā pi kho āvuso ariyasāvako sammādiṭṭhi hoti, ujugatā'ssa diṭṭhi, dhamme aveccappasādena samannāgato, āgato imaṁ saddhammaṁ.*

the three poisons as the roots (passion, aversion, and delusion) driving the five unskillful actions (killing, stealing, sexual misconduct, false speech, and intoxication) as stated in the five precepts. In response, Right View discerns these unskillful means and their roots clearly, leading to their abandonment.

For the second aspect, Sāriputta applies the formula of the Four Noble Truths to discern all fifteen subsequent aspects, including the discernment of:

(1) what is *dukkha*
(2) the origin or cause of *dukkha*,
(3) the cessation of *dukkha*, and
(4) the path of practice to the cessation of *dukkha*.

Following this formula, Sāriputta also explains one of the aspects—let's call it X—and discusses ways to practice Right View in that particular aspect. As the *sutta* mentions, true knowledge of the four noble truths can dissolve ignorance through the abandonment of passion, aversion, and the conceited view of "I am," as well as any underlying tendencies sustaining ignorance.[29] For example, regarding the four nutrients: "When, friends, a noble disciple understands nutriment, the origin of nutriment, the cessation of nutriment, and the way leading to the cessation of nutriment, in that way he is one of right view . . . and has arrived at this true Dhamma" (Bodhi 1995, 132–44).[30]

Sāriputta explains the meaning of the nutriments: physical food (*kabaliṅkāra āhāra*), contact (*phassa*), mental volition (*manosañcetanā*), and consciousness (*viññāṇa*), of which the cause is craving (*taṇhāsamudayā*), their cessation being brought about by overcoming craving (*taṇhānirodhā*) and by practicing the Noble Eightfold Path (*ayameva ariyo aṭṭhaṅgiko maggo āhāranirodhagāminī-paṭipadā*) (MN I, 47).

As the *sutta* depicts, Right View embodies the Four Noble Truths perspectives on self, others, and the world. The beginning of the *sutta* starts with defining Right View as wisely understanding (*pajānāti*) skillfulness, unskillfulness, and their roots. In this sense, to view things "right" or to be skillful is also to wisely understand: (1) how mind processes, such as mental qualities, thoughts, ideas, or behaviors, can be harmful and suffering-inducing, (2) their root causes, particularly delusion, hatred, and greed, and (3) the arising, changing, and ceasing of

29. As is mentioned in the *sutta*, MN I, 48: *so sabbaso rāgānusayaṁ pahāya paṭighānusayaṁ paṭivinodetvā asmīti diṭṭhimānusayaṁ samuhanitvā avijjaṁ pahāya vijjaṁ uppādetvā diṭṭhe va dhamme dukkhass' antakaro hoti.* (he, having abandoned the underlying tendency to passion, abolished the underlying tendency to aversion, extirpated the underlying tendency to the view of "I am," produces the true knowledge and puts end to *dukkha* in this very life.)

30. MN I, 47: *Yato kho āvuso ariyasāvako āhārañ-ca-pajānāti, āhāra samudayañ-ca pajānāti, āhāranirodhañ-ca pajānāti, āhāranirodhagāminī-paṭipadañ-ca pajānāti, ettāvatā pi kho āvuso ariyasāvako sammādiṭṭhi hoti.*

Table 7.1: Aspects of Right View in the *Sammādiṭṭhi-sutta*

16 Aspects of Right View	Brief Description According to the *Sammādiṭṭhi-sutta*
Skillful and unskillful	Discerning the unskillful roots of the three poisons, the five unskillful actions of the five precepts, the underlying tendency to existence of self, and choosing to abandon these unskillful views and actions as a skillful practice.
The four nutriments	Discerning the four nutriments (physical food, contact, mental volition, and consciousness) and the craving for them.
Dukkha	Discerning *dukkha* in the form of the eight types of suffering and the four noble truths.
Ageing and death	Discerning the 12th factor of dependent origination of ageing and death.
Birth	Discerning the 11th factor of dependent origination of birth.
Becoming	Discerning the 10th factor of dependent origination of becoming.
Clinging	Discerning the 9th factor of dependent origination of clinging.
Craving	Discerning the 8th factor of dependent origination of ageing craving.
Feeling	Discerning the 7th factor of dependent origination of feeling.
Contact	Discerning the 6th factor of dependent origination of contact.
Six sense bases	Discerning the 5th factor of dependent origination of six sense bases.
Name-and-form	Discerning the 4th factor of dependent origination of name-and-form.
Consciousness	Discerning the 3rd factor of dependent origination of consciousness.
Volitional formation	Discerning the 2nd factor of dependent origination of volitional formation.
Ignorance	Discerning the 1st factor of dependent origination of ignorance.
Defilements or outflows (*āsava*)	Discerning the defilements of sensual desire, being and ignorance.

these mental phenomena. For example, in a painful breakup, a Wrong View would involve continuously blaming the person for leaving, ruminating over memories, and retaliating against the person.

In contrast, one with Right View will see how all these resentful thoughts and volitions bring more suffering and perpetrate hatred based on emotional injury; such a person can then understand how forgiveness, compassion for self and others, and letting go of the past will gradually reduce suffering. For most people, it may sound like common sense to know what is good for oneself. However, a worldly person's mind "common sense" can be deluded, and a deluded mind is usually clouded by unwholesome thoughts and actions, leading them to pursue instant and temporary gratification at the cost of long-term suffering. For example, pursuing an unwholesome thought might provide an illusionary sense of control, or grasping an angry thought might make one feel powerful. However, these short-term gratifications always come with more suffering, a fact that an unskillful mind is ignorant of. Fostering Right View requires effort and practice to discern wholesome from unwholesome, to contemplate experience to know what is right, and to access support from the seven other paths.

7.3.1 Discussion of Right View in the *Kaccānagotta-sutta*

Approaching Right View from another angle, the Buddha taught a non-dualistic perspective in the *Kaccānagotta-sutta* (SN 12.15), as illustrated in the following excerpt: "This world, Kaccāna, for the most part depends upon a duality—upon the notion of existence (*atthitā*) and the notion of nonexistence (*natthitā*). But for one who sees the origin of the world as it really is with correct wisdom, there is no notion of nonexistence in regard to the world. And for one who sees the cessation of the world as it really is with correct wisdom, there is no notion of existence in regard to the world" (Bodhi 2000, 544).[31] This indicates that clinging to the absolute and immortal existence of a self, or rejecting self-existence, leads to duality as well as conflict. In fact, all sorts of conflicts in the world, including individual and social conflicts, are due to being unable to abandon the binary extremes and see the Middle Way. From the non-dualistic perspective, there is no ultimate existence, but it cannot be denied that the self "exists" as well. As mentioned before, in a world of dependent co-arising, self—which, of course, is merely a conventional term—is a product of causes and conditions, and, therefore, conditionally exists. This is the middle position that denies both extremes: self exists or does not exist.

31. SN III, 135: *Dvayānissito khvāyaṃ Kaccāna loko yebhuyyena atthi tañceva natthi tañ ca. Lokasamudayaṃ kho Kaccāna yathābhūtam sammappaññāya passato yā loke natthitā sā na hoti. Loka nirodhaṃ kho kaccāna yathābhūtaṃ sammapaññāya passato yā loke atthitā sā na hoti.*

In the *sutta*, the Buddha continued to discuss Right View as freedom from bondage: "This world, Kaccāna, is for the most part shackled by engagement, clinging, and adherence. But this one with right view does not become engaged and cling through that engagement and clinging, mental standpoint, adherence, underlying tendency; he does not take a stand about 'my self.' He has no perplexity or doubt that what arises is only suffering arising, what ceases is only suffering ceasing. His knowledge about this is independent of others. It is in this way, Kaccāna, that there is right view" (Bodhi, 2000, 544).[32]

One important characteristic of Right View pointed out in this *sutta* is freedom from any dogmatic and rigid attachment to the view or belief that "only this is right, all others are wrong" (Karunadasa, 2013, 34). In contrast, a Right View will reflect a flexible and open mindset that empirically examines different perspectives to find more beneficial and constructive ways of thinking (Lee 2022, 44). In Buddhism, all concepts and ideologies are only transitional guides to realizing goals, not for attaching or clinging to (Lee 2022, 44). Like rafts, concepts are constructed devices for crossing a "river" of a mental obstacle to reach a "destination" or understanding (Somaratne 2021, 42). For example: "George Lee" is a product of body, mind, culture, environment, and other conditions. Therefore, one can say "this is George Lee," as it is a conventional identity, but this "George Lee" is still just a label for a particular phenomenon. Clinging to the view that "George Lee" exists and to believe in its self-existence is wrong, as the phenomenon will disappear when the causes and conditions cease (i.e., the phenomenon of "George Lee" in the previous moment is different from the phenomenon of "George Lee" in this moment). On the other hand, clinging to the view that "George Lee" does not exist is also not right, as the phenomenon of "George Lee" provisionally and conceptually exists when the appropriate causes and conditions are available. Without veering towards the two extremes, seeing according to the Middle Way is having the mental flexibility that sees "George Lee" arise and pass away as a neutral phenomenon. This view understands how the two extremes make sense provisionally without becoming attached to either perspective.

7.4 The Cultivation of Right View

The previous section addressed the content of Right View as informed by some Early Buddhist *sutta*s and commentaries. While Right View may seem to be a straightforward goal and practice of the Buddhist path, the way to cultivate Right

32. SN III, 135: *Upāyupādānābhinivesavinibandho khāyaṃ Kaccāna loko yebhuyyena. Tañcāyam upāyupādānaṃ cetaso adhiṭṭhānābhinivesānusaya na upeti na upādiyati nādhiṭṭhāti attā me ti. Dukkham eva uppajjamānam uppajjati dukkhaṃ niriddhamānaṃ nirujjhati na kaṅkhati na vicikicchati aparapaccayā ñāṇam evassa ettha hoti. Ettāvatā kho Kaccāna sammādiṭṭhi hoti.*

View requires further consideration. In particular, is Right View a "view?" This question has led to some controversial viewpoints, which have had a large impact on how to cultivate Right View.

To revisit the translation of *sammā diṭṭhi* as Right View—the Pāli term *diṭṭhi* means view or opinion (usually with the negative connotation of clinging to view), while *sammā* refers to "proper," "complete," or "perfect." As a result, *sammā diṭṭhi* is commonly translated as Right View by some and as Perfect View by some others (Rahman et al. 2013, 72). In many Early Buddhist texts, such as the *Sammadiṭṭhi-sutta* and *Mahācattārīsaka-sutta*, the aim of the Buddhist path emphasized the importance of cultivating Right View and the abandonment of Wrong View (Fuller 2005, 16). These texts directly differentiate the views as "wrong" (*micchā;* Bodhi 1995, 936) and "right" (*sammā*; Bodhi 1995, 132). We believe this perspective implies two assumptions. First, Right View and Wrong View are in direct opposition, with Buddhist practice aiming to replace Wrong View with Right View. Second, Right View seems to be a type of correct or accurate belief based on the Buddhist teachings, such as making judgments based on *annica*, *anattā*, and *dukkha* (Gethin 2005, 24). As Gethin (2005, 24) further observes, the Vaibhāṣika school generally sees Right View as a correct understanding of the three marks of existence. From the translation and some Early Buddhist texts, Right View is generally considered as a view, opinion, attitude or proposition about the nature of things.

Fuller (2005) pointed out a different perspective and proposed another understanding of "views" in Early Buddhist teachings in his book on the notion of "view." In particular, Fuller (2005, 16) emphasized the fundamental idea in Early Buddhist texts that clinging to any "view" is Wrong View. Holding any view with attachment, including what has been taught as Right View in Buddhism, is a hindrance that leads to suffering and is against the goal of Buddhist practice. He asserted that the goal of the Buddhist path is not to cultivate Right View, or any view, but to reach a state of non-attachment, so that "the consequence of achieving right-view is that one does not hold any view". In other words, Right View is basically "non-grasped view", a complete transcendence of all views. Here, complete transcendence of all views also refers to being a visionary person who does not grasp any views. This idea is well expressed in the *Metta-sutta* as such: "Being endowed with a vision (*dassanena sampanno*) but not having taken up any views, a virtuous one discards desire for sensuality and thus would not return to the womb."[33] Here, being endowed with vision itself means being endowed with

33. Khp 9: *Diṭṭhiñ ca anupagamma—sīlavā dassanena sampanno—kāmesu vineyya gedhaṃ—nahi jātu ghabbaseyyaṃ punar eti.*

right view;[34] that is, not to grasp any view but being able to see the reality of the things as they are—all the phenomena are dependently originated. In essence, this is to conform to the Middle Path doctrine. Going one step further, the *sutta*s, such as the *Majjhe-sutta* (AN 6.61) and the *Tissametteyyamāṇavapucchā* (Sn 5.3), also remind us not only of the two extremes, but that one should not get caught up even in the middle of them: "One who, having known both extremes, is not stuck in the middle, we declare he is a great man who has escaped the seamstress here."[35]

One of the first proponents of "non-grasped view" is Gómez (1976, 137) who argued that considering Right View as a view can be an attachment to a theoretical understanding, thereby hindering the realization that all *dhamma*s, either conditioned or unconditioned, have no inherently existing or unchanging self. In essence, overtheorizing Buddhism is against the aim of practice (Gómez 1976, 138). Taking the teaching of *anattā* as an example, non-self does not refer to the annihilation of self or the denial of the existence of self; instead, non-self is the teaching of being non-attached to the notion of a permanent or unchanging "self," which always occurs in the context of the three characteristics of sentential existence. As we understand it, the root of the problem is not whether there is a self, but whether there is attachment to a notion of self (*attavāda-upādāna*). Using this rationale, holding Right View is not the key; however, a view based on the knowledge of Buddhist teachings while not being attached to the teaching is important. In turn, Gómez (1976, 140) proposed "no-view" as the true meaning of Right View in order to signify the importance of non-attachment in congruence with the teaching of anattā. Our interpretation of Right View aligns with the "no-view" proposed by Gómez, although we prefer to use the term "non-grasped view." First, the term "no-view" may suggest the view of annihilationism that rejects all views that fall into one of two extremes, which is contrary to Buddhist teachings. Furthermore, "non-grasped view" implies having views while not grasping or clinging onto them, which aligns with the teaching of the Middle Way. In other words, we want to emphasize that individuals who have attained Right View can still have views while also not being attached to them. This mental flexibility is highly important for counselors to understand the different perspectives of clients as well as for clients to become non-attached to their issues.

34. This is also well explained in the commentary: "Being endowed with vision means gradually being a virtuous one with supramundane virtues, and who perfects the right view belonging to the stream-entry path associated by supramundane virtue" (*anupubbena lokuttarasīlena sīlavā hutvā, lokuttarasīlasampayuttena eve sotāpatti maggasammādiṭṭhisaṃkhātena dassanena sampanno*) (KhpA 251).

35. Sn 1042: *So Ubh' anta-m-abhiññāya majjhe mantā na lippati taṃ brūmi mahāpuriso ti, so idha sibbanimaccagā*" ti; AN III, 399: *yo ubh'ante viditvāna majjhe mantā na limpati taṃ brūmi mahāpuriso ti, so 'dha sibbanim accagā ti*

Resonating with Fuller, Gethin (2004) used the Theravāda *Abhidhamma* to discuss Right View and Wrong View. He claimed that the Theravāda *Abhidhamma* never interpreted Right View as correct opinion or belief, or as based on theoretical understanding or direct experience (Gethin 2004, 24). He proposed that Wrong View is not essentially an inaccurate or wrong way of seeing and knowing things, but that it is a rigid and fixed holding on to a particular view. In other words, attachment to the concept of Right View is also a Wrong View, the reason being that a mind with ignorance and craving, the two main causes of suffering presented in the Early Buddhist *sutta*s, is inclined to grasp (Gethin 2004, 25). Instead of forming a "correct" viewpoint, the aim of practice should be to free oneself from attachment to all views (Gethin 2004, 25). For this reason, Gethin (2004) claimed, "perfect seeing is precisely the transcending of all viewpoints; Right View should not be understood as a view itself, but as freedom from all views" (20).

In support of the argument of "non-grasped view," one way that Gethin (2004, 25) defines Right View is to employ the perspective of *Dhammasaṅgaṇī,* which considers Right View as a "mental-concomitant of ordinary, sense-sphere, skillful consciousness." This kind of consciousness is a "direct awareness" of the nature of things that transcends any view or teaching (Gethin 2004, 25). The Buddhist teaching offers a route to cultivate such awareness of suffering, the arising of suffering, cessation of suffering, and the path to the liberation of suffering, while there is no meaning in holding on to the route itself.

One perspective that reconciles the debate on whether Right View is a view or a practice of "non-grasped view" is Ñāṇamoli and Bodhi's (1998, 7) idea, which is based on the *Mahāvedalla-sutta* (MN 43); that is, the development of Right View occurs at two sequential levels: listening to others (*parato ghosa)* and wise reflection (*yonisomanasikāra*). First, one starts learning about Right View conceptually (Ñāṇamoli and Bodhi 1998, 7). This intellectual comprehension of Right View, as in the studying of *sutta*s and commentaries, listening to *Dhamma* talks, or learning from other Buddhist practitioners, fosters concepts of Right View in the individual (Ñāṇamoli and Bodhi 1998, 7). This beginning step is important for nurturing motivation at the start and then continuing Buddhist practice (Ñāṇamoli and Bodhi 1998, 8). The second level is the experience of Right View (Ñāṇamoli and Bodhi 1998, 8). Such an experiential process relies heavily on one's immediate experience with various practices, such as meditation, contemplation, and other direct experiences to attain the realization of Right View (Ñāṇamoli and Bodhi 1998, 8). Ñāṇamoli and Bodhi compared the conceptual Right View to a hand grasping the concept, while the experiential approach is like letting one's eyes see the true nature of existence (Ñāṇamoli and Bodhi 1998, 8). If this position stands, the entrance to the Buddhist path would consist initially of the intellectual attainment of Right View, while the destination would be an embodiment of Right View through penetrative experiences. We can also describe Right View as approaching the middle state in which there is neither conflict nor attachment to any views.

We find the above argument convincing enough to understand the deeper meaning of Right View as the "non-grasped view." As stated in the *Upādiyamāna-sutta*, "Monk, if you cling to anything, you are in bondage to *Māra*. If you do not cling, you are free of the *Māra*."[36] If Right View is to grasp on to a certain view regardless of the nature of the view, such grasping can easily be driven by egoistic desires to support the existence of self and fulfill egoistic needs, which does not align with Early Buddhist teachings. The essence of Right View should be freedom or liberation from the desire to grasp onto a view.

Assuming "non-grasped view" is a valid description of Right View, the next question is: Can an individual let go of all views before forming any view? The problem is with fixed views, believing that only this is true and all other views are false,[37] such clinging being a combination of cognitive and emotional attachment that comes with bondage and suffering (Gethin 2004, 24). As pointed out in the previous section and in the *Kaccānagotta-sutta*, the flexibility of mind to be non-attached seems more important than the content of Right View itself. The ultimate solution of Right View is a non-attachment that can allow the mind to cultivate a direct awareness and penetration of the true nature of things. However, this process only marks the beginning and the end without delineating the steps in between.

A further question arises concerning whether we can conceptualize Right View as having different levels and steps towards its attainment. In fact, the idea of Nanamoli and Bodhi's concept on dividing Right View into levels may originate from the *Mahācattārīsaka-sutta* (MN 117), which discussed three levels of views:

> Therein, bhikkhus, right view comes first. And how does right view come first? One understands wrong view as wrong view and right view as right view: this is one's right view. "And what, bhikkhus, is wrong view? 'There is nothing given, nothing offered, nothing sacrificed; no fruit or result of good and bad actions; no this world, no other world; no mother, no father; no beings who are reborn spontaneously; no good and virtuous recluses and brahmins in the world who

36. SN III, 73: *Upādiyamāno kho bhikkhu baddho Mārassa anupādiyamāno mutti pāpimato ti.*

37. There had been many *śramana*s and *brāhamaṇa*s who held and propagated their views dogmatically, stating "*Idameva saccaṃ mogha maññaṃ*" (this is the only truth, everything else is false). Such a belief, in fact, is rigorously rejected in many early *sutta*s, such as the *Poṭṭhapāda-sutta* (DN 9), the *Sakkapañha-sutta* (DN 21), the *Aggaivaccha-sutta* (MN72) and the *Pañcattaya-sutta* (MN 102).

have realised for themselves by direct knowledge and declare this world and the other world.' This is wrong view. (Bodhi 1995, 934)[38]

From our perspective, the first level of Right View is knowing what is wrong or improper View; this is basically the view of annihilationism—an extreme—that denies the law of *kamma*, implying a deep delusion with how the world functions. Having such views are wrong or improper in the sense that they are neither beneficial to oneself nor to the outside world, but can cause harm to both oneself and others. After a practitioner identifies and relinquishes Wrong View, one can approach the two levels of Right View: "And what, bhikkhus, is right view? Right view, we say, is twofold: there is right view that is affected by taints, partaking of merit, ripening in the acquisitions; and there is right view that is noble, taintless, supramundane, a factor of the path" (Bodhi 2000, 934–35).[39]

As we read it, the Buddha explains here that the first type of Right View is a mundane practice that leads to being reborn in response to one's actions. The first level of Right View acknowledges *kamma* and understands the world correctly at a mundane level (or a "mundane Right View"), such as understanding good and bad as well as acknowledging one's parents. Although at this stage Right View is not the result of understanding the ultimate truth, it is an essential as well as a transitional step to acquiring certain wholesome concepts. The second type of Right View is described as a supramundane path fostering a taintless and noble state of mind. Such comparision implies that, in the two types of Right View, the supramundane path is more advanced than the mundane one, as it is an advancement along the noble path. According to the sequence of the Buddha's discourse, the attainment of Right View seems to follow the step-by-step process of: (1) understanding Wrong Views as Wrong Views, (2) practicing mundane Right View, and (3) practicing supramundane Right View. Informed by this *sutta*, we propose three steps to cultivate Right View:

(1) Realization of Wrong View (and its suffering);
(2) Intellectual understanding of Right View;
(3) Experiential cultivation of Right View.

38. MN III, 71–72:*Tatra, bhikkhave, sammādiṭṭhi pubbaṅgamā hoti. Kathañ ca bhikkhave, sammādiṭṭhi pubbaṅgamā hoti? Micchādiṭṭhiṁ: micchādiṭṭhīti pājānāti, sammādiṭṭhiṁ: Sammādiṭṭhīti pajānāti, Sā 'ssa hoti sammādiṭṭhi. Katamā ca bhikkhave, micchādiṭṭhi? Na'tthi dinnaṁ, na'tthi yiṭṭhaṁ, na'tthi hutaṁ, na'tthi sukaṭadukkaṭānaṁ kammānaṁ phalaṁ vipāko, na'tthi ayaṁ loko, na'tthi paro loko, na'tthi mātā, na'tthi pitā, na'tthi sattā opapātikā, na'tthi loke samaṇabrāhmaṇā sammaggatā sammāpaṭipannā ye imañ ca lokaṁ parañ ca lokaṁ sayaṁ abhiññā sacchikatvā pavedentīti; ayaṁ bhikkhave micchādiṭṭhi*

39. MN III, 72: *Sammādiṭṭhiṁ p'ahaṁ bhikkhave, dvayaṁ vadāmi. Atthi, bhikkhave, sammādiṭṭhi sāsavā puññabhāgiyā upadhivepakkā; atthi, bhikkhave sammādiṭṭhi ariyā anāsavā lokuttarā maggaṅgā.*

In the first proposed step, Wrong View (and its subsequent suffering) is driven by craving and ignorance. An uncultivated mind is inclined to attach to different Wrong Views, such as believing in an inherently existing self or soul, perceiving entities in life (e.g., love or possessions) as permanent, or seeing suffering as a source of happiness (e.g., taking the short-term pleasant feeling of eating unhealthy food as happiness while neglecting the suffering and negative consequences associated with it). Another important characteristic of Wrong View is that, regardless of the content of the view, the individual takes the view as "my view," thereby clinging on to it, defending it, and rejecting other possible views (Somaratne 2021, 32). As pointed out by Gethin (2004) and Fuller (2005), such clinging to view is an obstacle on the path and leads to cognitive and emotional suffering. Therefore, perhaps the first step is to identify clinging to Wrong Views and suffering in order to develop the motivation to change.

The four common Wrong Views, as examined by Gethin (2004, 20) in the *sutta*s are listed as follows:

(1) Self-identity view (*sakkāya diṭṭhi*)
(2) View of permanence (*sassata-diṭṭhi*)
(3) View of annihilation (*uccheda-diṭṭhi*)
(4) View of inefficacy of action (*akiriya-ditthi*).

The categorization of Wrong Views can be used as a reference and reminder of how an individual inaccurately understands the nature of things. Understanding these common false views can help practitioners mindfully identify them, see the suffering associated with them, and then make the choice to abandon them. For example, when one believes his or her health should remain the same regardless of aging, one is attached to a view of permanence (*sassata-diṭṭhi*). As the person grows, ages, and their bodily function deteriorates, clinging to the view of permanence can manifest as the unacceptance of reality, such as blaming oneself and others or denying the fact of aging by forcing one's body to perform. These thoughts and behaviors can result in a huge cognitive and emotional burden. But being mindful of the suffering motivates one to examine one's view and contemplate whether the physical body is actually permanent, thereby noticing one's inaccurate view.

The second proposed step is the intellectual understanding of Right View. This is the beginning of the journey on the Buddhist path that can lead to the gradual abandonment of Wrong View and intellectual attainment of Right View. This process usually requires at least a preliminary level of faith (*saddhā*), learning (by listening [*sotaṃ odahati*] or reading), remembering (*dhāreti*), examining the meaning (*atthaṃ upaparikkhati*), and reflective acceptance of reality (*dhammā nijjhānaṃ khamanti*) as mentioned in the *Caṅkī-sutta* (MN 95). Through reading, listening to *Dhamma* talks, and intellectual reflection and analysis, one can gradually develop a knowledge base for Right View and the dangers of Wrong View. Applying this attitude of Right View in life can build a foundation for further advancement on the path. Using the same example as before, conceptually understanding that the body is an impermanent entity that we hold on to, arising and ceasing based on different causes and conditions, can help to foster an intellectually Right View. Although it may not lead to non-attachment nor resolve emotional issues, this cognitive attainment is likely to cultivate more acceptance by seeing and knowing more of reality, and this practice can be a gradual process to continually develop Right View from a mundane level to a supramundane level.

The final proposed step is the experiential cultivation of Right View, which can be considered the ultimate direction of practice. Through repeated wise reflection, which is also *vipassanā* (insight) meditation itself, one can advance on the path through direct experiences and penetration to the true nature of things, leading to the unattached middle point that avoids all extreme views. In contrast to the previous step, this realization is unbounded by concepts and intellectual attainment. The product should align with Gethin's (2004, 25) proposed direct awareness in which there is a spontaneous mental state to see and know things as they are. This realization of Right View is a sign of wisdom, which is also defined as attainment of stream-entry (*sotāpatti*) in the *sutta*s. Simply put, stream entry refers to the point when a practitioner enters the stream towards *Nibbāna*, meaning the untainted Right View is established. It is by this establishment that accurate practice begins. In other words, the path begins from here. We can understand that until then, all the practices being carried out are no more than trials. The other remaining paths, as explained in the *Magga-saṃyutta*, will be cultivated gradually after attaining Right View. Intellectual Right View, which is usually gained by learning, is the entry point and the key to all other Noble Paths because the practice of each of the Noble Paths reciprocally fosters the experiential cultivation of Right View. The mind state of Right View can lead to becoming non-attached to one's body and truly seeing and knowing its nature of arising and ceasing, thereby becoming able to accept it effortlessly. Moreover, this mind state naturally discerns how suffering arises from clinging to the concept of permanence and a body, perceives how the causes of craving and ignorance occur, understands the path to cessation through non-attachment, and appreciates the path of practice to non-attachment.

After reviewing the core concepts of Right View and discussing the path of cultivation, the next section switches gear to discuss the psychological correlates and applications of the Buddhist Right View.

7.5 View and Right View According to the Perspective of Psychology

The development of a healthier view is a common result of treatment in many theoretical orientations in psychology, especially in cognitively based counseling models. CBT, for example, is one of the most common psychotherapeutic methods that is rooted in the writings of the Greek stoic philosopher Epictetus; he believed that "men are not moved by things, but by the view they take of them" (Hofmann 2012, 5). This simple yet powerful statement highlights the essential principle of CBT: our cognition and interpretation of things play a crucial role in determining our emotional and behavioral responses (Beck 2011, 228). Driven by this paradigm, CBT has the core treatment goal of identifying and modifying client's cognitive distortions so that the client can "critically examine whether his or her response to a situation is justified" (Hofmann 2012, 17). That is, CBT can help clients formulate adaptive views on events based on objective facts and valid assumptions so as to foster proper responses to reality (Beck 2011, 287). In our view, both CBT and Buddhism posit that suffering originates from problematic views and hence interventions should focus on modifying such problematic beliefs. However, the definition of reality according to CBT is different from that of Buddhism.

In CBT, reality is generally referred to as external events, so one treatment goal, the "right" view of CBT, is designed to help clients differentiate their internal thoughts and cognitive appraisals from the external environment (Hofmann 2012, 16). In contrast, reality in Buddhism concerns the law of things; that is, dependent co-arising, impermanence, non-self, dukkha, and the Right View to see the nature of reality (Somaratne 2021, 71). Even though both CBT and Buddhism aim to see and know reality, the implications of what reality is are fundamentally different. From our understanding, the Buddhist path of cultivation uses the Right View to foster a paradigm shift and eventually become non-attached to views, while CBT emphasizes seeing external reality more objectively and reasonably. Such a contrast impacts the different approaches to therapeutic treatment.

Another major model of contemporary psychotherapy that has gained significant recognition over the past two decades is Acceptance and Commitment Therapy (ACT). Although it is thought of as a third wave CBT, ACT has a somewhat different perspective regarding interventions. ACT emphasizes that human beings rely heavily on verbally ascribed functions to interact with the world, and intervenes by transforming such functions embedded in a client's language—an intervention based on relational frame therapy (Webster 2011, 309). We will give an example based on a common ACT technique: the verbally ascribed function of self-blame manifests as highly critical inner voices saying "you are useless." A technique to counteract such inner statements is repeating "you are useless" as a song, repeating it until it loses its power; alternatively, one can thank its presence while not taking the voice seriously. Another key assumption of ACT is to see psychological problems as products of psychological rigidity and holding on too tightly to thoughts, a sense of self, rules, or any other things in life (Twohig 2012, 499). The key treatment goal is to help a client develop psychological flexibility, "which is the ability to fully contact the present moment and the inner experiences that are occurring, without needless defense, and, depending upon the context, persisting or changing in the pursuit of goals or personal values" (Twohig 2012, 501). In this way, ACT also helps clients develop a more flexible view of events while easing one's cognitive rigidity (Webster 2011, 311).

It is difficult not to associate the Buddhist concept of clinging with the ACT concept of psychological flexibility. In fact, the founder of ACT, Steven Hayes, wrote an article in which he discussed the relationship between ACT and Buddhism. In the article, Hayes (2002, 58–66) discussed several parallels between the two schools of thought, such as assumptions about the ubiquity of human suffering and the source of suffering as attachment, the importance of acceptance and mindfulness, and the position of valued action in psychological well-being. The main divergence Hayes noticed is the assumption of the sense of self (Hayes 2002, 65). In short, although ACT believes in a transcendent sense of self that is susceptible to change, there is also a stable, unchangeable, and immutable "I" in the present moment (Hayes 2002, 65). As we see it, this perspective may offer a little taste of non-self while not fully exercising the psychological flexibility to see the sense of self as a dependently co-arising phenomenon which arises, changes, and ceases according to causes and conditions. In other words, there seems to still be an inherently existing "I" in ACT, although this sense of self is far more fluid and changeable in comparison to that in many theoretical orientations. If this understanding is correct, the Right View of non-self in Buddhism is different from the "right" view of psychological flexibility when developing a transcendent sense of self in ACT.

Reviewing the theoretical assumptions of CBT and ACT shows us that changing a client's view is a common intervention. In fact, many other theoretical orientations also aim to foster certain more adaptive or realistic views in clients. For example, humanistic and existential therapies help clients foster a view of life based on the four dialectical existential givens (*life and death*, *community and isolation*, *freedom or determinism*, and *meaning or absurdity*) and then choose a preferred way of living (Bland, 2020). While there are plenty of successful intervention models in psychology, dialectical behavioral therapy (DBT) fosters a view known as "wise mind" to integrate the emotional and rational mind in order to see the wisest option at any given moment (Sakdalan, Allan, and Gupta 2014, 114). After briefly revisiting these theoretical orientations, we can see the commonality in fostering certain views in clients for their benefit, while the nature of the view is largely dependent on the theoretical assumption of the particular orientation. In other words, each paradigm has its own assumption of "right" view. This common and customary intervention to foster views in clients suggests that it is highly reasonable for the Buddhist counseling process to also foster Right View in clients.

Interestingly, regardless of the success of mental health treatments based on the previously mentioned theoretical orientations, there is a clear trend to integrate Buddhist wisdom, including Right View, into the treatment. This trend can be seen in professional psychology in which mindfulness, a secular adaptation of Right Mindfulness that makes minimal use of Buddhist ethics and wisdom, has significantly influenced the mental health treatment model over the past three decades. However, an increasing number of voices have cast doubt and criticized such an "out-of-context" adaptation in which certain components have been extracted from Buddhism to formulate a solitary intervention. In particular, some scholars are concerned that this process of adaptation might distort certain important Buddhist teachings and that there is a lot more valuable wisdom Buddhism can contribute to psychological interventions. For instance, Van Gordon and Shonin (2020) developed a meditation awareness training (MAT) intervention with reintegrated components of Buddhist ethics and wisdom added to the framework, while Negi and his team (2014) developed cognitively-based compassion training (CBCT) as a mind training program based on Tibetan Buddhist meditation practices involving wisdom and compassion. These interventions have yielded clear empirical support as well as recognition from the professional field, suggesting the increasing acceptance of the integration of Buddhist wisdom in psychological interventions.

The increasing integration of views in interventions, and the rising acceptance of Buddhist wisdom, is perfect timing for the use of Right View as a core intervention. The next section will examine one way of achieving such an inclusion in more detail.

7.6 Implications of Right View for Buddhist Counseling

Assuming that the development of Right View is the core intervention in Buddhist-inspired counseling, we can now go a step further by emphasizing wise reflection or attention (*yonisomanasikāra*) as a key part of the process to help a client develop Right View.

Yonisomanasikāra, which is translated in different ways (such as wise reflection, wise attention, proper attention, proper reflection, proper mental engagement, and so on), is a cognitive technique for investigating the root causes of a phenomenon in order to generate penetrative insight in accord with the true nature of things. Fundamentally, it relates to the contemplation of the three marks of existence, namely, *annica*, *anattā*, and *dukkha*, which is of utmost importance to the practice of the Noble Eightfold Path. As the *Mahāvedalla-sutta* (MN 43) pointed out, the development of Right View relies on two conditions: (1) learning from others and (2) wise reflection.[40] In contrast, unwise reflection is a mental engagement which does not accord with the true nature of things. For example, viewing a self in non-self (*Anattani attaṃ ti*), viewing permanence in impermanence (*anicce niccaṃ ti*), viewing suffering as happiness (*dukkhe sukhaṃ ti*), and viewing impure as pure (*asubhe subhaṃ ti*) (MA i, 64).

There are two potential questions here: how do we assess Right View, and how do we intervene and help a client practice wise reflection in order to attain Right View? In this section, we will propose an interpretation of Right View for Buddhist counseling assessment and integrate the proposed three-step process to foster Right View together with the three means of gaining wisdom in order to provide an intervention model based on Right View.

While a worldly individual may not be fully able to establish Right View, it is possible to use this mental flexibility as a reference to interpret the Right View for Buddhist counseling. Right View, in terms of dwelling on an unattached middle path, is skillfully applicable in any field. In simple words, it is not to attach or cling to two opposite views but to stay in between, having not been attached to the middle point either—when there is no attachment to a view, there are no conflicts, only concordance. For example, a person, perhaps a client, may have faith in a creator god, which is considered as unskillfulness in Buddhism because attachment to this view will lead to suffering. A counselor with Right View will not have any conflicting views, although they will skillfully adopt a view for the welfare of the client, which goes beyond and becomes non-attached to the extremes of whether there is a creator god or not. In other words, the counselor's Right View is only germane to the suffering of their client instead of any need or desire to prove oneself right.

For that reason, we propose to understand Right View in Buddhist counseling at a worldly level as such: in a given moment with the current causes and conditions, Right View is the flexibility of the mind—free of all attachments—that focuses on the solution to a problem and leads to appropriate actions manifested in more wholesome thoughts, speech, and behaviors. In other words, this significance implies flexibility in listening to a client while not being attached to their own particular view, and skillfulness in choosing a perspective and action conducive to intervening in any client's presenting problem at any given moment. To measure such a view, we have developed the self-perceived Right View Scale (see Table 7.2).

40. M I, 294: *dve kho āvuso paccayā sammādiṭṭhiyā uppādāya: parato ca ghoso yoniso ca manasikāro. Ime kho āvuso dve paccayā sammādiṭṭhiyā uppādāyāti.*

Table 7.2: Self-Perceived Right View Scale

Self-Perceived Right View Scale

Directions: The following statements reflect the ways in which we view life, the world, and ourselves. Rate the degree to which you agree or disagree with each statement using the following scale (e.g., 1 = strongly disagree and 5 = strongly agree). There is no right or wrong answer. Do not spend too much time on any one statement and do not leave any unanswered.

No.	Items	Strongly disagree	Slightly disagree	Disagree	Slightly agree	Strongly agree
1.	Everything in life, including relationships, health, achievements, thoughts, emotions, or problems, are impermanent.	1	2	3	4	5
2.	I have no problem accepting changes in life.	1	2	3	4	5
3.	There are certain things that I have no control over in life.	1	2	3	4	5
4.	I believe I can control most of the things in life as long as I try.*	1	2	3	4	5
5.	Life itself inevitably involves suffering.	1	2	3	4	5
6.	I am willing to accept suffering when it arises.	1	2	3	4	5
7.	For every problem I encounter, there are always different causes and conditions for its occurrence.	1	2	3	4	5
8.	I can understand the causes and conditions giving rise to or sustaining a problem.	1	2	3	4	5
9.	I can see things as they are without rejecting, distorting, or fabricating them.	1	2	3	4	5
10.	Every decision has consequences, both for my mind and the external world.	1	2	3	4	5
11.	I am responsible for how I think, how I speak, and how I act.	1	2	3	4	5

(continued on p. 166)

Table 7.2: (*continued*)

No.	Items	Strongly disagree	Slightly disagree	Disagree	Slightly agree	Strongly agree
12.	How I think, how I speak, and how I act directly influence how I feel.	1	2	3	4	5
13.	I don't have to hold on to an identity according to others' definition of me.	1	2	3	4	5
14.	I don't have to hold on to an identity according to my definition of myself.	1	2	3	4	5
15.	The sense of "I" is just an experience.	1	2	3	4	5
16.	I know who I am and I live my life sincerely according to who I am.*	1	2	3	4	5
17.	I realize that some of my views, opinions, or concepts can make me suffer.	1	2	3	4	5
18.	I am always assertive in what I think is right.*	1	2	3	4	5
19.	I am satisfied with what I have.	1	2	3	4	5
20.	I am peaceful and happy the way I am.	1	2	3	4	5

Grouping:
Impermanence: Q1–4.
Suffering: Q5–6.
Dependent co-arising: Q7–9.
Kamma: Q10–12.
Non-self: Q13–16, 19–20.
Clinging to view: Q17–18.
* Reverse scoring

7.6.1 Self-Perceived Right View Scale

Based on our discussion of Right View, it would be helpful to develop a measurement scale to evaluate a client's attainment of Right View in order to gauge their progress in counseling in relation to this very important construct. However, one definition of Right View is "non-grasped view," which is difficult to measure in a simple way, so we have aimed instead for a measure of "self-perceived" Right View; that is, clients can self-report their intellectual understanding of this construct. As a supplement to the third component of the Right View intervention (see below), the aim of this scale is to evaluate treatment progress in a practical way. In terms of procedure, clients will be instructed to rate their agreement on the twenty items using a 5-point Likert scale from 1 (strongly disagree) to 5 (strongly agree).

7.6.1.1 Item Development of Self-Perceived Right View Scale

In formulating the items on the self-perceived Right View scale (SPRVS), several key Buddhist teachings on Right View were used. The scale is divided into six components: (1) impermanence: Q1–4, (2) suffering: Q5–6, (3) dependent co-arising: Q7–9, (4) *kamma*: Q10–12, (5) non-self: Q13–16, 19–20, and (6) clinging to views: Q17–18. Here is a brief rationale for each component.

Impermanence. The teaching of impermanence is included because it is one of the fundamental Buddhist teachings: all conditioned phenomena are impermanent (*sabbe saṅhārā aniccā*) (Dhp 277). The Dhp (277) further signifies: "When one is able to see this reality with one's own wisdom, one becomes able to turn away from suffering. This itself is the path for ultimate purification."[41] The items here aim to measure the client's ability to know and see the impermanent nature of things.

Suffering. Suffering represents the first of the four noble truths. In early Pāli canonical texts, accepting the reality or *dhamma*, including impermanence, suffering and no-self, is called "*dhammanijjhānakkhantī*" (reflective acceptance of the *dhamma*), which can be considered a sign of Right View. These items represent one's ability and willingness to reflectively accept suffering as it is.

Dependent co-arising. Dependent co-arising, as discussed in early chapters, is a fundamental teaching. We attempt to measure a client's ability to see reality as it is through the lens of dependent co-arising. Doctrinally speaking, this itself is the practice for gaining knowledge via insight (*vipassanā ñāṇa*). One is fully able to see things as they are, which means one has gained insight termed "*yathābhūtañāṇadassana*" (knowledge and vision of things as they really are).

---

41. Dhp 277: *sabbe saṅkhārā aniccā ti yadā paññāya passati atha nibbindati dukkhe esa maggo visuddhiyā*

In transforming this key concept into a scale item, we also integrated a sense of "wise reflection" (*yonisomanasikāra*) in order to measure a client's capacity to skillfully reflect on the dependent co-arising nature of phenomena.

Kamma. Another way to develop Right View is by understanding the teaching of *kamma*. For one is responsible for one's thoughts, speech, and actions, not others. The first two verses of the *Dhammapada* say the same thing while adding "among the three, mind is forerunner."

Non-self. Non-self is another key doctrine in Early Buddhist teachings. Our attempt to measure non-self is by evaluating a client's flexibility in either defining oneself or allowing others to define oneself by a fixed and rigid notion.

Clinging to View. Holding onto any view can bring suffering, which is not what the Buddha taught. When one realizes the suffering that arises from clinging to view, one is able to let go of such clinging. These items measure a client's flexibility in holding onto views, assuming that the more flexible they are, the less clinging to a view they would have.

With this scale, Buddhist counselors can administer it regularly to evaluate the progress of clients. The next section will address our interpretation of Right View with regard to a practical treatment model for Buddhist counseling.

7.6.2 Component 1: Cultivation of a Buddhist Counselor

One of the first tasks of a Buddhist counselor is to be able to understand Right View and Wrong View, including its manifestations, common classifications, and ways to cultivate Right View. In Buddhism, a wise and righteous friend (*kalyāna mitta*) plays an important role in helping each other overcome ignorance and develop Right View, this friendship even being described by the Buddha in the *Upaḍḍha-sutta* (SN 45.2) as the whole of the holy life,[42] correcting the Venerable Ānanda who held that having a wise and righteous friend (*kaḷyāṇa mitta*) is half of the holy life. To become a wise and righteous friend, one has to practice the Noble Eightfold Path, starting with Right View, as it is said in the *Magga-saṃyutta*: "When a bhikkhu has a good friend, a good companion, a good comrade, it is to be expected that he will develop and cultivate the Noble Eightfold Path."[43] When applying this concept to Buddhist counseling, the Buddhist counselor should start with learning and experiencing Right View in order to embody this important Buddhist wisdom. For a specific learning model, the *Saṅgīti-sutta* (DN 33) mentioned three ways of gaining wisdom, including wisdom gained through think-

42. SN V, 2: *Sakalam eva hidam Ānanda brahmacariyaṃ yad idaṃ kalyāṇamittatā.*
43. SN V, 2: *Kalyāṇamittassetam Ānanda bhikkhuno pāṭikaṅkham kalyānasahāyassa kalyāṇasampavaṅkassa ariyam aṭṭhaṅgikam maggam bhāvessati ariyam aṭṭhaṅgikam maggam bahulikarissati.*

ing (*cintāmayā paññā*), wisdom gained through learning (*sutamayā paññā*), and wisdom gained through cultivation (*bhāvanāmayā paññā*). As a process of mind cultivation, a Buddhist counselor can apply this model by: (1) acquiring Buddhist wisdom via the study of Buddhism and listening to *Dhamma* talks, (2) wisely thinking, reflecting, and contemplating on their meanings and applying the intellectual wisdom in personal life, and (3) mental development through consistent practice that is Right Mindfulness. This is a crucial beginning to help Buddhist counselors develop a solid intellectual and experiential reservoir in sharing their knowledge on Right View and guiding clients to practice it, thereby preparing oneself to be a "wise and righteous friend" to walk with a client on the Buddhist path.

7.6.3 Component 2: Raising Awareness of Wrong Views and Its Suffering in Clients

The knowledge and experience of the Buddhist counselor can be used to help the client identify the potential Wrong Views contributing to their suffering. As counseling is different from teaching, bluntly pointing out a client's Wrong View can come across as judgmental and invalidating, making them defensive and depriving them of the chance to be listened to and understood, even causing harm to their psychological well-being. But it must be emphasized that while this component requires Buddhist counselors to have a basic understanding of Wrong Views, including being able to identify them in clients, they also have to be empathic about the client's suffering caused by their ignorance, gradually reflecting upon and examining it to raise the client's awareness. Consider the following case example:

> Sally is a 32-year-old Chinese woman who lost her father when she was ten years old. Her fiancé died one year previously in a tragic car accident. In the counseling room, she presented with a depressed mood, exhaustion, and hopelessness and said, "All the important men in my life have left me. I think it's a curse, a curse that will never stop . . . This pain is so overwhelming that I cannot see any way out. I just feel . . . no matter what I do, this depressing pain will always be here."

In this example, Sally used categorical terms like "always" and "never" to describe her view that all important men leave her, resulting in her feeling trapped in depression, and implying the rigid opinion that these two events are permanent factors in her life. This is also a deluded view of permanence (*sassata-diṭṭhi*), which has formed and ossified in an impermanent world due to her previous life challenges. To provide Buddhist counseling, it is crucial to compassionately listen to her suffering and understand why she sees the world and events this way. It is important to validate her feelings and empathize with her pain and sadness. At the same time, part of the intervention is to try pointing out Wrong View skillfully without judgment or rejection:

> Sally: "This depression will always be here."
>
> Buddhist counselor: "It seems like what you conclude from your experience is that this depressing pain is always with you, almost like it's permanent. Is that right?" (*Pointing out client's view.*)
>
> Sally: "That's right, it does feel permanent. I can't really recall a time that I wasn't depressed."
>
> Buddhist counselor: "How does it feel seeing depression as a permanent experience?" (*Exploring suffering arising from Wrong View.*)
>
> Sally: "It's even more depressing to think this way." (Said with a bitter smile.)
>
> Buddhist counselor: "So just seeing depression as permanent brings even more suffering than the depression itself. (*Reflecting the suffering aggravated by the view.*) In fact, seeing things as permanent can be a painful thought." (*Moving forward to explore the view.*)

In this dialogue with the client, the counselor used reflections to raise the client's awareness of: (1) the view she held on to, and (2) the suffering created from holding on to this view. Inside the counselor's mind, they mentally identified the client's suffering as a view of permanence and hence pinpointed the effect of holding on to this view. At this stage, the Buddhist counselor does not have to start with didactics, because teaching concepts or ideas may not synchronize with the client's emotional experiences when more skillful and emotionally sensitive engagement is required.

7.6.4 Component 3: Intellectual Learning

To begin the journey towards Right View, intellectual and conceptual learning can be a good starting point. Buddhist counselors can use various ways to "teach" Right View according to the client's cognitive level, emotional states, openness to learning, and rapport with the counselor. Again, to "teach" may not be exactly like taking out a textbook to show the client *sutta*s and commentaries on Right View; instead, it requires flexibility and skillfulness to provide knowledge, use contemplative questions, initiate dialogue, or use other ways to disseminate the message.

CBT is widely known for its psychoeducation component, which offers a systematic and structured approach for educating clients about the nature of illness, including its treatment modality, as well as providing other relevant resources. In Buddhist counseling, we coined the term "Buddho-education" to describe a parallel process. Buddho-education can be the optimized sharing of Buddhist teachings or even a mini-*Dhamma* talk, the sharing of articles or paragraphs (e.g., sharing quotes from Venerables Thich Nhat Hanh, Ajahn Brahm, or Hin Hung), providing short handouts and going through them with clients, telling relevant Buddhist stories, using reflective or contemplative questions, or other creative ways. A crucial consideration is that counseling is much more about the process instead of the content: the key to Buddho-education is *how* to do it at that given moment. For example, one has to consider the amount of information, the style of presentation, the timing of sharing such knowledge, and the ability to adapt in response to a client's immediate needs at that counseling moment. We will use the same example to illustrate this point:

> Sally: "But my depression has always been here, right? I tried many things, but it just doesn't go away. It feels pretty permanent to me."
>
> Buddhist counselor: "Let's talk about permanence for a second . . . if you don't mind me asking, how do you make sense of your loss of two important men in your life?"
>
> Sally: "Huge losses . . . losses that I have no control over. There is no pain as great as having the most important person in your life ripped away from you . . . one after another . . . and I still remember how I tried so hard to treasure moments with them and made sure they were safe and healthy, especially my fiancé . . . but now they're gone."
>
> Buddhist counselor: "If these uncontrollable losses convey a lesson about life, what would it be?" (*Trying to introduce the view of impermanence.*)
>
> Sally: "I guess . . . life is out of one's control? No matter how much I try to hold on to people or things, they can still disappear!"
>
> Buddhist counselor: "That's an insightful way to describe it. Certain things, regardless of their importance, are out of our control. One way to name this lesson in life is impermanence." (*Buddho-education on impermanence through labeling the phenomenon.*)
>
> Sally: "Impermanence?"
>
> Buddhist counselor: "Yes, impermanence. There are certainly things and people that we have no control over—they can come, they can change, or they can leave. While we may not be able to control them, we can be in control of our perspective on them." (*Buddho-education on impermanence using minimal and lay term didactics.*)
>
> Sally: "How so?"
>
> Buddhist counselor: "Let me ask you a question. What if depression is as impermanent as any other thing in life?" (*Buddho-education on impermanence using a question for reflection.*)

In this dialogue, the Buddhist counselor used a few ways to teach the intellectual Right View of impermanence in order to provide the client with a new perspective. The next component will discuss how to use reflection and contemplation to reach a deeper understanding.

7.6.5 Component 4: Reflection and Contemplation

During reflection and contemplation, Buddhist counselors must process, analyze, and discuss the selected part or aspect of Right View with clients in order to help them self-reflect and contemplate to gain insights. Buddhist counselors can apply basic counseling skills, such as paraphrasing, reflection on meanings, contemplative questions, or other means to reach the same goal. This is a process of personal inquiry based on Buddhist teachings. Some key points are to help clients see patterns as well as causes and effects of thoughts and behaviors, note the arising and ceasing of experiences of suffering, raise awareness of mind states that are less painful, and focus back on the present moment without dwelling on the past or future. Let us return to the previous example:

> Buddhist counselor: "Let me ask you a question. What if depression is as impermanent as any other thing in life?"
>
> Sally: "Let me see if I understand what you mean. If I can lose my important ones in life, I can lose my depression too?"
>
> Buddhist counselor: "What do you think?"
>
> Sally: "I guess I understand the logic, but I've never thought of it this way." (She pauses for a few seconds, with relief on her face). "I think I agree with what you mean, but I'm not sure what to do, since I can't remember what it's like not to be depressed."
>
> Buddhist counselor: "Did you notice, when you thought about the possibility that depression might be impermanent, that there was relief on your face for a second?" (*Bringing the client's mind back to the present moment.*)
>
> Sally: "That's right, there was a moment of relief . . . but moments with my fiancé come up again and sweetness turns into bitterness in a flash."
>
> Buddhist counselor: "What you're saying is that you are more relieved when you stayed in the present moment. Then you notice how images arise and they attract your attention. When you dwell on these images, depressive feelings arise again." (*Reflecting on cognitive processes to raise client's awareness.*)
>
> Sally: "I guess this is what happens. All of it happens so fast. I guess that's why I am sad all the time . . . it's hard for me to resist those memories as I miss him so much."
>
> Buddhist counselor: "Would you like to try Buddhist practice to see if it helps?"

In this segment, the counselor deepened the exploration of Right View by (1) bringing the client back to the present moment and (2) reflecting how painful experiences arise and cease. This analysis helped the client gain insight into the fact that depression may not be as permanent and static as she previously believed.

7.6.6 Component 5: Experiential Practice

Last but not least, as pointed out in the *Kālāma-sutta* (AN 3.65), the key to liberation is to reach realization through direct knowledge. Relying on reports (*mā anussavena*), legends (*mā paramparāya*), traditions (*mā itikirāya*), scriptures (*mā pīṭakasampadānena*), by logical conjecture (*mā takka hetu*), by inference (*mā nayahetu*), by analogies (*mā ākāraparivitakkena*), by acceptance through pondering views (*mā diṭṭhinijjhānakkhantiyā*), by probability (*mā bhabbarūpatāya*), and by the thought that "this is our teacher" (*mā samaṇo no garu*) to attain knowledge requires careful reflection and understanding; a student of Buddhism should not blindly take these sources of knowledge as the only truth. In other words, experiential practices are an essential step on the path. There are many ways of using experiential practices as interventions, especially different forms of meditation, in the cultivation of Right View. To develop an experiential learning of Right View, it is crucial for clients to develop a regular cultivation practice as a form of mind training, such as mindfulness of their bodily states, feelings, and mental acts in daily life, then finally progressing to the development of wise reflection upon reality. Wise reflection fosters the cognitive capacity to investigate the root causes of phenomena, such as knowing and seeing that suffering arises from attachment and craving to sensual pleasures, the egoistic desire to grasp onto a self-identity in daily encounters, as well as learning how to become non-attached to unwholesome thoughts. Applying this approach to Buddhist counseling and the case study above, a Buddhist counselor can guide the client in practicing breathing meditation (*ānāpānāsati*) by first calming her mind and raising awareness of her bodily movements as well as the activity and fabrications of her mind. After that, more advanced guidance can prompt her to notice how particular mental states arise and pass away, followed by the arising of other mental states, thereby reaching the experiential conclusion that mental events are always impermanent (Anālayo 2018, 145). By firmly grounding her mind on the object of meditation in the present moment (e.g., the in- and out-breaths), the client can gradually learn to pause her dwelling on memories of her father and fiancé or her worries about losing other important ones in the future. With this foundation, the client can gain mental clarity and stability to discern that her depressive thoughts are impermanent, thus viewing them as a temporary experience constructed according to various causes and conditions that are themselves susceptible to change.

Buddhist counselors can also apply the methods taught in the *Vitakkasaṇṭhāna-sutta* (MN 20) to help clients remove distracting thoughts. In particular, Buddhist counselors can guide their clients to practice the following, with each technique being adapted to the case example:

1. **Thought substitution** (*aññaṃ nimittaṃ manasikātabbaṃ*). Intentionally replacing an unwholesome thought with a wholesome one to eliminate the former, such as using a compassionate view to replace a depressive thought, or recollecting the image of her grandmother embracing her. At that point, the client can settle her mind with the object.
2. **Reflecting drawback** (*ādīnavo upaparikkhitabbo*). Should distracting thoughts prevail, a practitioner can examine how the thoughts are unhelpful and distress-provoking, thereby letting the thoughts dissipate. In other words, examine the thoughts leading to suffering and contemplate the danger and drawback of such thoughts. Acknowledge and then let go of the unwholesome thoughts in order to avoid fueling such cognitive tendencies. In practice, the counselors can guide the client above to just acknowledge her unwholesome thoughts and avoid grasping on to them by visualizing herself standing on top of a mountain watching the thoughts flowing by, like a river, or sitting on a train looking out of the window and seeing the thoughts passing by like the scenery Counselors can help clients reflect on how holding onto these thoughts can only result in unpleasant feelings, and explaining how these thoughts are unhelpful regardless of their validity. For example, one can have the valid thought "I am losing hair and I have a big belly," but grasping onto or ruminating on this thought only brings distress, shame, and frustration. Seeing the drawbacks of the thought can allow clients to choose to not attach to it.
3. **Thought ignoring** (*asatiamanasikāro āpajjitabbo*). Another technique is to ignore an unskillful thought. It is similar to shutting our eyes or looking away when we see horrible images that our mind selectively ignores, withholds attention from, or lets go of certain thoughts. For example, if a client thinks: "My depression will never end," the counselor can invite client to simply see it as a thought which will cease by itself and "look away" to other experiences or more productive thoughts. The counselor may also use a visualization exercise and invite client to visualize being like a firm and steady mountain in mindfulness practice, letting any thought pass like a cloud. Regardless of how many clouds pass, nothing can disturb the tranquility and stability of a mountain.
4. **Thought reflection** (*vitakkasaṅkhārasaṇṭhānaṃ manasikātabbaṃ*). Pause and inquire into the root causes of the thought. This requires a process of experiential reflection in which one needs to be disinvested in the thought, metacognitively examining the causes for it. Buddhist

counselors may examine the craving beneath the thought and the Wrong View implicit in them. For example, the frequent emergence of recollections of the fiancé and inclination to grasp on to them represent a strong clinging to the relationship. Every time the memories arise, the client's craving for love and security as well as her aversion to loneliness and sadness led to her grasp on to the pleasant memories, although such memories quickly turn into grief and mourning. This insight can help the client gain a more thorough understanding of how her clinging is one of the major causes for her depression.

5. **Thought crushing** (*cittaṃ abhiniggaṇhitabbaṃ*). This method of removing distracting thoughts has caused some controversy among scholars, as it is difficult to find a similar description of this method in this *sutta*. Other *sutta*s do not generally teach such a forceful and suppressive method. This method advises the use of willful physical actions (e.g., clenched teeth, or the tongue pressing on the palate) to crush a disturbed mind state. In CBT, there is a strategy known as "thought stopping" that involves strong clapping by the client or the therapist to forcefully stop a negative thought, and then deliberately stopping one's thoughts or behaviors. Another common behavioral technique is called "progressive muscle relaxation" (PMR) and involves a two-step process to tighten a group of muscles and then let go, releasing the tension. PMR emphasizes paying attention to bodily sensations and the process of tightening and relaxing the muscles, feeling the release of tension, instead of focusing on cognitive events. These two psychological techniques resonate with the thought crushing method. If we focus on the physical aspect of this technique to relax thoughts, there can be other potential applications, such as physical exercises, mindfully cleaning up a place, planting and gardening, or at least trying to stop the thought by physically going somewhere. For example, when the client's depressive thoughts become uncontrollable, the counselor can create a loud sound with a singing bowl, practice mindful stretching with the client, or even sing or play music to induce strong physical stimulation. Using the physical sensations as anchors, one can ease the grasping of unwholesome thoughts. Afterwards, it is important to let the client fully immerse into the present moment and attend to a more neutral, or even pleasant, experience.

In effect, while clients learn to master or relax the unwholesome thoughts, Buddhist counselors play a caring and responsive role along the way and flexibly choose different techniques to facilitate clients' awareness.

7.7 Conclusion

In comparison with common theoretical orientations in psychology, Buddhist counseling is a theoretical orientation based on non-self, with the core intervention helping the client adopt the Right View in order to see the dependently co-arising nature of a self-notion. This chapter on interventions discussed the essence of Right View as the right understanding of Buddhist teachings and reality, taught a deeper analysis to see Right View as non-view, and demonstrated one way to use it as an intervention. Right View is a non-attached perspective that relinquishes holding on to views, thereby preventing the effort to sustain any extremes or contradictions. It involves surrendering to the present moment, thereby flexibly and skillfully reaching the correct understanding in a given situation. While on this middle path, a sense of peace arises through "sitting back" and disengaging to observe, accept, and understand a phenomenon.

Right View is the entry point to the Noble Eightfold Path, which means that the true practice of Buddhism begins from here, not before this. This is the essential underlying wisdom that makes all subsequent spiritual endeavors meaningful. In response to the frenetic effort to apply Right Mindfulness in psychological interventions over the last three decades, we also hope that this chapter initiates a turning point in which Right View can be seen as a necessary component in the application of Right Mindfulness, as it is for the other seven Noble Paths. The next chapter explores ways that a counseling practitioner can successfully incorporate such a component into their therapeutic practice in more detail.

8

Early Buddhist Teachings as a Complete Model of Theoretical Orientation

The penultimate chapter of this book aims to demonstrate an application of the complete theoretical orientation of our Buddhist-inspired model of counseling. This chapter briefly summarizes the theory-informed model of Buddhist teaching and psychology and uses a case vignette to illustrate how it might be employed in practice.

8.1 The Complete Model

Table 8.1 briefly summarizes the five components of a theoretical orientation for Buddhist counseling discussed in this book together with suggested applications:

To further illustrate the practicality of the proposed theoretical orientation for Buddhist counseling, this chapter will focus on a hypothetical case vignette woven together using actual information from various clients. The process of counseling will follow a common three-step model consisting of assessment, conceptualization, and intervention, and this process will integrate the components of the theoretical orientation. First, let us understand the client's background.

Anson Lau (pseudonym) is a 49-year-old Chinese man, born and raised in Hong Kong. He completed secondary school in Hong Kong and worked as a bank teller for a few years. Afterwards, his family supported his studies and he earned a bachelor's degree in fine art at an Australian university. He returned to Hong Kong after completing his degree and has been working as a graphic designer since then. Anson identifies himself as an atheist, but he is open to Buddhist teachings. He was self-referred to the Buddhist counseling center because he felt depressed, was lost without a direction in life, found work meaningless, and had relationship problems with his girlfriend.

Upon meeting Anson in the first session, I was struck by his handsome appearance and youthful-looking face that belied his chronological age. Even so, he was also clearly lacking in energy, had difficulty concentrating, and looked

Table 8.1: The Proposed Theoretical Framework for a Buddhist-Inspired Counseling Model

Dimension	Integration of Buddhism	Proposed Applications
Basic Philosophy	Dependent co-arising is the key principle in understanding human nature and the world.	Dependent co-arising can be transformed into practical assessment tools and counseling techniques to raise clients' awareness of the multiple causes and conditions that sustain the experience of suffering.
Central Theoretical Constructs of Human Nature and Human Motivation	Under the law of dependent co-arising, the self does not possess an inherently existing nature. Driven by craving and ignorance, the human mind clings on to the notion of self through subjective configurations, which is the core cause of suffering. Thus, attaining the realization of non-self can cause suffering to cease.	Based on the teaching of non-self, the overarching treatment goal for Buddhist counseling is the realization of non-self, or the liberation from clinging to the notion of self.
Theory of Human Development	Mundane human growth, maturation, and development are not the primary concerns of Buddhism; rather, it is liberation from suffering. With this as an end goal, the Buddhist understanding of human development can be considered as a process of mind cultivation towards non-self.	To gauge a client's advancement in mental cultivation, use evaluation scales to measure particular domains and attainments.

(continued on p. 179)

Table 8.1: (*continued*)

Dimension	Integration of Buddhism	Proposed Applications
Psychological Dysfunction	The primary dysfunction or symptom that interferes with well-being is *dukkha*, the main causes of which are ignorance as delineated in the twelve factors of dependent co-arising as well as craving as stated in the four noble truths. Craving and ignorance can manifest as different desires, urges, and cognitive events in daily interactions. Ignorance and craving fuel clinging to the notion of self, resulting in mental suffering.	The proposed conceptualization model based on craving, clinging, and expectations offers an easily understood framework to comprehend and analyze the suffering of clients. The treatment goal is to foster awareness and insights of client's clinging to the notion of self, thereby practicing to reduce or liberate from such clinging. In layman's terms, the goal is not for clients to disown or destroy the notion of self but to let them realize the notion of self does not define who they are.
Interventions and Techniques	The Noble Eightfold Path provides the rationale for an overarching set of interventions, with Right View, the forerunner of the eight paths, being the core intervention.	The five components in developing Right View in Buddhist counseling. Moreover, a variety of techniques can be used to supplement the intervention of Right View, such as Buddho-education, meditation guidance, contemplative dialogues, reflection questions, and other counseling skills.

sad. When asked about what brought him to counseling, he responded with some hesitation, saying: "I'm not sure what to tell you . . . is everything confidential here?" The counselor assured Anson of confidentiality and validated his feelings of difficulty and awkwardness in opening up to a stranger. Afterwards, Anson said, "I have a girlfriend (aged thirty-six) whom I've been dating for twelve years. However, I . . . I've been having an affair. I should say I have been having some affairs here and there. I wasn't like that before dating this girl, but somehow, I started cheating, again and again, after dating her. She has always been so kind to me and has faith in me . . . I know, I'm such a horrible person! I'm such a f—— bastard!" Anson looked down and started blaming himself, clearly feeling lots of frustration.

Anson's father was a successful businessman whom Anson described as "a very traditional Chinese father" that was distant, harsh, and unwilling to share emotions, but worked very hard to ensure financial stability at home. His mother was a housewife who aligned with her husband's view that a son should obey and respect his elders while also carrying on the family name to make his parents proud. These highly critical parents had very high expectations of him as their only son, hoping for him to become a medical doctor or other professional in a respectable field. However, Anson described himself as an artistic person who had always loved drawing and painting from a young age; he disliked most of the traditional academic subjects. His parents took his interest in art as an excuse to be "lazy." Anson said, "I still remember how my mother always said that I was fat, lazy, and useless. She was right that I was pretty useless and I only liked to eat. Even kids at my school called me 'fat-boy.' During my teenage years, I started to lose weight and I also started to hate anyone who was fat! I would never let myself gain so much weight again! Around secondary five, I finally became fitter and I wasn't sure if that was the reason, but I did feel like I had more friends once I wasn't a 'fat-boy' anymore, you know." Anson's father had a stroke five years ago and has had many conflicts with his mother since then. Although Anson's family always lived together, he described their relationship as distant and estranged.

Anson said he found his job very "boring" and "meaningless." He described his colleagues as "dull and nice" and that he could not really chat with others during work. The job did not require much creativity and many original ideas; rather, it was a somewhat mechanical job designing textbooks and school publications according to fixed formats. He felt that he couldn't do any real artwork at any of the jobs he held over the past eighteen years. To cope with this boredom and dissatisfaction, he put in a minimal effort at work and chatted with girls on a dating app during office hours. When asked what would be meaningful for him, he said, "When I was in Australia, I was a totally different person. I worked extremely hard day and night to complete my projects. My tutors were very encouraging and I was able to be creative and artistic in my work. I was very motivated when I graduated and thought I could become a successful artist in Hong Kong. The reality is, art is worthless to Hong Kongers. Everyone only talks about money. It is a cultural desert in which artists can only live by quitting being artists." Seeing his melancholic attitude resulting from his work, the counselor became curious whether he had any dreams or aspirations. His response to the question was, "I wish I could be a successful artist who publishes illustrated books. Of course, I know it's an unrealistic dream."

Among all the issues Anson brought up, he stated that the main reason he sought counseling was his relationship with his girlfriend. Anson disclosed that the reason he had multiple affairs is because of his girlfriend's body shape. Anson said, "Whenever I get physically close with my girlfriend, I become mentally and physically immobilized, because I think she is too fat. My mind will keep comparing her body to other girls who have a great body shape. This kind of thinking makes it very hard for me to get close to her. However, we do get along very well as friends. She is a very kind girl who is very accepting of me. Besides my parents, she is the kindest person to me in my life and I don't want to lose her. But . . . even though she doesn't know about my cheating, I keep hurting her behind her back . . . I'm really stuck right now. I'm getting old and I know I should marry her. However, I don't know how to be in a marriage without sex and I am so afraid of hurting her if I tell her 'I don't want to have sex with you because you are fat.' So I keep running away and finding ways to distract myself . . . just like with those other girls . . . and then I feel even more guilty. I don't know what to do now." Anson started crying and used expletives to blame himself.

8.2 Building a Foundation for Buddhist-inspired Counseling

Like all types of counseling, building a solid therapeutic relationship and alliance characterized by trust, empathic attunement, genuine curiosity, and safety is the key to success. As Anson presented with much shame and guilt, the counselor took a non-judgmental stance and tried to understand his various psychological defenses behind which he is suffering. It was also important to acknowledge the Anson's tremendous courage to talk about his "bastard" behaviors and willingness to be vulnerable, which one can feel extremely ashamed to share with another human being. In response to his harsh self-criticism, the counselor gently reflected the occurrence of such comments to the client, such as, "It has only been twenty minutes since getting to know you and you've used more than half of the time to criticize yourself for what you've done. I see how you are critical of yourself and I can imagine how painful it is to choose to see yourself as a 'sinful person' every day." Getting to know Anson and building a more conducive environment characterized by acceptance and empathy constituted the first step of the therapeutic journey.

8.3 Buddhist-Inspired Counseling Assessment

Informed by dependent co-arising, the assessment tasks for a Buddhist counselor are to: 1) learn about the client's suffering, and 2) collect information about causes and conditions contributing to such suffering. Using the dependent co-arising exercise (Figure 3.1), a Buddhist counselor can create dialogue with Anson in a naturalistic way while aiming to collect relevant information. For example, knowing that Anson suffers most in his relationships and at work, a Buddhist-inspired counseling approach can make use of the following systematic questions:

- **Family**
    - Tell me about your family.
    - How would you describe your relationship with your father/mother/sister? How would you describe your father/mother as a person/parent?
    - What was it like for you growing up in your family?
    - What are your family's expectations of you? How do you feel about that?
- **Relationships**
    - How did you meet your girlfriend? How did you guys start dating?
    - What words would you use to describe your girlfriend?
    - When was the first time you noticed a problem? When there is a problem, how do you guys handle it?
    - What comes up in your mind when you get closer to your girlfriend? And then what do you do?
    - How did you start using those dating apps? How did you feel after those encounters?
- **Work**
    - Could you describe your typical workday to me?
    - What would be a good working environment for you?
    - What are your aspirations at work? Does your job support those aspirations?
    - What do you think about when you find your work unsatisfying?
- **Clinging**
    - If you were a friend of Anson who knows him very well, how would you describe him to me?
    - What adjectives would you use to describe yourself?
    - In reflection upon your life story, what makes you who you are today?
    - What labels or definitions have you adopted for yourself?

These questions and process yielded a variety of internal and external conditions contributing to Anson's suffering. First of all, Anson's main suffering was an overwhelming sense of depression and loneliness together with a lack of control and meaning in life. In collaboration with the Buddhist counselor, he was able to identify external conditions as the stressful dynamic of living in Hong Kong, pressure from his family and friends to make more money, his financial burden, a girlfriend whom he loved emotionally but was physically repulsed by, a highly critical mother who lived with him, and an unchallenging work environment which nevertheless provided him with financial security. As for clinging, he became aware that he habitually criticized and blamed himself while lacking the motivation to change, had resisted growing up and accepting life's dissatisfactions, his enjoyment of sensuality, his idealized expectation of a romantic partner whom he could be emotionally and sexually satisfied with, and his strong need for recognition and acceptance.

Another assessment strategy is to gauge Anson's development of mind as seen on the scale of mindfulness cultivation (Table 5.2). A further intervention and essential technique to help the client develop Right View is meditation. In Buddhist counseling, the Buddhist counselor collaborates with a client to develop a meditation practice as an ongoing process of mind training. Guidance in meditation also helped Anson develop an effective mindfulness practice. For example, guiding Anson to be mindful of the in- and out-breaths and raising awareness of his body and thoughts assuaged his urge for sensuality and cultivated mental distance from thoughts and images that gave rise to depression. In another example, the counselor guided Anson to meditate on any drawings he made and fostered his awareness by noticing his senses to manage his guilt and irritability. In the first session, the counselor administered the scale as a baseline measure of Anson's mindfulness level and then administered it regularly during subsequent sessions to track his development.

8.4 Buddhist-Inspired Counseling Conceptualization

After collecting information from Anson, the counselor proceeded with a case conceptualization to understand the causes and conditions contributing to his suffering. Based on the conceptualization model in Figure 6.1, a comprehensive understanding of Anson's suffering is as follows.

With this conceptualization, we can be more specific about the intervention of Right View when formulating a treatment plan. First, the Buddhist counselor was able to work with Anson to develop a mindfulness practice to calm his mind and nurture clarity and stability by observing his thoughts and urges with more mental distance. Second, the counselor could help Anson identify his Wrong Views as well as the craving and ignorance driving such views. Third, the counselor was able to collaborate with Anson to develop both an intellectual and experiential Right View of his suffering in relationships and work.

Table 8.2: Conceptualization of Anson

Components of Conceptualization	Application to Anson
Reality	Anson's perceived reality is far from perfect, although his actual conditions suggest otherwise given that his girlfriend accepts and loves him as he is, providing him with needed love and security. However, for him, the relationship does not fulfill his idealistic expectations of sexual satisfaction due to her being seen as "fat," which also triggers Anson's aversion towards his mental image of himself as "fat boy Anson." As for work, the external conditions of Hong Kong make it very difficult to be an artist and his work does not challenge him to develop his artistic potential or earn him any recognition.
Expectations	Anson expects romantic love to be a perfect way to satisfy his needs for acceptance, security, intimacy, and sexual fulfillment, and he expects this satisfaction to be lasting. He also expects work to be an ideal way to help him actualize his potential in art and earn recognition so that he can feel accepted and valued.
Suffering	Seeing permanence in impermanence (feeling stuck in depression). Seeing self in non-self (clinging onto his self-notion as a "vulnerable and evil" person). Seeing pleasure in *dukkha* (dwelling in sensuality). Not getting what he wants (failing to have his ideal life). Association with what he dislikes (having to deal with an undesirable environment).
Self-notion	Anson seems to have fabricated a self-notion as a weak, timid, and inferior person who cannot handle conflicts and become independent, so he tries to avoid conflicts and relational problems by dwelling on sensual pleasure. Perhaps partly due to his childhood experiences of being rejected due to his body weight, his perceived failure of being a son recognized by his parents, and teasing from his peers, this sense of "I" believes that people will not accept him the way he is. His harsh self-criticism is also likely to be an internalization of harsh criticism from his parents as well as bullies during his school years. Moreover, his mother's overprotection may have deprived him of the confidence and autonomy to make decisions in life and resolve conflicts with others. In the face of conflicts with his mother, classmates, and later with colleagues at work, his usual coping skill is to hide or run away, which may account for his frequent job change, his avoidance of the need to address the sexual issues with his

(continued on p. 185)

Table 8.2: (*continued*)

Components of Conceptualization	**Application to Anson**
	girlfriend, and his dwelling in sensuality to distract himself from life's dissatisfactions. It seems as if Anson does not feel he can be in control of anything. In addition to his self-view of clinging to his self-notion, there are two potential Wrong Views here. First, he mistakenly believes he can find sustainable happiness via affairs, such actions however only bringing him transient happiness and burdensome feelings of guilt, self-criticism, and loneliness. Second, he sees permanence in impermanence by believing that romantic relationships can sustain and satisfy his emotional and physical needs, while his work and potential can only be recognized based on his experience in Australia. When such attempts at love and work fail, instead of accepting the impermanent nature of such sought-after satisfactions, he continually pursues alternatives by pursuing fantasies of love and work, resulting in repeated failures and wounds. One of the very few things he felt he is accepted for is his physical appearance after he matured, and so he has worked very hard to keep his fit body shape in order to be liked and accepted, thereby dealing with his overwhelming fear of becoming "fat boy Anson" again and being teased and rejected. Deep inside he is yearning for love, acceptance, and security. The pursuit of his ideals and perfection may be a response to the deep insecurity he feels and fears, hence his wishes for everlasting and unchangeable love and acceptance in his relationships and at work.
Cravings	Craving for existence.

8.5 Buddhist-Inspired Interventions

The intervention phase employs the previously proposed five-components of Right View as the core intervention and adds other Noble Paths as part of the treatment.

8.5.1 Component 1: Cultivation of a Buddhist Counselor

In the process of counseling, it is important for the Buddhist counselor to reflect on their own view regarding affairs and infidelity. If there is strong aversion, counselors should certainly become mindful of it and seek supervision or consultation if needed, as such feelings will impede the development of a therapeutic alliance and compassion for this client. Noticing one's mental factors arising in the counseling process is an important awareness for Buddhist counselors. Moreover, as mentioned in the last chapter, it is important for such counselors to continue their meditation practice and learning of Buddhism in order to effectively identify Anson's Wrong Views and cravings.

8.5.2 Component 2: Raising Awareness of Wrong Views and Their Cause of Suffering

As stated in the *Sabbāsava-sutta* (MN 2), only one who knows and sees can overcome cankers (*āsava*), not by the one who does not know and see (Bodhi 1995, 91–92).[1] This statement emphasizes the importance of awareness of one's problems as an important precondition in overcoming them. Part of Anson's suffering was driven by his clinging to certain views, including "A love relationship is a lasting and sustainable way to satisfy emotional and sexual needs," "Work is a place where I can always fully actualize my potential and earn recognition" (view of permanence in impermanence), "I am weak and vulnerable and I need security and love, or else I will ditch whoever makes me feel unfulfilled and then keep looking" (view of self in non-self), and "affairs can bring me happiness" (view of happiness in suffering). There are different ways that a Buddhist counselor can help a client reflect upon such wrong views and their associated suffering. For example, the counselor started with reflections on the view of permanence in impermanence, such as: "You talked quite a lot about how happy you were in Australia, and that the tutors really valued your work, while you came across as frustrated and disappointed when your supervisors in Hong Kong could not do the same for you. It seems like part of you knows that things are different in

1. MN I, 7: *Jānato ahaṁ bhikkhave passato āsavānaṁ khayaṁ vadāmi, no ajānato no apassato.*

Hong Kong, but the other part of you keeps expecting things to be the same, is that right?"

Furthermore, for the view of self in non-self, and knowing that Anson is an artist, the counselor invited Anson to draw "Fat Boy Anson" on a piece of paper. Anson was then asked to describe both the drawing and its portrayal of himself, after which he was invited to share his thoughts and feelings that arose during the creation of these pictures:

> Anson: "I find it difficult to look at the picture of Fat Boy Anson."
>
> Buddhist counselor: "What was your mind telling you when you drew it?"
>
> Anson: "Ah . . . there is an inner voice that keeps saying things like 'So fat,' 'Such an ugly face,' 'He should lose weight,' 'What a lazy bastard,' and so on like that."
>
> Buddhist counselor: "That's a lot of harsh criticisms! I see how your mind is actively engaging with this picture while really wanting to resist it, hating it so much." (*Pointing out unwise reflection.*)
>
> Anson: "You're right, I really hate him! I don't want him to be part of me . . . but sometimes I think he still lives inside me."
>
> Buddhist counselor: "What you're saying is, this fat boy Anson is an inner part of you . . . I would like to ask you: have you been holding on to him, like memories of him, images of him, or some reminders about him, as part of you?"
>
> Anson (pondering for a few seconds and sighing): "I think I've been holding on to this part of me. Sometimes I think it might be why I hate fat people so much. It might be because I hate this part of me that I have been holding on to. It might be because I hate this part of me so much. Maybe that ugly fat boy image and those awful memories are very much imprinted in me, like I need to remember exactly what that is like so I can make sure I don't fall back into it again."

To examine the view of happiness in suffering, the Buddhist counselor can explore the client's experience when having affairs, as the following dialogue illustrates:

> Buddhist counselor: "What makes you use dating apps to find sexual partners?"
>
> Anson: "Well . . . sometimes I'm bored, sometimes I'm lonely . . . I guess most of the time I'm bored and I want to find something fun to do."
>
> Buddhist counselor: "I see, boredom is a big trigger. So which part of the process brings you the most enjoyment?" (*Exploring the sukha.*)
>
> Anson: "When I was younger, I had lots of fun chatting with girls. There were so many very attractive girls and everything was so easy. But honestly, I soon realized that it was not as fun as it seems."
>
> Buddhist counselor: "How so?"

Anson: "The chatting was fun, the sex was fun . . . but it doesn't really change anything." (*The client suddenly appeared sad and looked down at the floor.*)

Buddhist counselor: "You seem to be upset when talking about it. Can you tell me more?"

Anson: "You know, everything was exciting at the beginning . . . but somehow I didn't quite enjoy the sex, not to mention feeling empty and guilty afterwards . . . it was like I felt even more lonely after the sex, and I soon blamed myself for having affairs again."

Buddhist counselor: "Let me see if I understand this correctly. So the sex was actually not as satisfying as you thought it would be, and it was followed by the consequence of more loneliness, emptiness, guilt, and self-blame." (*Reflecting on the dukkha in sukha.*)

Anson: "That's right."

Buddhist counselor: "It sounds like there is more suffering than happiness." (*Reflecting on the dukkha in sukha.*)

Anson: "Yes . . . but I guess I just forget about it when I'm bored."

Buddhist counselor: "So again, boredom is the trigger, and at such moments you choose to focus on the excitement while neglecting the fact that more suffering will come as a consequence. That sounds pretty painful to be in a cycle like that." (*Reflecting on the dukkha in sukha.*)

These verbal interventions of the Buddhist counselor make use of counseling microskills to identify the client's Wrong Views and the suffering associated with them, thereby raising his awareness of the risks involved in such a belief system.

8.5.3 Component 3: Intellectual Learning

After identifying Anson's Wrong View, the counselor raised his level of awareness of how these views are unskillful, thereby nurturing insights into more accurate views. In this section, the Buddhist counselor continues fostering an intellectual Right View of impermanence.

In the session, the counselor used Buddho-education and shared a quote with Anson from Thich Nhat Hanh: "Impermanence does not necessarily lead to suffering. What makes us suffer is wanting for things to be permanent when they are not." The counselor then invited Anson to read it and share his thoughts:

Buddhist counselor: "What do you think about this quote?"

Anson (pondering for a few seconds): ". . . It makes sense."

Buddhist counselor: "How would you relate this to your current situation?"

Anson: "It reminded me of our conversation on how I keep wanting things to stay the same when it's good, like my time in Australia."

Buddhist counselor: "That's a good insight. What do you think about the concept of impermanence?"

Anson: "Is it like . . . eventually we will lose everything and there's nothing we can do about it?"

Buddhist counselor: "Well, that might be part of it, but impermanence is more of a reminder that things keep changing. The bad news is, things are impermanent; you can lose something and be depressed about it unless you are able to accept the reality. The good news is, things are impermanent. Depression cannot stay forever because everything changes, including depression."

Anson: "Hahaha, really?"

Buddhist counselor: "Of course! You also said we can't control things. Do you think there are things that can be controlled?"

Anson: "I'm not sure . . . I don't seem to be able to control things in my life."

The Buddhist counselor realized that Anson showed some insight but struggled to acquire Right View experientially, so the counselor decided to use the following contemplative exercise to foster this realization.

8.5.4 Component 4: Reflection and Contemplation

Besides using dialectical means to reflect and contemplate, the Buddhist counselor used the following Table 8.3 to help the client gain Right View about impermanence and to examine things that can be controlled. The table has four quadrants divided into whether an event is controllable and whether the event is an external (conditions in external environment) or internal condition (conditions within the five aggregates). This exercise aims to cultivate a client's capacity to accept what cannot be changed, to change what can be changed, and to discern the difference between the two. Together with the concept of internal and external conditions, the Buddhist counselor worked with Anson to write down or describe the conditions and had a conversation on whether they are controllable or not.

After exploring such questions, the client started to gain insights into the fact that there are certain things he could control within the parameters of impermanence. This experience was empowering for him in the sense of accepting what cannot be changed and valuing what can be changed. What was especially rewarding for Anson was finding controllable events that were easy and simple enough for him to execute. The success in such control further motivated him to practice this new way of thinking.

Table 8.3: Controllable Conditions Exercise

Please fill in the suffering at this moment in each box provided	Internal conditions (e.g. thoughts and emotions)	External conditions (e.g. environment)
Uncontrollable Events	Boredom. Pop-up thought of "It's so damn boring! I want to have some fun!" Physical urge to gain excitement.	Unchallenging work environment. Distant colleagues.
Controllable Events	Taking mindful breaths. Thinking about the negative consequences of another affair, such as the possibility of losing his girlfriend, the loneliness afterwards, and the self-blame. Engaging in other tasks, such as side jobs. Drawing and painting again.	Thinking whether to delete the dating apps. Initiate conversations with others, such as colleagues, friends, or girlfriend. Prepare interesting and suitable books or magazines for the office. Volunteer for charitable organizations on the design aspect of projects.

Besides that, the Buddhist counselor continued to use artwork to help Anson develop Right View. In particular, using Anson's talent and interest in drawing, the counselor invited Anson to draw a picture on the themes of impermanence, introspection, depression, and other relevant topics. The counselor then had discussions with Anson about the contents and experience of drawing in order to foster insights into his craving and self-notion.

In the next session, Anson showed up looking devastated, saying that his girlfriend caught him chatting with a girl on the dating app, after which the couple had a conflict. Upon processing the event with Anson, the counselor invited Anson to draw a picture of him and his girlfriend. In this creative process, Anson realized that he was very afraid of losing his girlfriend, that he actually had a lot of love for her, and that he would not want to live a life without her. With this awareness, the counselor processed more deeply what craving or yearning did to satisfy Anson in relationships, especially given that loneliness was the key cause of his suffering. Being with his girlfriend brought acceptance and security, but his inability to have sex with her brought an overwhelming sense of loneliness, which made him turn to affairs for satisfaction, as if such relationships could fill the dark hole in his heart. However, he realized that affairs could never fill the emptiness, only pulling him away from his girlfriend. At the end of the session, Anson decided to delete his dating app and try to reconcile with his girlfriend.

Knowing that one root cause of suffering for Anson was his clinging to the self-notion as the "fat boy" who is not worthy of love and acceptance, the counselor thought of one technique to help him detach from that self-notion, called "A Little Emptiness Exercise." Consequently, the counselor prepared an A4 piece of paper, a pen, and some sticky notes in different colors to help him project the notion of self through an experiential exercise. This visualization involved this procedure:

1. Instruct the client to draw a stick figure to represent himself (Figure 8.1). This piece of paper represents the emptiness of self while the drawing of the stick figure represents the subjective configuration of the self-notion.
2. Prompt the client to examine the labels that people have imposed on him and to write each label on a post note. Invite the client to stick the post note on the peripheral areas of the stick figure. Process the client's feelings and thoughts on the labels.
3. Instruct the client to explore the labels that they have internalized and imposed on him. Again, invite the client to stick the post note on the stick figure but this time putting the post notes in the core area. Invite the client to take a moment to observe the stick figure which represents their notion of self and to examine whether this "Anson" yearns for or resists certain labels. Steps 2-3 experientially brings out the essence of

dependent co-arising to help the client realize how different conditions shape and sustain a notion of self.

4. Provide the client with the choice to decide whether he or she wants to let go of certain labels. Then instruct the client to mindfully take them off and then process the feelings in doing so. Afterwards, prompt the client to add desirable labels, encouraging them to experience the feelings of the new "Anson." This step aims to help the client realize the impermanence of the notion of self and cultivate the mental flexibility to understand the potential for change.
5. In the final step, instruct the client to mindfully take off the stickers one by one and acknowledge each label with respect. After putting all the post notes aside, the counselor says, "Let's take a look at this paper and the empty stick figure for a second. Experience what it is like to be free of any labels, of any expectations, of any yearnings, or of any disturbances. Feel the freedom and peaceful state that accompanies it. Experience the emptiness . . . (pause for a few seconds) . . . I want you to now contemplate a question: what if I do not need to be Anson anymore, what would happen?" This final step aims to provide an experiential moment for the contemplation of non-self, thereby helping the client realize the suffering that arises from clinging to a self-notion and the peaceful feelings and potentiality of letting go of the desire to hold onto a self-notion.

Figure 8.1: "A Little Emptiness Exercise" Illustration

In response, Anson was expected to gain more understanding of how his loneliness and fear of rejection of his self-notion urged him to cheat, realizing that he might not have to hold so tightly on to this identity.

Another important step in the treatment was to address his main presenting problem: physical and psychological aversion towards the body of his girlfriend. He froze when he became physically close to his girlfriend, although he did not have any problem with other girls. This confusing experience resulted in many doubts, worries, and self-blame. The counselor tried to explore the background cognitive events of such behavior more thoroughly in order to trace potential reasons and find solutions.

> Buddhist counselor: "What comes to your mind when you're physically close to her?" (*Exploring cognitive events.*)
>
> Anson: "I think . . . a girl should not be this way . . . I compare her body to other girls and I feel uncomfortable. Then I usually go away or freeze. I think she feels hurt by me doing that."
>
> Buddhist counselor: "Let's come back to that moment. Did your mind say anything else?" (*Exploring cognitive events.*)
>
> Anson: "That's fat . . . That's not right . . . that's lazy . . . she shouldn't be this way."
>
> Buddhist counselor: "Lazy? It's interesting that the label 'lazy' came up."
>
> Anson (pondering for a few seconds): "Maybe she reminds me of how fat I was . . . people kept saying I was lazy and useless. My parents kept forcing me to study, but I didn't like the subjects, so I got very bad grades. Then they gave up on me. I think I was never recognized as someone who could handle problems and, in fact, I've been escaping from various responsibilities for years."
>
> Buddhist counselor: "It seems like you've used your parents' definition and treatment of you to define yourself as "weak" and "lazy." This label has given you lots of suffering and made you feel that you have to run away from problems. Is that how you want to keep defining yourself?" (*Identifying notion of self and how clinging to it causes suffering.*)
>
> Anson: "No! I do want to change. I've had enough of it. I want to stop running away from problems . . . but I just don't know how."

Initially, Anson held tightly onto the self-view of "fat boy Anson" as a weak and unlovable person and tried hard to receive love and acceptance in work and relationships. After several sessions of exploration, Anson was able to gain insight into how his physical rejection of his girlfriend as well as his aversion to all fat people may be related to his holding on to the "fat boy Anson" identity. This insight helped him detach from this existing view and flexibly foster a new, more wholesome, and realistic view of himself and his relationship, thereby getting closer to a Right View or non-grasped view. This new and more wholesome view can also foster compassion for his girlfriend.

8.5.5 Component 5: Experiential Practice

Finally, and perhaps most importantly, it was necessary to invite Anson to experience a Buddhist-inspired practice. This is usually carried out using different types of meditation together with a Buddhist counselor in session. For example, Anson was dwelling on his conceptual proliferations of the past and launched a ruminative self-blame game that made his mind lose touch with reality. His mood was going downhill, his body seemed lethargic, and his voice was soft and bitter. The counselor tried to use an experiential mindfulness practice to help him recenter his mind in the present moment.

> Buddhist counselor: "What do you like to do?"
>
> Anson: "Me?" (Pausing for a few seconds.) "I like playing basketball."
>
> Buddhist counselor: "Really? I like that too! What position do you play?"
>
> Anson: "Well, I used to play power forward or even center, but now that I'm getting old, usually I just make far shots." (This conversation went on for about three minutes during which the client evinced more energy.)
>
> Buddhist counselor: "Let's pause for a moment and notice the process here. You talked faster, had more energy in your speech, and your eyes opened much wider. What happened at this moment?" (*Somatic reflection to bring Anson's mind back to the present moment.*)
>
> Anson: "That's right! When talking about basketball, I felt much more energetic and felt less depressed."
>
> Buddhist counselor: "This moment is an important point of awareness that lets you know that what you choose to focus on directly influences your mood, and that you actually have the power to disengage from those ruminative thoughts and re-center your mind on the present moment." (*Reflecting the Right View mind state by staying in the present moment.*)

Benefiting from guided mindful breathing during the session, Anson began to become more aware of moments in which he was beset by conceptual proliferations. He was more motivated to practice mindful breathing by himself and he was able to foster more mental distance from the thoughts that proliferated, thereby nurturing his potential to disengage from depressive thoughts and images as well as re-center his mind on neutral or pleasant aspects in his body and environment in the present moment.

As measured by the mindfulness scale, Anson developed strong stability and clarity of mind after eight sessions of counseling. In the sessions before and after meditating with Anson, the counselor provided guidance to help Anson deepen his practice, such as correcting his seating posture and helping him sustain mindfulness on an object of meditation. To address his aversion towards his girlfriend, the counselor also used a visualization exercise for a more in-depth experiential practice. First, the counselor used mindful breathing to help Anson become more aware of his body and mind and sustain mindfulness on his in-and-out breaths. Second, the counselor invited Anson to recall moments of physical closeness with his girlfriend and notice the unpleasant feelings and perceptions that arose in the process. At that moment, Anson would maintain a meditative state with his eyes closed while verbally communicating his experiences to the counselor. In the visualization, Anson noticed unpleasant mental feelings, perceptions of "fat" and "lazy," and a strong feeling of resistance just by touching his girlfriend's arms. Third, the counselor experimented with Anson to guide him to slow down the thinking process and visualize himself touching her hands and other non-sexual parts of the body, although Anson's aversion stayed the same. Fourth, the counselor invited Anson to look at the warm smile on his girlfriend's face. Anson said that the aversion and resistance in the body suddenly stopped and he was able to feel compassion radiating to him from his girlfriend, conveying a message of love and acceptance. The counselor then guided Anson to visualize walking closer to his girlfriend. Without the counselor's guidance, Anson imagined hugging his girlfriend, thanking her, apologizing to her, after which he burst into tears. At that moment, the counselor invited Anson to be mindful of his bodily sensations and any resistance. Interestingly, Anson described that the tension and resistance in his body dissolved and he was able to visually hold his girlfriend tight without any aversion.

After the meditation, Anson realized that his love for his girlfriend and his feelings of receiving acceptance and compassion from her were keys to dissolving his aversion towards his undesirable body image of himself and his girlfriend. A mundane skillful means that he could act on was to take some deep breaths during any moment of resistance and shift his attention to something warm and loving, such as his girlfriend's smile. Anson also claimed that he was done running away from conflicts and he would try to face this difficulty with his girlfriend and foster a stable relationship with her until the end of his life. Although he might not have reached an ultimate Right View and liberated himself completely from his present suffering, the path towards the Right View was able to help him reduce a significant amount of suffering and recover from clinical-level depression.

8.6 Conclusion

This chapter integrated the entire theoretical orientation into a counseling case as a demonstration of Buddhist teaching in action. To reiterate an important message of this book, Early Buddhist teachings possess sufficient source information to develop a standalone theoretical orientation for professional counseling. This Buddhist counseling approach is supplemented by the traditional counseling framework and associated techniques, while the direction of treatment and clinical decisions are all driven by core Buddhist teachings, especially those arising from non-self and Right View. However, this book is just one effort in developing a Buddhist theoretical orientation, so we encourage scholars and practitioners from other Buddhist schools and traditions to develop specific theoretical orientations for counseling according to their interpretations of Buddhist teachings. In this way, we can better apply Buddhist teachings to the field of professional counseling. The next step would then be for researchers to conduct empirical studies on this model and make modifications and adaptations in order to make Buddhist counseling an evidence-based treatment of choice. This endeavor will likely benefit millions of individuals who are affiliated with Buddhism, as well as provide hope for the establishment of a culturally congruent treatment approach to match clients' specific backgrounds and needs.

Bibliography

Primary Sources (Pāli)

Aṅguttara-nikāya. Vol. i. Edited by A. K. Warder. London: PTS, 1961.

Aṅguttara-nikāya. Vol. ii. Edited by Richard Morris. London: PTS, 1976.

Aṅguttara-nikāya. Vol. iii. Edited by E. Hardy. London: PTS, 1976.

Aṅguttara-nikāya. Vol. iv; v. Edited by E. Hardy. London: PTS, 1958.

Dhammapada. Edited by O. Von Hinuber and K. R. Norman. Oxford: PTS, 1995.

Dhammapada-aṭṭhakthā (*The commentary on the Dhammapada*). Vol. i. Edited by H. C. Norman. London: PTS, 1970.

Dīgha-nikāya. Vol. i. Edited by T. W. Rhys Davids and J. Estlin Carpenter. London: PTS, 1975.

Dīgha-nikāya. Vol. ii. Edited by T. W. Rhys Davids and J. Estlin Carpenter. London: PTS, 1966.

Dīgha-nikāya. Vol. iii. Edited by J. E. Carpenter. London: PTS, 1976.

Dhammasaṅgaṇī. Edited by. Edward Muller. London: PTS, 1978.

Iti-vuttaka. Edited by Ernst Windisch. London: PTS. 1975.

Khuddaka-pāṭha: *Together with It Commentary* (*Paramatthajotikā* I.). Edited by Helmer Smit. London: PTS, 1978.

Majjhima-nikāya. Vol. i. Edited by V. Trenckner. London: PTS, 1979.

Majjhima-nikāya. Vol. ii; iii. Edited by Robert Chalmers. London: PTS, 1977.

Saṃyutta-nikāya. Vol. i. Edited by F. L. Woodward. London: PTS, 1977.

Saṃyutta-nikāya. Vol. ii. Edited by M. Leon Feer. London: PTS, 1989.

Saṃyutta-nikāya. Vol. iii. Edited by M. Leon Feer. London: PTS, 1975.

Saṃyutta-nikāya. Vol. iv. Edited by M. Leon Feer. London: PTS, 1990.

Saṃyutta-nikāya. Vol. v. Edited by M. Leon Feer. London: PTS, 1976.

Sutta Nipāta. Edited by Dines Andersen and Helmer Smith. London: PTS, 1913.

Udāna. Edited by Paul Steinthal. London: PTS, 1982.

Vibhaṃga. Edited by Rhys Davids. London: PTS, 1978.

Primary Sources (English Translations)

Bodhi, Bhikkhu. *The Connected Discourses of the Buddha: A New Translation of the Saṃyutta Nikāya*. Translated by Bhikkhu Bodhi. Boston: Wisdom Publications, 2000.

Bodhi, Bhikkhu. *The Middle Length Discourses of the Buddha: A Translation of the Majjhima Nikāya*. Translated by Bhikkhu Bodhi. Boston: Wisdom Publications, 1995.

Bodhi, Bhikkhu. *The Numerical Discourses of the Buddha: A Complete Translation of the Aṅguttara Nikāya*. Translated by Bhikkhu Bodhi. Boston: Wisdom Publications, 2012.

Walshe, Maurice. *The Long Discourses of the Buddha: A Translation of the Dīgha Nikāya*. Translated by Maurice Walshe. Boston: Wisdom Publications, 1995.

Secondary Sources

Abeysekara, Ananda. "Buddhism, Power, Modernity. Gathering Leaves and Lifting Words: Histories of Buddhist Monastic Education in Laos and Thailand." *Culture and Religion* 12, no. 4 (2011): 489–97.

Amaro, Ajahn. "Unshakeable Well-Being: Is the Buddhist Concept of Enlightenment a Meaningful Possibility in the Current Age." *Mindfulness* 10, no. 9 (2019): 1952–56. https://doi.org/10.1007/s12671-019-01179-7.

American Counseling Association. "20/20: Consensus Definition of Counseling." ACA (WEBusage), 2014. Accessed October 2, 2024. https://archive.counseling.org/docs/david-kaplan's-files/consensus-definition-of-counseling.docx?sfvrsn=4383304b_2.

Anālayo, Bhikkhu. *Satipaṭṭhāna: The Direct Path to Realization*. Kandy: Buddhist Publication Society, 2010.

Anālayo, Bhikkhu. "The Role of Mindfulness in the Cultivation of Absorption." *Mindfulness* 10, no. 11 (2019): 2341–51. https://doi.org/10.1007/s12671-019-01206-7.

Anālayo, Bhikkhu. *Satipaṭṭhāna Meditation: A Practice Guide*. London: Windhorse Publication, 2018.

Arbel, Keren. *Early Buddhist Meditation: The Four Jhānas as the Actualization of Insight*. New York: Routledge, 2017.

Ash, Marcia, Timothy Harrison, Melissa Pinto, Ralph DiClemente, and Lobsang Tenzin Negi. "A Model for Cognitively-Based Compassion Training: Theoretical Underpinnings and Proposed Mechanisms." *Social Theory & Health* 19, no. 1 (2021): 43–67. https://doi.org/10.1057/s41285-019-00124-x.

A-Tjak, Jacqueline G. L., Michelle L Davis, Nexhmedin Morina, Mark B Powers, Jasper A. J. Smits, and Paul M. G. Emmelkamp. "A Meta-Analysis of the Efficacy of Acceptance and Commitment Therapy for Clinically Relevant Mental and Physical Health Problems." *Psychotherapy and Psychosomatics* 84, no. 1 (2015): 30–36.

Basten, Christopher, and Stephen Touyz. "Sense of Self: Its Place in Personality Disturbance, Psychopathology, and Normal Experience." *Review of General Psychology* 24, no. 2 (2020): 159–71.

Beck, Judith S. *Cognitive Behavior Therapy: Basics and Beyond*. 2nd ed. New York: Guilford Press, 2011.

Benish, Steven G., Stephen Quintana, and Bruce E. Wampold. "Culturally Adapted Psychotherapy and the Legitimacy of Myth: A Direct-Comparison Meta-Analysis." *Journal of Counseling Psychology* 58, no. 3 (2011): 279–89.

Bianco, Simone, Paolo Barilaro, and Arianna Palmieri. "Traditional Meditation, Mindfulness and Psychodynamic Approach: An Integrative Perspective." *Frontiers in Psychology* 7 (2016): 552–62.

Bland, Andrew M. "Existential Givens in the COVID-19 Crisis." *The Journal of Humanistic Psychology* 60, no. 5 (2020): 710–24.

Böge, Kerem, Inge Hahne, Niklas Bergmann, Katja Wingenfeld, Marco Zierhut, Neil Thomas, Thi Minh Tam Ta, Malek Bajbouj, and Eric Hahn. "Mindfulness-Based Group Therapy for In-Patients with Schizophrenia Spectrum Disorders—Feasibility, Acceptability, and Preliminary Outcomes of a Rater-Blinded Randomized Controlled Trial." *Schizophrenia research* 228 (2021): 134–44.

Bodhi, Bhikkhu. *The Great Discourse on Causation: The Mahānidāna Sutta and Its Commentaries*. 2nd ed. Kandy: Buddhist Publication Society, 1995.

Bodhi, Bhikkhu, and Nanamoli, Bhikkhu. *The Discourse on Right View: The Sammaditthi Sutta and Its Commentary*. Sri Lanka: Buddhist Publication Society, 1998.

Bodhi, Bhikkhu. "The Noble Eightfold Path: The Way to the End of Suffering." *Access to Insight (BCBS Edition)*, November 30, 2013, http://www.accesstoinsight.org/lib/authors/bodhi/waytoend.html.

Borchert, Thomas A, and Mark Michael Rowe. *Educating Monks: Minority Buddhism on China's Southwest Border*. Honolulu: University of Hawaii Press, 2017.

Bornaetxea, Fernando Rodríguez, David Alvear Morón, Antonio Arrébola Gil, and Andrew Alexander Hastings Molloy. "Construction Of Reality or Dependent Origination? From Scientific Psychotherapy to Responsible Attention." *Contemporary Buddhism* 15, no. 2 (2014): 216–43.

Britton, Willoughby B., Jared R. Lindahl, B. Rael Cahn, Jake H. Davis, and Roberta E. Goldman. "Awakening Is Not a Metaphor: The Effects of Buddhist Meditation Practices on Basic Wakefulness: Meditation and Wakefulness." *Annals of the New York Academy of Sciences* 1307, no. 1 (2014): 64–81.

Brown, Daniel, and Jack Engler. "The Stages of Mindfulness Meditation: A Validation Study." *The Journal of Transpersonal Psychology* 12, no. 2 (1980): 143–93.

Canda, Edward R, and Sachiko Gomi. "Zen Philosophy of Spiritual Development: Insights about Human Development and Spiritual Diversity for Social Work Education." *Journal of Religion & Spirituality in Social Work* 38, no. 1 (2019): 43–67.

Cardaciotto, LeeAnn, James D. Herbert, Evan M. Forman, Ethan Moitra, and Victoria Farrow. "The Assessment of Present-Moment Awareness and Acceptance." *Assessment* 15, no. 2 (2008): 204–23.

Chia, Jack Meng-Tat. "Toward a Modern Buddhist Hagiography: Telling the Life of Hsing Yun in Popular Media." *Asian Ethnology* 74, no. 1 (2015): 141–65.

Chaplaincy Innovation Lab. "Buddhist Chaplaincy." Accessed October 13, 2022. https://chaplaincyinnovation.org/resources/faith-tradition/buddhist-chaplaincy.

Cox, Collett. "Dependent Origination: Its Elaboration in Early Sarvastivadin Abhidharma Texts." In *Researches in Indian and Buddhist philosophy: Essays in Honor of*

Professor Alex Wayman, edited by Ram Karan Sharma, 119–41. Delhi: Motilal Banarsidass, 1993.

陳慶餘 (Ching-Yu Chen).〈癌末病人死亡恐懼之臨床情境：臨床佛教宗教師參與靈性照顧〉.《台灣醫學》18, no. 1 (2014): 115–25.

Crago, Hugh. "Counselling and Psychotherapy: Is There a Difference? Does It Matter?" *Australian and New Zealand Journal of Family Therapy* 21, no. 2 (2000): 73–80.

Chaudhuri, Rachita. *Buddhist Education in Ancient India*. Kolkata: Punthi Pustak, 2008.

Crosby, Kate. "The Inheritance of Rāhula: Abandoned Child, Boy Monk, Ideal Son and Trainee." In *Little Buddhas: Children and Childhoods in Buddhist Texts and Traditions*, edited by Vanessa R. Sasson, 97–123. Oxford: Oxford University Press, 2013.

Davidson, Richard J., Daniel J. Goleman, and Gary E. Schwartz. "Attentional and Affective Concomitants of Meditation: A Cross-Sectional Study." *Journal of Abnormal Psychology* 85, no. 2 (1976): 235–38.

Davidson, Richard J., and Daniel J. Goleman. "The Role of Attention in Meditation and Hypnosis: A Psychobiological Perspective on Transformations of Consciousness." *International Journal of Clinical and Experimental Hypnosis* 25, no. 4 (October 1977): 291–308. https://doi.org/10.1080/00207147708415986.

Deatherage, Gary. "The Clinical Use of 'Mindfulness' Meditation Techniques in Short-Term Psychotherapy." *Journal of Transpersonal Psychology* 7, no. 2 (1975): 133–43.

DeCou, Christopher R., Katherine Anne Comtois, and Sara J. Landes. "Dialectical Behavior Therapy Is Effective for the Treatment of Suicidal Behavior: A Meta-Analysis." *Behavior Therapy* 50, no. 1 (2019): 60–72.

Dessein, Bart. "The Significance of the Buddhist 10-Membered Formula of Dependent Origination." *Asian Philosophy* 24, no. 1 (2014): 1–13. doi:10.1080/09552367.2014.867639.

Dippmann, Jeffrey. W. Review of *Little Buddhas: Children and Childhoods in Buddhist Texts and Traditions*, edited by Vanessa R. Sassoon. *Choice* 50, no. 12 (August 2013): 2248.

Dobkin, Patricia L., Julie A. Irving, and Simon Amar. "For Whom May Participation in a Mindfulness-Based Stress Reduction Program Be Contraindicated?" *Mindfulness* 3, no. 1 (2011): 44–50.

Murguia, Edward, and Kim Diaz. "The Philosophical Foundations of Cognitive Behavioral Therapy: Stoicism, Buddhism, Taoism, and Existentialism." *Journal of Evidence-Based Psychotherapies* 15, no. 1 (2015): 37–50.

Ellis, Gabriel. 2020. "Dependent Origination as Emergence of the Subject – A Cognitive-Psychological Approach." Contemporary Buddhism 21 (1–2): 263–83. doi:10.1080/14639947.2021.1988214.

Feliu-Soler, Albert, Joaquim Soler, Juan V. Luciano, Ausiàs Cebolla, Matilde Elices, Marcelo Demarzo, and Javier García-Campayo. "Psychometric Properties of the Spanish Version of the Nonattachment Scale (NAS) and Its Relationship with Mindfulness, Decentering, and Mental Health." *Mindfulness* 7, no. 5 (2016): 1156–69.

Fond-Harmant, Laurence, and Mihaela Gavrila-ardelean. "The Contribution of the Human Development Theory for the Education and Mental Health of the Child." *Journal Plus Education / Educatia Plus* 14 (May 2, 2016): 174–81.
Fiedler, Fred E. "The Concept of an Ideal Therapeutic Relationship." *Journal of Consulting Psychology* 14, no. 4 (1950): 239–45.
Frank, Jerome D., and Julia B. Frank. *Persuasion and Healing: A Comparative Study of Psychotherapy*. 3rd ed. Baltimore: Johns Hopkins University Press, 1991.
Freud, Sigmund. "A Differentiating Grade in the Ego." In *Group Psychology and the Analysis of the Ego*, translated by James Strachey, 101–9. Boni and Liveright, 1922. https://doi.org/10.1037/11327-011.
Fuller, Paul. *The Notion of Ditthi in Theravada Buddhism*. London: Routledge, 2005.
Fung, Kenneth. "Acceptance and Commitment Therapy: Western Adoption of Buddhist Tenets?" *Transcultural Psychiatry* 52, no. 4 (August 2015): 561–76. https://doi.org/10.1177/1363461514537544.
Gauthier, Tina Jitsujo. "Hope in the Midst of Suffering: A Buddhist Perspective." *Journal of Pastoral Theology* 26, no. 2 (2016): 133–37.
Gehart, Diane R. *Mastering Competencies in Family Therapy: A Practical Approach to Theories and Clinical Case Documentation*. 2nd ed. Belmont, CA: Brooks/Cole, Cengage Learning, 2014.
Gehart, Diane R. *Theory and Treatment Planning in Counseling and Psychotherapy*. 2nd ed. Boston, MA: Cengage Learning, 2016.
Gethin, Rupert. "Wrong View (micchā-di Hi) and Right View (sammā-diṭṭhi) in the Theravada Abhidhamma." *Contemporary Buddhism* 5, no. 1 (2004): 15–28.
Gethin, Rupert. *The Foundations of Buddhism*. Oxford: Oxford University Press, 1998.
Gomez, Luis O. "Proto-Mādhyamika in the Pāli Canon." *Philosophy East & West* 26, no. 2 (1976): 137–65.
Hansen, James C., Richard R. Stevic, and Richard W. Warner. *Counseling: Theory and Process*. 4th ed. Boston: Allyn and Bacon, 1986.
Harrington, Anne, and John D. Dunne. "When Mindfulness is Therapy: Ethical Qualms, Historical Perspectives." *The American Psychologist* 70, no. 7 (2015): 621–31.
Harter, Susan, and William M. Bukowski. *The Construction of the Self: Developmental and Sociocultural Foundations*. 2nd ed. New York: Guilford Press, 2012.
Harvey, Peter. *An Introduction to Buddhism: Teaching, History and Practice*. 2nd ed. Cambridge: Cambridge University Press, 2013.
Hattie, John. *Self-Concept*. Hillsdale, NJ: L. Erlbaum Associates, 1992.
Hayes, Steven C. "Buddhism and Acceptance and Commitment Therapy." *Cognitive and Behavioral Practice* 9, no. 1 (2002): 58–66.
Hayes, Steven C., Kirk Strosahl, and Kelly G. Wilson. *Acceptance and Commitment Therapy: An Experiential Approach to Behavior Change*. New York: Guilford Press, 1999.
Ho, S. Shaun, Yoshio Nakamura, Meroona Gopang, and James E. Swain. "Intersubjectivity as an Antidote to Stress: Using Dyadic Active Inference Model of Intersubjectivity to Predict the Efficacy of Parenting Interventions in Reducing Stress—through the

Lens of Dependent Origination in Buddhist Madhyamaka Philosophy." *Frontiers in Psychology* 13 (2022): 806755.

Hofmann, Stefan G. *An Introduction to Modern CBT [electronic resource] : Psychological Solutions to Mental Health Problems*. Chichester, West Sussex, UK; Malden, MA: Wiley-Blackwell, 2012.

Husband, Richard W. "Can an Eclectic Position be Sound?" *Psychological Review* 41, no. 4 (1934): 368–80. https://doi.org/10.1037/h0072841.

Hunter, Murray. "Dependent Origination as a Natural Governing Law." *Contemporary Readings in Law and Social Justice* 4, no. 2 (2012): 116–77.

Huxter, Malcolm John. "Mindfulness as Therapy from a Buddhist Perspective." In *Innovations and Advances in Cognitive Behaviour Therapy*, 43–53. 1st ed. Bowen Hills, Qld: Australian Academic Press, 2007.

Hyland, Terry. "McMindfulness in the Workplace: Vocational Learning and the Commodification of the Present Moment." *Journal of Vocational Education & Training* 67, no. 2 (2015): 219–34.

Ivey, Allen E., Mary Bradford Ivey, and Lynn Simek-Downing. *Counseling and Psychotherapy: Integrating Skills, Theory, and Practice*. 2nd ed. Englewood Cliffs: Prentice-Hall, 1987.

James, William. *The Principles of Psychology*. Cambridge, MA: Harvard University Press, 1890.

Jones-Smith, Elsie. *Theories of Counseling and Psychotherapy: An Integrative Approach*. 2nd ed. Thousand Oaks, CA: SAGE, 2016.

Jones, Dhivan Thomas. "New Light on the Twelve Nidānas." *Contemporary Buddhism* 10, no. 2 (2009): 241–59.

Jonutytė, Kristina. "Beyond 'Bad' Buddhism: Conceptualizing Buddhist Counseling in Ulan-Ude, Buryatia." *Journal of Global Buddhism* 21 (2020): 261–76.

Kabat-Zinn, Jon. "An Outpatient Program in Behavioral Medicine for Chronic Pain Patients Based on the Practice of Mindfulness Meditation: Theoretical Considerations and Preliminary Results." *General Hospital Psychiatry* 4, no. 1 (April 1982): 33–47.

Kabat-Zinn, Jon. "Mindfulness-Based Interventions in Context: Past, Present, and Future." *Clinical Psychology* 10, no. 2 (2003): 144–56.

Kabat-Zinn, Jon. *Full Catastrophe Living: Using the Wisdom of Your Body and Mind to Face Stress, Pain and Illness*. New York: Delta Trade Paperbacks, 1991.

Kabat-Zinn, Jon. "Some Reflections on the Origins of MBSR, Skillful Means, and the Trouble with Maps." *Contemporary Buddhism* 12, no. 1 (2011): 281–306.

Kaplan, Uri. *Monastic Education in Korea: Teaching Monks about Buddhism in the Modern Age*. Honolulu: University of Hawaii Press, 2020.

Karunadasa, Yakupitiyage. *Early Buddhist Teachings: The Middle Position in Theory and Practice*. Hong Kong: Centre of Buddhist Studies, HKU, 2013.

Karunadasa, Yakupitiyage. *The Theravada Abhidhamma: Its Inquiry into the Nature of Conditioned Reality*. Hong Kong: Centre of Buddhist Studies, HKU, 2010.

Karunadasa, Yakupitiyage. "Buddhist Psychology of Philosophy." How Buddhism Looks at Philosophical and Psychological Views and Theories. Class lecture at Buddha-Dharma Centre of Hong Kong, China, June 21, 2019.

Karunadasa, Yakupitiyage. "*Theravāda Abhidhamma: Origins and Development*." Paññatti Class lecture at Buddha-Dharma Centre of Hong Kong, China, May 14, 2019.

Karunadasa, Yakupitiyage. *The Theravada Abhidhamma: Its Inquiry into the Nature of Conditioned Reality*. Hong Kong: Centre of Buddhist Studies, HKU, 2010.

Kelly, Brendan D. "Beyond Mindfulness: Buddhist Psychology and the Abhidharma." *Journal of Spirituality in Mental Health* 25, no. 1 (2023): 71–82.

Kim, Jookyoung. "Consideration of the Applicability of Person-centered Therapy to Culturally Varying Clients, Focusing on the Actualizing Tendency and Self-actualization—from East Asian Perspective." *Person-Centered & Experiential Psychotherapies* 17, no. 3 (2018): 201–23.

Koul, Rekha, Geeta Verma, and Vanashri Nargund-Joshi. *Science Education in India: Philosophical, Historical, and Contemporary Conversations*. Singapore: Springer, 2019.

Lee, Kin Cheung. *The Guide to Buddhist Counseling*. London: Routledge, 2022.

Lee, Kin Cheung (George). "Introduction to a Buddhist Counselling Technique Based on Early Buddhist Teachings: Mind Moment Analysis." Contemporary Buddhism 21, no. 1–2 (2020): 241–62.

Lee, Kin Cheung (George), and Chez Kuang Ong. "The Satipaṭṭhāna Sutta: An Application of Buddhist Mindfulness for Counsellors." *Contemporary Buddhism* 19, no. 2 (2019): 327–41.

Lee, Kin Cheung (George), Alice Oh, Qianru Zhao, Fang-Yi Wu, Shiyun Chen, Thomas Ong Diaz, and Chez Kuang. "Buddhist Counseling: Implications for Mental Health Professionals." *Spirituality in Clinical Practice* 4, no. 2 (2017). 113–28.

Lee, Kin Cheung (George), and Jessica Lut Ki Tang. "Note, Know, Choose: A Psychospiritual Treatment Model Based on Early Buddhist Teachings." *Spirituality in Clinical Practice* 10, no. 2 (2023): 150–67.

Li, Deming, Jiuhong Xu, Fang Liu, Xinjing Wang, Huanhuan Yang, and Xinli Li. "Alcohol Drinking and the Risk of Chronic Kidney Damage: A Meta-Analysis of 15 Prospective Cohort Studies." *Alcoholism, Clinical and Experimental Research* 43, no. 7 (2019): 1360–72.

Linehan, Marsha. *Cognitive-Behavioral Treatment of Borderline Personality Disorder*. New York: Guilford Press, 1993.

Liu, Wei. "Recognition of, and Beliefs about, Causes of Mental Disorders: A Cross-sectional Study of US and Chinese Undergraduate Nursing Students." *Nursing & Health Sciences* 21, no. 1 (2019): 28–36.

Los Angeles County Department of Mental Health. "Infancy, Childhood & Relationship Enrichment Initial Assessment." MH-645. May 4, 2023. https://file.lacounty.gov/SDSInter/dmh/1069490_MH-645InfancyChildhoodAssessment2-20-20fillable.pdf.

Spalek, Mark, and Basia Spalek. *Integrative Counselling and Psychotherapy*. London: Routledge, 2019.

McCartney, Mark, Sarah Nevitt, Annette Lloyd, Ruaraidh Hill, Ross White, and Rui Duarte. "Mindfulness-Based Cognitive Therapy for Prevention and Time to Depressive Relapse: Systematic Review and Network Meta-analysis." *Acta Psychiatrica Scandinavica* 143, no. 1 (2021): 6–21.

McWilliams, Spencer A. "Contemplating a Contemporary Constructivist Buddhist Psychology." Review of *New Horizons in Buddhist Psychology: Relational Buddhism for Collaborative Practitioners,* edited by Maurits G. T. KweeChagrin. *Journal of Constructivist Psychology* 24, no. 3 (2011): 268–76.

Meares, Russell. "The Conversational Model: An Outline." *American Journal of Psychotherapy* 58, no. 1 (2004): 51–66.

Murdock, Nancy L. *Theories of Counseling and Psychotherapy: A Case Approach*. 4th ed. New York: Pearson, 2017.

Mookerji, Radhakumud. *Ancient Indian Education: Brahmanical and Buddhist.* 4th ed. Delhi: Motilal Banarsidass, 1989.

Nakagawa, Yasuyoshi. "The Child as Compassionate Bodhisattva and as Human Sufferer/Spiritual Seeker: Intertwined Buddhist Images." In *Nurturing Child and Adolescent Spirituality: Perspectives from the World's Religious Traditions*, edited by K. M. Yust et al., 33–42. Lanham, MD: Rowman & Littlefield, 2006.

Nārada, Thera. *Buddhism in a Nutshell.* 1st ed. Sri Lanka: Buddhist Publication Society, 2013.

Neale, Miles. "McMindfulness and Frozen Yoga: Rediscovering the Essential Teachings of Ethics and Wisdom." Accessed September 1, 2022, https://static1.squarespace.com/static/5a8e29ffcd39c3de866b5e14/t/5b5303d91ae6cf630b641909/1532167130908/McMindfulness.pdf (site discontinued).

Negi, Lobsang Tenzin, Thaddeus W. W. Pace, B. Alan Wallace, Charles L. Raison, and Eric L. Schwartz. "Effects of Eight-Week Meditation Training on Hippocampal Volume: A Comparison of Mindful Attention Training and Cognitively-Based Compassion Training." *Journal of Alternative & Complementary Medicine* 20, no. 5 (May 2014): A24. https://doi.org/10.1089/acm.2014.5059.abstract.

Nelson-Jones, Richard. *Nelson-Jones' Theory and Practice of Counselling and Psychotherapy*. 6th ed. London: SAGE Publications Ltd, 2015.

Ng, Siu-man, King Wo Chow, Hi Po Lau, and Qi Wang. "Awareness Versus Un-Clinging: Which Matters in Mindfulness?" *Contemporary Buddhism* 18, no. 2 (2017): 277–91.

Nupponen, Ritva. "What Is Counseling All About: Basics in the Counseling of Health-Related Physical Activity." *Patient Education and Counseling* 33, S1 (1998): S61–67.

Paris, Joel. "How the History of Psychotherapy Interferes with Integration." *Journal of Psychotherapy Integration* 23, no. 2 (2013): 99–106.

Panos, Patrick T., John W. Jackson, Omar Hasan, and Angelea Panos. "Meta-Analysis and Systematic Review Assessing the Efficacy of Dialectical Behavior Therapy (DBT)." *Research on Social Work Practice* 24, no. 2 (2014): 213–23.

Piaget, Jean. "Part I: Cognitive Development in Children—Piaget Development and Learning." *Journal of Research in Science Teaching* 2, no. 3 (September 1, 1964): 176–186. https://doi.org/10.1002/tea.3660020306.

Piet, Jacob, and Esben Hougaard. "The Effect of Mindfulness-Based Cognitive Therapy for Prevention of Relapse in Recurrent Major Depressive Disorder: A Systematic Review and Meta-Analysis." *Clinical Psychology Review* 31, no. 6 (2011): 1032–40.

Poehlmann-Tynan, Julie, Ashleigh Engbretson, Abra B. Vigna, Lindsay A. Weymouth, Cynthia Burnson, Carolyn Zahn-Waxler, Amita Kapoor, Emily D Gerstein, Kerrie A.

Fanning, and Charles L. Raison. "Cognitively-Based Compassion Training for Parents Reduces Cortisol in Infants and Young Children." *Infant Mental Health Journal* 41, no. 1 (January 2020): 126–44. https://doi.org/10.1002/imhj.21831.

Poznanski, Joseph J., and Jim McLennan. "Conceptualizing and Measuring Counselors' Theoretical Orientation." *Journal of Counseling Psychology* 42, no. 4 (1995): 411–22.

Poznanski, Joseph J., and Jim McLennan. "Becoming a Psychologist with a Particular Theoretical Orientation to Counselling Practice." *Australian Psychologist* 38, no. 3 (2003): 223–26.

Tengland, Per-Anders. "Psychoanalysis, Humanistic Psychology, and Positive Mental Health." In *Mental Health: A Philosophical Analysis*, 35–45. Dordrecht: Springer, 2001. https://doi.org/10.1007/978-94-017-2237-7 3.

Rahman, Azhar Bin Abdul, Mohd Nizam Sahad, and Suhaila Abdullah. "The Concept of Right View in Buddhism from the Islamic Perspective." *Procedia, Social and Behavioral Sciences* 91 (2013): 72–77.

Reddy, M. S., and Starlin M. Vijay. "Empirical Reality of Dialectical Behavioral Therapy in Borderline Personality." *Indian Journal of Psychological Medicine* 39, no. 2 (2017): 105–8.

Reddy, Sheethal D., Lobsang Tenzin Negi, Brooke Dodson-Lavelle, Brendan Ozawa-de Silva, Thaddeus W. W. Pace, Steve P. Cole, Charles L. Raison, and Linda W. Craighead. "Cognitive-Based Compassion Training: A Promising Prevention Strategy for At-Risk Adolescents." *Journal of Child and Family Studies* 22, no. 2 (February 2013): 219–30. https://doi.org/10.1007/s10826-012-9571-7.

Revatadhamma, Sayadaw. *The First Discourse of the Buddha: Turning the Wheel of Dhamma*. Boston, MA: Wisdom Publications, 1997.

Robertson, Donald. "Rational Emotion in Stoicism and CBT." In *The Philosophy of Cognitive-Behavioural Therapy (CBT)*, 71–99. 2nd ed. London: Routledge, 2020.

Rogers, Carl Ransom. "A Theory of Therapy, Personality, and Interpersonal Relationships, as Developed in the Client-Centered Framework." New York: McGraw Hill, 1959.

Rehm, Jürgen, Kevin D. Shield, Narges Joharchi, and Paul A. Shuper. "Alcohol Consumption and the Intention to Engage in Unprotected Sex: Systematic Review and Meta-Analysis of Experimental Studies." *Addiction* 107, no. 1 (2012): 51–59.

Rungreangkulkij, Somporn, and Wiwat Wongtakee. "The Psychological Impact of Buddhist Counseling for Patients Suffering from Symptoms of Anxiety." *Archives of Psychiatric Nursing* 22, no. 3 (2008): 127–34.

Sakdalan, Joseph Allan, and Rajan Gupta. "Wise Mind-Risky Mind: A Reconceptualisation of Dialectical Behaviour Therapy Concepts and Its Application to Sexual Offender Treatment." *The Journal of Sexual Aggression* 20, no. 1 (2014): 110–20.

Salisbury, Justin. "Client-Centered Therapy Versus Rational Emotive Behavior Therapy: Applications in Adjustment-to-Blindness Training." *Journal of Blindness Innovation and Research* 11, no. 1 (2021). https://doi.org/10.5241/11-196.

Sanford, Monica, and Nathan Jishin Michon. "Buddhist Chaplaincy." *Oxford Research Encyclopedias*. New York: Oxford University Press, 2019.

Sasson, Vanessa R. "Buddhism and Children." *Child Abuse & Neglect* 38, no. 4 (2014): 593–99.

Schmidt, Andreas T. "The Ethics and Politics of Mindfulness-Based Interventions." *Journal of Medical Ethics* 42, no. 7 (2016): 450–54. https://doi.org/10.1136/medethics-2015-102942.

Sears, Richard W. *The Sense of Self.* London: Palgrave Macmillan, 2016.

Segal, Zindel V., J. Mark G. Williams, and John D. Teasdale. *Mindfulness-Based Cognitive Therapy for Depression: A New Approach to Preventing Relapse*. New York: Guilford Press, 2002.

Shah, Monica. "Acceptance-Based Therapies and Asian Philosophical Traditions: Similarities and Differences in the Concept of Acceptance." *Journal of Rational-Emotive and Cognitive-Behavior Therapy* 39, no 1 (2020): 1–13.

Shamdasani, Sonu. "Towards Transcultural Histories of Psychotherapies." *European Journal of Psychotherapy & Counselling* 20, no. 1 (2018): 4–9.

Shulman, Eviatar. "Early Meanings of Dependent-Origination." *Journal of Indian Philosophy* 36, no. 2 (2008): 297–317.

Shonin, Edo, William Van Gordon, and Mark D. Griffiths. "The Emerging Role of Buddhism in Clinical Psychology: Toward Effective Integration." *Psychology of Religion and Spirituality* 6, no. 2 (2014): 123–37.

Shonin, Edo, William Van Gordon, and Mark D. Griffiths. "Meditation Awareness Training (MAT) for Improved Psychological Well-Being: A Qualitative Examination of Participant Experiences." *Journal of Religion and Health* 53, no. 3 (2014): 849–63.

Shonin, Edo, William Van Gordon, Thomas J. Dunn, Nirbhay N. Singh, and Mark D. Griffiths. "Meditation Awareness Training (MAT) for Work-Related Wellbeing and Job Performance: A Randomised Controlled Trial." *International Journal of Mental Health and Addiction* 12, no. 6 (2014): 806–23.

Sik, Hin Hung. "Dharma Therapy: An Intervention Program with Mindfulness as One of Its Key Components." In *New Horizons in Buddhist Psychology: Relational Buddhism for Collaborative Practitioners*, edited by Maurits G.T Kwee, 353–72. Chagrin Falls: Taos Institute Publications, 2010.

Sik, Hin Hung, and Jennifer Yim. "Dharma Therapy: A Buddhist Counselling Approach to Acknowledging and Enhancing Perspectives, Attitudes and Values." In *International Perspectives in Values-Based Mental Health Practice,* edited by Drozdstoy Stoyanov, Bill Fulford, Giovanni Stanghellini, Werdie Van Staden, and Michael T. H. Wong, 305–12. New York: Springer, 2021.

Singh, Sukhdev. "Brahma." *Journal of International Women's Studies* 22, no. 5 (2021): 474–75.

Skrzynski, Carillon J., and Kasey G. Creswell. "Associations Between Solitary Drinking and Increased Alcohol Consumption, Alcohol Problems, and Drinking to Cope Motives in Adolescents and Young Adults: A Systematic Review and Meta-analysis." *Addiction* 115, no. 11 (2020): 1989–2007.

Soggie, Neil A. *Logotherapy: Viktor Frankl, Life and Work.* Lanham: Rowman & Littlefield, 2016.

Somaratne, G. A. *The Buddha's Teaching: A Buddhistic Analysis*. Singapore: Palgrave Macmillan, 2021.

Spinhoven, Philip, Marloes J Huijbers, Johan Ormel, and Anne E. M Speckens. "Improvement of Mindfulness Skills During Mindfulness-Based Cognitive Therapy Predicts Long-Term Reductions of Neuroticism in Persons with Recurrent Depression in Remission." *Journal of Affective Disorders* 213 (2017): 112–17.

Srichannil, Chomphunut, and Seamus Prior. "Practise What You Preach: Counsellors' Experience of Practising Buddhist Counselling in Thailand." *International Journal for the Advancement of Counselling* 36, no. 3 (2013): 243–61.

Sue, Erica Smith. *Buddhist Voices in School: How a Community Created a Buddhist Education Program for State Schools*. Rotterdam: Sense Publishers, 2013.

Sumanacara, Ashin. "The Experience of Dukkha and Domanassa among Puthujjanas." *Journal of Buddhist Ethics* 26 (2019): 109.

Sumanacara, Ashin. "Do the Arahant and the Buddha Experience Dukkha and Domanassa?" *Buddhist Studies Review* 36, no. 1 (2019): 53–70.

Sun, Jessie. "Mindfulness in Context: A Historical Discourse Analysis." *Contemporary Buddhism* 15, no. 2 (2014): 394–415.

Sun, Shufang, Alison M. Pickover, Simon B. Goldberg, Jabeene Bhimji, Julie K. Nguyen, Anna E. Evans, Bobbi Patterson, and Nadine J. Kaslow. "For Whom Does Cognitively Based Compassion Training (CBCT) Work? An Analysis of Predictors and Moderators among African American Suicide Attempters." *Mindfulness* 10, no. 11 (2019): 2327–40.

Tamura, Yoshirō. *Japanese Buddhism: A Cultural History*. Tokyo: Kosei Publishing Co., 2000.

Thapaliya, Suresh, Kapil Dev Upadhyaya, Rohan Borschmann, and Kuppili Pooja Patnaik. "Mindfulness Based Interventions for Depression and Anxiety in Asian Population: A Systematic Review." *Journal of Psychiatrists' Association of Nepal* 7, no. 1 (2018): 10–23.

Thích, Nhất Hạnh. *Planting Seeds: Practicing Mindfulness with Children*. Berkeley, CA: Parallax Press, 2011.

Thích, Nhất Hạnh. *A Pebble for Your Pocket: Mindful Stories for Children and Grown-Ups*. Rev. ed. Berkeley, CA: Plum Blossom Books, 2010.

Tirch, Dennis, Laura R. Silberstein-Tirch, and Russell L. Kolts. Buddhist Psychology and Cognitive-Behavioral Therapy: A Clinician's Guide. Reprint edition. New York: Guilford Press, 2016.

Trungpa, Chogyam. *The Truth of Suffering and the Path of Liberation*. London: Shambhala, 2009.

Twohig, Michael P. "Acceptance and Commitment Therapy: Introduction." *Cognitive and Behavioral Practice* 19, no. 4 (2012): 499–507.

Uthayaratana, Tanaphong, Nattasuda Taephant, and Kullaya Pisitsungkagarn. "Four Noble Truths Based Problem Solving: A Therapeutic View." *Mental Health, Religion & Culture* 22, no. 2 (February 2019): 119–29. https://doi.org/10.1080/13674676.2018.1512565.

Vajiranana, Parawahera. *Buddhist Meditation: In Theory and Practice: A General Exposition According to the Pāli Canon of the Theravada School*. 3rd ed. Kuala Lumpur, Malaysia: Buddhist Missionary Society, 1987.

William Van Gordon, and Edo Shonin. "Second-Generation Mindfulness-Based Interventions: Toward More Authentic Mindfulness Practice and Teaching." *Mindfulness* 11, no. 1 (2019): 1–4.

William Van Gordon, Edo Shonin, Alex Sumich, Eva C. Sundin, and Mark D. Griffiths. "Meditation Awareness Training (MAT) for Psychological Well-Being in a Sub-Clinical Sample of University Students: A Controlled Pilot Study." *Mindfulness* 5, no. 4 (2014): 381–91. https://doi.org/10.1007/s12671-012-0191-5.

William Van Gordon, Edo Shonin, and Mark D. Griffiths. "Buddhist Emptiness Theory: Implications for Psychology." *Psychology of Religion and Spirituality* 9, no. 4 (2017): 309–18.

William Van Gordon, Edo Shonin, Thomas J. Dunn, Campayo, Javier Garcia, and Mark D. Griffiths. "Meditation Awareness Training for the Treatment of Fibromyalgia Syndrome: A Randomized Controlled Trial." *British Journal of Health Psychology* 22, no. 1 (2017): 186–206. https://doi.org/10.1111/bjhp.12224.

Wasantha Priyadarshana. "Buddhism as a System of Psychotherapy." *The Smaratungga Journal of Buddhist Studies and Education* 1, no. 1 (2017): 35–47.

Walpola, Piyal L., D. Y. Walpola, I. C. Walpola, and T. Toneatto. 2017. "Mapping the Mind: A Model Based on Theravada Buddhist Texts and Practices." *Contemporary Buddhism* 18 (1): 140–64. https://doi.org/10.1080/14639947.2017.1307575.

Webster, Mark. "Introduction to Acceptance and Commitment Therapy." *Advances in Psychiatric Treatment* 17, no. 4 (2011): 309–16.

Weragoda, Sarada Thero. *Treasury of Truth Illustrated Dhammapada*. Taiwan: Buddha Dharma Education Association Inc., 1993.

Wolff, Sabine, and Anna Auckenthaler. "Processes of Theoretical Orientation Development in CBT Trainees: What Internal Processes Do Psychotherapists in Training Undergo as They 'Integrate'?" *Journal of psychotherapy Integration* 24, no. 3 (2014): 223–37.

World Health Organization. *ICD-10: International Statistical Classification of Diseases and Related Health Problems: Tenth Revision*, 2nd ed. Geneva: World Health Organization, 2004. https://apps.who.int/iris/handle/10665/42980.

Wu, Bonnie Wai Yan, Junling Gao, Hang Kin Leung, and Hin Hung Sik. "A Randomized Controlled Trial of Awareness Training Program (ATP), A Group-Based Mahayana Buddhist Intervention." *Mindfulness* 10, no. 1 (2019): 1280–93. https://doi.org/10.1007/s12671-018-1082-1.

Xue, Keqiao 薛克翹. 佛教與中國文化 [Buddhism and Chinese Culture]. Beijing: Zhongguo huaqiao chubanshe, 1994.

Yang, Xun, Fangfang Tian, Handi Zhang, Jianguang Zeng, Taolin Chen, Song Wang, Zhiyun Jia, and Qiyong Gong. "Cortical and Subcortical Gray Matter Shrinkage in Alcohol-Use Disorders: A Voxel-Based Meta-Analysis." *Neuroscience and Biobehavioral Reviews* 66, no. 1 (2016): 92–103.

Yavuz, K Fatih, and Zülal Çelik. "Introduction to Acceptance and Commitment Therapy." *Klinik psikofarmakoloji bülteni* 29, no. 1 (2019): 360–61.

Yim, Jennifer. "Dharma Therapy: Buddhist Spiritual Counselling: A Healing Journey from Suffering to Happiness." PowerPoint presentation presented at the MaMa Charitable Foundation Symposium: Buddhist Counselling Instigating Insight into the Healing Process, Hong Kong, China, December 8–9, 2018.

Index

Note: Page numbers in **bold** refer to figures and tables.

www.ingramcontent.com/pod-product-compliance
Ingram Content Group UK Ltd.
Pitfield, Milton Keynes, MK11 3LW, UK
UKHW021838100926
8556IPUK00004B/412

9 789888 876846